RELIGION AND POLITICS IN SOUTHEAST ASIA

RELIGION AND POLITICS IN SOUTHEAST ASIA

Proceedings of the Conference
on Religious and Cultural Drivers
and Responses to Political
Dynamics in Southeast Asia

Held at Pace University
November 8, 2019

Edited by Amy Freedman

PACE UNIVERSITY PRESS   NEW YORK

Photo Credits: Susy Tekunan, taken at the "Tauhid Parade" in Jakarta, Indonesia in September 2019.
The march was calling for the primacy of Islam in Indonesia.

The article "A Righteous Intervention: Megachurch Christianity and Duterte's War on Drugs in the Philippines" by Jayeel Cornelio and Ia Marañon is reprinted with permission from the *International Journal of Asian Christianity*.

☉ Paper used in this publication meets the minimum requirements of American National Standard for Information Sciences–Permanence of Paper for Printed Library Materials, ANSI Z39.48–1984

TABLE OF CONTENTS

INTRODUCTION

Amy Freedman

This volume comes out of a conference held at Pace University on November 8, 2019. The title of the conference was "Religious and Cultural Drivers and Responses to Political Dynamics in Southeast Asia." The goal of the conference was to reach across academic disciplines and address some of the interesting phenomena occurring at the nexus of religion and politics. In academia, scholars often spend most of their time within their own fields: political scientists talk to political scientists, historians to historians, religious studies scholars to religious studies scholars, and so on. I thought it would be fruitful to bring together a more diverse group of people who are interested in the overlapping trends in Southeast Asia and to see how different fields of study fit together.

This has been a tumultuous few years in the region: elections were held in 2019 in Thailand and Indonesia; the year before in Malaysia and Cambodia. While Southeast Asia enjoyed a democratic moment after the 1997 financial crisis, more recent trends have gone in the other direction: extra judicial killings in the Philippines, state-assisted genocide in Myanmar, one-party rule in Cambodia, military rule in Thailand, and anti-tolerant and anti-liberal behavior and politicking in Indonesia. The thinking behind the call for papers for this conference was the question of whether these dynamics are being driven by elites within the top circles of political and religious power, or if what is happening is a response to popular sentiment from the bottom up? In other words, are elites steering these trends and if so, to what end? Or, are we seeing renewed populism and leaders who are simply reflecting the growing conservatism and divisiveness in society? If it is the latter, what else should we be watching for in terms of how cultural dynamics have changed? Have religious practices and values, in particular, changed or become more salient? In early waves of democratization, religious organizations such as the Catholic Church played a role in challenging autocratic rule, but what about now? Are religious groups clearly on one side of these dynamics or the other? Are Christian, Buddhist, and Muslim leaders and organizations standing up to power grabs by the state, or are they cheering or promoting this occurrence, and why? Can or do political institutions such as legislatures, the monarchy, or the bureaucracy affect what happens, and in what way? These were the organizing questions behind the conference. This volume does not pretend to answer all of these questions. Instead, the chapters here offer us ways to think about these overarching questions.

The introductory chapter lays out current trends in the region, and then the chapters go into detail and look at Thailand, Cambodia, Indonesia, and the Philippines. The concluding chapter draws out the implications of this research and suggests further avenues of study.

Current Trends in Southeast Asia

Indonesia

After making a successful transition to democracy between 1998 and 2004, Indonesia has increasingly seen a worsening of political, religious, and personal freedoms. Since the 2017 Jakarta governor's race, religion has become a potent part of the electoral process. In the gubernatorial race in 2017, incumbent Governor, Basuki Tjahaja Purnama, popularly known as Ahok, lost to Anies Baswedan, former Minister of Education. Ahok is a Chinese and a Christian, a double minority in a country of Muslims and local ethnicities. During the course of the campaign, Ahok was accused of blasphemy for quoting a passage of the Quran he said demonstrated that it is permissible for Muslims to vote for non-Muslims. Hard-line Islamist groups charged that he misrepresented the holy book and they mobilized massive street protests against Ahok and mounted a highly effective social media campaign to turn support against him. Ahok lost the election and was then charged in court and convicted of the blasphemy charges. He served two years in prison for the alleged offense (Freedom House 2019b). In Indonesia, the use of blasphemy charges has increased over the last few years and we are seeing that police and the courts are now more willing to convict on these religious charges.

Additionally, we are seeing increased harassment of religious minorities like Ahmadiyah and Shiite communities and LGBTQ individuals. Media and press freedoms are also under assault, the arrest and death of journalist Muhammad Yusum who died in police custody in 2018 for investigating illegal land grabs by a palm oil company demonstrates the increasing danger of holding political and economically powerful actors accountable (Freedom House 2019b).

The entwining of religion and politics continued with the 2019 elections. The Presidential race was a repeat of the 2014 contest between Joko Widodo (Jokowi) and former general Prabowo Subianto. Although Jokowi won in 2014 and was leading in early polls, after the religiously charged governor's race in Jakarta he felt a need to shore up his religious support and he picked former Nadhtul Ulama head and former chair of the national Ulama Council (MUI), Ma'ruf Amin (BBC 2019).

Jokowi's choice of running mate in the 2019 presidential election prompted concerns about his commitment to religious freedom. His pick, Ma'ruf Amin, is an Islamic cleric known for controversial fatwas as chairman of the Majelis Ulama Indonesia (MUI), the Indonesian Ulama Council. Under his leadership, MUI issued fatwas against Shia Islam and Ahmadiyya, as well as the 2016 fatwa declaring that Ahok, the former governor of Jakarta, insulted the Quran, paving the way for Ahok's 2017 blasphemy conviction (Arifianto 2019). Prabowo marshalled support from religious hard liners who had been instrumental in Ahok's defeat, and who spearhead the newly organized groups "Defending Islam" and "Alumni 212." Although Jokowi won the election, hard line religious groups have not gone away. The use of blasphemy laws against real and perceived enemies is becoming more and more common, and the introduction of laws in the Parliament to further marginalize minority communities looks like it will continue into the future.

Thailand

After years of political instability in Thailand between pro-Thaksin (redshirted protesters) and anti-Thaksin (yellow shirted protesters) forces, in 2014 the military carried out a coup against then Prime Minister (and Thaksin's sister) Yingluck Shinawatra. While coups have been used repeatedly in Thailand, this one was accompanied by more repression than usual. Opposition groups and individuals have been subject to arrest, legal harassment, and reeducation campaigns. Civil Society groups, the press, and activists are closely monitored, and indoctrination efforts are aimed at opposition groups and have become part of the school curriculum. Since 2014, the military has exercised almost unprecedented levels of political and social control (Freedom House 2019e). The junta put off elections repeatedly. Finally, the military held elections in the spring of 2019.

While the opposition Pheu Thai party (Thaksin and Yingluck's former party) won the most votes, no party won an absolute majority. Since the upper house is made up solely of appointed (by the military) seats, it was hardly surprising that pro-military parties in the lower and upper houses combined claimed victory and chose General Prayuth Chan-ocha to continue in his role as Prime Minister (BBC News 2019; Peck 2019).

The other center of power in Thailand is the monarchy. In 2016 the much-revered king, King Bhumibol Adulyadej, or Rama IX, passed away. Crown Prince Maha Vajiralongkorn ascended to the throne and the official coronation was in October 2017. Rama X lacks the reverence and legitimacy of his father, but he has none-the-less begun consolidating his power. He has taken control of the Crown Property Bureau (thus controlling the budget and funds of the monarchy), he approved the military-backed 2018 Constitution which allows the king to rule Thailand even while outside the country without needing to appoint a regent. The king disqualified his sister from running as a candidate for Prime Minister and has two army units in Bangkok under his direct control. In fall of 2019, the king fired his newly appointed "Royal Consort" and dismissed six senior palace officials (Westerman 2019). Alone, none of these moves seems terribly significant, but taken together they send a signal that the king is creating his own networks of power and is willing to sideline those not in agreement with him.

Thai nationalism has traditionally centered on powerful symbols and broad consensus on the significance of territorial sovereignty (Thailand was never formally colonized), Buddhism, and the monarchy. The military has often acted in the name of protecting the Thai nation from instability. King Bhumibol's long reign allowed him to cultivate a sense of unity within the nation. The monarch is the sworn patron of Buddhism and thus is central to Thai culture. The Thai nation, monarchy, and Buddhism became intertwined during the 19th and 20th centuries. Since the 2014 coup, Buddhism's relationship to the political sphere is being reassessed. After seizing power, the military junta set up a National Reform Council with a religious committee led by former Thai senator Paiboon Nititawan and former monk Mano Laohavanich. Calls for reform were spearheaded by right-wing activist monk Phra Buddha Issara, who had close ties with junta leader Prayuth Chan-ocha, and was known for his role as a leader of the anti-Thaksin/anti-Yingluk protests in Bangkok that led to the coup (Tan 2016).

State influence over several aspects of Thai Buddhism increased under military rule. In 2015, the National Reform Council (members of which were selected by the military and then formally appointed by the king) made several proposals to give the state greater control over Buddhism and leadership within monasteries. These changes include oversight of temple finances and registration mechanisms for monks, and frequent rotation of abbots among temples. The explanation for these reforms was that they were necessary to curb corruption and to police the monks' bad behavior. Top monks in Thailand are organized into the Sangha Supreme Council, and the Council has come under scrutiny the last few years because of an alleged tax evasion scandal against one of their senior members, Somdet Chuang. New laws passed by the junta allow the government to appoint the supreme patriarch, taking the power away from the Council. The junta gave a list of possible names to the new king, and Rama X chose a new supreme patriarch. In the spring of 2018, several monks were arrested and defrocked. The monks were accused of various crimes. One of those arrested was Phra Buddha Issara. While it is not totally clear what the motives were behind these arrests, one possible explanation is that the military and the king want to ensure that religious figures don't become an independent source of power (Wongcha-um 2018). Anthropologist Jim Taylor argues that the arrests were the "ruling palace regime" trying to consolidate royalist power by eliminating non-royalist high-ranking monks (Taylor 2018). Although Phra Buddha Issara was a supporter of the military and the monarchy, it may have been feared that he had too much independent power and this was a preemptive move to consolidate political and religious control. A new king with weak popular support, and a former general serving as Prime Minister without genuine legitimacy derived from a legal rational electoral process means that there is a need for a new basis of legitimacy for both the political institutions and the institution of the monarchy. Buddhism may play a role in reasserting new forms of nationalism and state control.

Philippines

Rodrigo Duterte won the presidency of the Philippines in the 2016 election and soon after launched his war on drugs. Since 2016, estimates are that more than 20,000 people have been killed in extrajudicial actions for suspicion that they were using or selling illegal drugs (Willis

2019). Freedom House and Human Rights Watch have detailed the abuses of power and the worsening state of civil rights and liberties in The Philippines. While freedom of the press and freedom of association and assembly still exist in the country, over the last several years the climate for voices and groups critical of the government has become more and more dangerous. Lawsuits, arrests based on bogus tax violations, or supposed corruption, or drug charges, overt intimidation, and even assassination, have been levied against Duterte's critics (Freedom House 2019d).

More than 80% of Filipinos are Catholic and despite sexual abuse revelations, and other local scandals, Catholic iconography and Christian values are intrinsically linked to Philippine identity, values, and beliefs. The Church played a significant role in the people's power movement in the 1980s to oust dictator Ferdinand Marcos. Before Duterte's election, it would have seemed inconceivable for a national leader to not only be dismissive of Catholic or Christian values, but to be actively hostile to the Church, the Pope, and even God. After the Pope's 2017 visit to the Philippines, Duterte publically insulted him, and he has mocked saints and is reported to have said: "Who is this Stupid God?" (Willis 2019).

Even worse, four priests have been killed for their willingness to speak out against Duterte and the drug war. Given the Church's history in the Philippines, it is surprising that the Church has been somewhat slow to offer a louder dissenting voice. However, increasingly, individual clergy are emerging in opposition to Duterte. In response, the president has continued to go after the church questioning the legitimacy of the institution. Duterte is pressuring religious leaders to take sides, they are either with him and his framing of the drug war as a moral crusade, or they are against him and thus are suspect themselves of supporting, or even using drugs. It is worth noting here that Duterte has convinced the Philippine people of his righteousness and the morality of his drug war. His approval ratings have gone as high as 80%, and in midterm elections in 2019, all 12 contested senate seats were won by Duterte's allies (Willis 2019). One of the things which is profoundly different about the Philippines in 2020 (compared to the 1980s) is the increasingly large number of people who attend evangelical churches. Over time, the Catholic Church has lost its near monopoly on religious life in the Philippines. Today, millions of Filipinos worship in megachurches. These churches, in general, are more conservative and have been supporting Duterte's war on drugs.

Malaysia

Malaysia, like other countries in Southeast Asia, has seen its fair share of race baiting and religious politics. While there is not a chapter in this volume dedicated to Malaysia, religion, ethnicity and politics are very much intertwined. After more than 60 years in power, the ruling coalition was defeated in the 2018 general elections. Pakatan Harapan (PH) defeated the United Nasional Malays Organisation (UMNO) and the Barisan Nasional (BN). Under the leadership of former UMNO Prime Minister Mahathir Muhammad, Pakatan Harapan won the election by promising comprehensive political reforms to clean up corruption and promote a new model of interethnic and interreligious political cooperation. BN's defeat came about as a result of the 1Malaysia Development Berhad (1MBD) scandal involving Prime Minister Najib Razak. The 1MBD, a state run investment firm, was started to facilitate infrastructure development plans. Initially, it owned power plants and began planning a new financial district in Malaysia's capital Kuala Lumpur. It then branched out, investing in films and other pet projects of officials. The fund soon amassed significant debt, about $12 billion, instead of foreign investment. Much of the money raised was allegedly embezzled or laundered and went to help Najib's electoral plans and line political elites' pockets. The US Justice Department said that more than $4.5 billion went through fraudulent shell companies to corrupt officials (Burroughs and Kahn 2019). By 2018, public anger over the allegations helped defeat BN at the polls.

Ironically, it was long time UMNO insider, Mahathir, who helped bring the opposition coalition to power. Mahathir broke with UMNO over Najib's involvement in 1MDB. The opposition had long championed a slate of political reforms to end highly restrictive policies on assembly, political speech, and improve accountability and independence of the judiciary. Once in power, Pakatan initiated legislation to reform draconian sedition and assembly laws, and to repeal anti-fake news laws used to stifle opposition speech. However, many of these reforms were stymied in Parliament and hampered by push back from conservative elements within the new ruling coalition (Freedom House 2019c). More progressive groups in Malaysia had hoped for a radical shift in tone and practice away from ethnic and religious politics. However, this fragile coalition didn't last fragile coalition didn't last, Mahathir resigned in late February 2020 when several members of the ruling coalition pulled out and joined a new block of Malay parties in Parliament.

A new coalition of Islamic and Malay parties is pushing back against policies perceived as anti-Islamic or as too tolerant of diversity and significant change , and this coalition is now in power.

The new Muslim-Malay majority may now flex their muscle against minorities and they may not need these other groups to remain in power. The Selangor temple riot and subsequent mobilization against the International Convention on the Elimination of All Forms of Racial Discrimination demonstration showed speedy mobilization of hardline groups (Cook 2019).

It may be too soon to know how the new realignment will fare when they need to compete in elections, we may now see a return of ethnicized and polarized politics based on identity. If so, conservative Islamic groups will come out the winners, and the considerable portion of the country which is not Muslim or which does not wish to see the primacy of conservative Islam, will lose out.

Cambodia

Cambodia was never a bastion of democracy, but over the last few years it has devolved into a one-party state. Hun Sen has consolidated his power and the power of the Cambodian People's Party (CPP). The 2018 elections were not an exercise in democracy. Opposition parties were not allowed to compete, their leaders were jailed, or exiled ahead of the campaign. Independent media and civil society organizations were muzzl (Freedom House 2019a). Most of the Cambodian population is Buddhist, but about 2% are Muslim. Most Muslims are ethnically Cham. The government is devoting resources to promoting Buddhism, Buddhist holidays are celebrated more actively, and more state money is going to education and training for both monks and lay persons. Hun Sen also hosted an iftar celebration in Phnom Penh for 5,000 Muslims (US Department of State 2018). Increased government attention on religion mirrors increased government control over society writ large. Hun Sen is willing to use both carrots (money and personal attention) and sticks (arrests, lawsuits, harassment) to get different elements of society to fall into line. Religious groups are no exception.

Religion and Politics

There is extensive literature on the relationship between religion and politics. Some of the most enduring questions in the study of government and politics have to do with the relationship between religious practice and the state. Prior to the enlightenment, rulers often derived their power and legitimacy by claiming their links to God and religion. Enlightenment thinking began to question both man's place in the universe as separate from God and question the divine rule of king. Writings from diverse thinkers such as Locke, Descartes, and Kant reflect an era from the 1620s to the 1780s in which cultural and intellectual forces in Western Europe emphasized reason, analysis, and individualism rather than traditional lines of authority (Freedman 2019a). More recent political science literature argued that as the world became more "modern" (industrialized and looking more like the "West"), it would become more secular than religious (Berger 1979). Much of this literature used as its starting point the perceived trend in Western Europe in the late twentieth century where church attendance and religious practice and belief fell dramatically. However, this link between modernity and weakening religiosity was not broadly true in the United States until very recently (Cox and Jones 2017), nor has it been the case in Southeast Asia. Predictions of secularization were so off base that Berger wrote a retraction of his earlier work in 1996, finding that his and others' assumptions about increasing secularization would have been better characterized as "pluralization." Instead of norms and practices going only in a secular direction, religious practice has instead become more diverse. In Southeast Asia, despite economic growth and industrialization, religious identification and religious practice have not disappeared, and in many instances, religious observance has increased and become more orthodox and more entwined with the state. There are a number of reasons for this: increased literacy resulted in more people who were able to read the Quran and access religious teachings directly. Rapid changes in communication tools increased access to religious ideas through radio, TV, cassette tapes, CDs. and DVDs, and of course the internet and social media have now expanded access even further and more cheaply (Hefner 2000). Additionally, increased travel to the Middle East and other religious centers, and the increased involvement of the state into religious affairs (building mosques, regulating religious practices like the Haj, etc.) resulted in greater religious practice, not less (Freedman 2019a).

If industrialization does not necessarily lead to secularization, what does that mean for politics? Does democracy require religious tolerance or should religion take a back seat? Not necessarily. Gabriel Almond and

Sidney Verba's (1963) work *The Civic Culture* described the characteristics of a political culture that enabled nations to implement and sustain democratic processes. In their work, Almond and Verba see culture as driving politics. Particular cultural characteristics support particular political arrangements. Key among Almond and Verba's "democratic" characteristics are trust in institutions of government, an aware and participatory public, and the requirement that elites and the public hold democratic values and support democratic processes. Almond and Verba's characterization of "democratic values" came out of Lasswell's personality traits of a 'democrat' (Lasswell 1948). These traits include the following: the willingness to play by the rules of the game (the loser in an election has to be willing to accept their loss and not take up arms against the victor or ignore the results); a certain level of tolerance for those whose ideas might different from one's own; an "open ego" or a warm and inclusive attitude towards other human beings, a capacity for sharing values with others; and a multi-valued rather than a single-valued orientation to produce trust in others (Almond and Verba 1965).

Almond and Verba's work initiated a host of studies by others finding that these traits were missing in many or most developing (and non-democratic states). Pye and Verba (1965) argued that many people in these nations were unaware and uninvolved in politics and had parochial and hierarchical views more supportive of autocratic forms of government. Yet, the next period of democratization called this into question. The (so-called) "third-wave" of democratization took hold in the late 1980s in Taiwan, South Korea, and the Philippines; then came the transitions in Eastern Europe after the fall of the Soviet Union in 1990, and the more recent reforms in Southeast Asia after the 1997 financial crisis. This last period of transitions brought down authoritarian rule in Indonesia, weakened it in Malaysia, and ushered in short-lived political reforms in Thailand. Many of these societies did not have the traits supposedly required for democracy to endure. This incongruence would supposedly make the political systems unstable and more likely to break down (Almond and Verba 1963, 20). While imperfect, democracy in most of Eastern Europe, and certainly in Taiwan and South Korea has endured and most of these countries are rated as "free" by Freedom House's evaluations of political, economic, and social freedoms. Even in Southeast Asia, democracy has not completely disappeared

(Freedman 2019b). Looking at the region it is hard to see culture as the key independent variable driving either democracy or autocracy. If this were the case, it would be hard to argue that culture somehow changed in a fundamental enough way to account for rapid political changes *to democracy* and then *away from it*, in such short periods of time. Survey research bears this out. Surveys consistently find a majority of Southeast Asians support democracy.

World Values Surveys give us a good deal of information about public attitudes and values relating to democracy. The results of the World Values Surveys and separate surveys done in Indonesia (Indonesia was not surveyed in Wave 6), the Philippines, Thailand, and Malaysia demonstrate that although respondents say they favor democracy, public opinion is lukewarm on values that undergird democracy. Respondents across several countries report high levels of support for democracy and respond that democracy is the best way to organize politics. Yet, large numbers of people surveyed prioritize "maintaining order" over giving people more say in government, and both of these answers dwarf "maintaining freedom of speech" (a key element in a democracy) as a priority.

Table: **World Values Surveys, Wave 5 (2006) & Wave 6 (2012)**
v. 62 (responses are from 2012, except for Indonesia, which are from 2006)

Which priority is most important to you?				
	Philippines	Thailand	Malaysia	Indonesia
Maintaing order in the nation	42.2	31.7	59.1	60.4
Giving people more say in important government decisions	21.8	23.0	17.7	9.0
Fighting rising prices	27.0	33.0	19.0	21.4
Freedom of Speech	8.9	9.0	4.2	6.4
No Answer	0.1	3.3	0	2.8

V130: Wave 5 & Wave 6

I'm going to describe various types of political systems and ask what you think about each as a way of governing this country; having a democratic system:	Philip-pines (2001)	Philip-pines (2012)	Thailand (2006)	Thailand (2012)	Malaysia (2006)	Malaysia (2012)	Indo-nessia (2006)
Very Good	27.9	33.9	44.9	68.3	43.5	47.8	54.5
Fairly Good	53.8	40.9	47.3	23.5	48.1	44.9	36.4
Bad	15.3	17.5	6.8	5.5	6.6	5.5	2.1
Very Bad	2.2	6.5	0.5	2.3	1.7	1.8	0.9
No Answer	0.8	0.1	0.4	0.4	0.1	0	1.5
Don't Know	0	1.1	0	0	0	0	4.6

Note. Percentages may not equal 100% due to rounding.

V140: Wave 6 (2012)

How important is it for you to live in a country that is governed democratically?	Philippines	Thailand	Malaysia
1 - Not at all important	5.0	0.3	0.2
2	0.7	0.3	0.1
3	0.6	0.6	0.2
4	2.5	1.6	0.8
5	9.6	7.4	3.6
6	7.0	10.0	8.6
7	7.3	8.9	8.8
8	9.9	11.8	19.8
9	7.5	10.1	12.2
10 - Absolutely important	49.4	47.0	45.8
No Answer	0.5	2.0	0

Note. Percentages may not equal 100% due to rounding.

A similar question was asked in the Institute of Southeast Asian Studies (ISEAS) 2017 survey in Indonesia. Respondents were asked if democracy was the best form of government for Indonesia: 79.8% agreed that democracy was the best form of government, 4.7% disagreed, and 15.5% neither agreed nor disagreed (ISEAS).

The ISEAS survey also asks Indonesians their views on the role of Islam, and the answers are important. Forty-nine percent of people thought that the government should prioritize Islam over other religions, 37% thought that Islamic religious leaders should play a very important role in politics, 41% thought that regions should be allowed to implement shari'a law at the local level, 39% thought that shari'a law should be implemented throughout Indonesia, 63% thought that blasphemy against Islam should be punished more severely, 58% thought that when voting in elections it was important to choose a Muslim leader, and 36% responded that Islam should be Indonesia's only official religion (ISEAS). These responses demonstrate that attitudes about democracy and religiosity do not neatly reflect Western beliefs and assumptions (Freedman 2019b). The surveys also show that perhaps two things are happening in tandem: Indonesians increasingly see religion as an important part of their identity and want politics to be a reflection of this, and more conservative and hard line religious leaders are able to use religious appeals and make identity and religious politics a divisive or wedge issue for electoral purposes. In playing up Islamic values, identity, and fear of violations of this identity and value system, a politician can come to power democratically and then chip away at, or dismantle, rights and protections for those outside this majority (ISEAS).

If one part of the relationship between religion and politics is how beliefs and values shape people's political outlook and preferences, there is also literature that flips the independent variable. What if it is something about political institutions (systems, laws, and processes), and political elites who shape religion? Many political scientists take an institutionalist approach; that the nature of political institutions is shaping and constraining behavior of citizens. For example, Jokowi may genuinely be a reform-minded leader, but because of his need to maintain support in parliament for his agenda (in his first term) and to keep control over his government, he was forced to water down his initial pledge of promoting tolerance and protecting civil rights. Moreover, his need to win reelection led him to choose a conservative Islamist as his running mate. The effectiveness of the campaign against Ahok in the Jakarta governor's race demonstrated how potent identity and religious politics could be in sway-ing elections. Perhaps this phenomenon is simply a scaling up of local dy-namics that have been under way for more than 10 years. Michael Buehler has shown that local politicians chose to adopt shari'a laws not because (or not just because) they are pious Muslims, but because it enables them access to the zakat (religious tithing) to benefit from patronage networks that help them reward supporters and maintain their positions of power. It is possible that promoting greater piety and favoring of Islam is more an instrument to win elections and maintain support than an end unto itself (Buehler 2008).

In this view, politicians are trying to capitalize on growing religiosity to maintain political power. In Indonesia, there is intrinsic support among many for Islam having a place in the public sphere. But, people also say they value democracy and civil rights. Politicians are using this to shape and carry out their campaign. Yes, there are vigorous and mostly free and fair elections in Indonesia, but candidates are using competitive elections simultaneously with increased use of blasphemy laws to stifle and delegit-imize some candidates running for office. Underlying public opinion about the importance of Islam is making this a viable electoral strategy, but it is ultimately the elites using this strategy to influence political behavior and results (Freedman 2019b).

In Malaysia, religion and politics have been intertwined since inde-pendence. The Malay population is overwhelmingly Muslim, the Indian population mostly Hindi, and the Chinese are Buddhist, Christian, or Con-fucian. Politics has largely been organized along ethnic lines, but this has often resulted in religion getting brought in as well. For years PAS, the Islamic Party of Malaysia, was one of the largest and most successful oppo-sition groups. In order to compete against the PAS's message of morality and the importance of Islamic values and laws, the ruling party, UMNO, began more active promotion of Islamic practice and values in the 1980s. This meant more oversight and larger budgets to the religious ministries (under control of the Prime Minister), and it meant increasingly outspoken policies granting primacy to Islam. It also meant that the state become the arbiter and funder of Islamic organizations. This was a way in part to counter the appeals of PAS as an electoral strategy, and it allowed the state to take effective control of religion. With the recent electoral shake up in Malaysia, it is not clear what direction the country will go in the relationship between religion and politics.

It matters who is running for office, who leaders surround themselves with, and what they choose to do after taking office. Elites who find that they can gain power by playing on underlying attitudes such as a desire for order, a mistrust of others, and group affiliation that views minorities as less than or unequal to the majority, find that it is possible to make political changes detrimental to democracy. In the Philippines, Duterte empowers the police to engage in extrajudicial killings and makes the Philippines even more dangerous for journalists. Duterte made no secret of his desire to shut down critics or his disdain for following the rule of law. And, he has the highest public approval ratings for a Philippine leader in many years. His decision to frame his drug war as a moral crusade against undesirable elements of society has made it hard for the Church to push back on his actions. It is only belatedly now (from some in the Catholic Church hierarchy, and even fewer in Megachurches) that the church is trying to reclaim that moral argument and put forth an alternate morality based on human dignity and worth for all.

Thailand's situation also reflects a similar but more blatant phenomenon. Elites in the military and within the bureaucracy of the monarchy had hoped they could hold power through nominally democratic means. However, in relatively fair elections from 2001 to 2006, and again in 2011, Thaksin Shinawatra, and then his sister Yingluck Shinawatra, won. Support for the Shinawatras threatened and undermined the more traditional elite alliance of bureaucrats, the military, and the monarchy. Unable to win power through elections, judicial activism, or mass protest activity, the military took matters into its own hands in 2014 and carried out a coup. The aftermath of this coup was a far more draconian curtailing of political and civil rights than at any time in Thailand since the 1970s. There is nothing in the World Values Survey data that indicates lower levels of support for democracy. If anything, the opposite is true; prior to the coup there were higher levels of support for democracy in Thailand than in neighboring countries and lower levels of support for "order" as the highest priority in the country. Only through brute force and now the rewriting of the political rules of the game (the new constitution) have antidemocratic elites been able to hold on to power. Religious values and practices have not changed dramatically In Thailand in the last ten years, yet the political landscape has. Military leaders in the junta and government today have vigorously promoted new morality campaigns to encourage harmony and good citizenship. While these campaigns may have a Buddhist flavor to them, the goal appears to be political rather than spiritual (Styllis 2018; Tongsakulrungruang 2018).

Plan of this Volume

There are six chapters included in this volume: three on Indonesia, one each on Cambodia, Thailand, and the Philippines. Each chapter asks a question related to the topic of religion and politics and looks at what the drivers are of current dynamics. How can we understand the current relationship between religion and politics? Who or what is driving change? For example, is increased religious conservatism among millions of Indonesians at the root of the new Islamic activism in politics? Or, are elites using religion for their own political power and interests? What explains the new state interest in oversight of Buddhism in Thailand? How might the roles of the king and the military be changing in Thailand? How should we think about megachurches in the Philippines and their political positioning in response to Duterte's policies? Information in the chapters helps us offer some answers.

Chapter two is by Christopher Ankersen. His work on Thailand examines "culture in action." While political elites make rules that support their interests and power, it is not enough to maintain a complex system of legitimacy. Rulers need normative power, and that is what Ankersen's research interrogates. How are military leaders, political elites (with a great deal of overlap between the two groups), and the monarchy trying to create and solidify normative power? Ankersen's chapter examines the "inequality regime" being perpetuated in Thailand today. He looks at how a set of ideas, beliefs, norms, and institutions exist in Thailand to rationalize, legitimize, and perpetuate systems of inequality. Elites are the ones who stand to lose if the system is challenged or overturned. In this system, the monarchy is a source of idealized power. The king is an amalgam of religious and secular power; he is the epitome of Hindu and Buddhist piety from above, and the embodiment of popular sovereignty from below (Ankersen, Ch. 2). The king's legitimacy derives in part from his sacredness. Rama X needs the myths and veneer of holiness even more than his father, since he is lacking that accumulated history. Given recent actions of the king, we are seeing indications that he is consolidating control over economic, military, and political power, not just ideological power. Ankersen's chapter gives us persuasive reasons for this behavior.

William Noseworthy's chapter on Cambodia presents an interesting look at Hun Sen's relationship to the Cham Muslim community. He finds that Hun Sen has cultivated close ties to the Grand Mufti and in return, the Muslim community has continued to support Hun Sen and his party, despite their minority status and weak protections from violations of their economic interests. Hun Sen's growing authoritarianism has weakened all other centers of power, but that does not mean he no longer feels a need to maintain links to Cambodia's diverse communities, and his ties to the Cham Muslims are one example of how he works to do so.

Chapter four by Lussier, Azca, Ikhwan and Kustiningsih looks at the link between religious practice and political participation in Yogyakarta, Indonesia. Their research looks at how ordinary people's religious lives shape their political activities. Their study looks at both Muslim and Christian communities. Yogyakarta is known for religious tolerance and so this work looks at if religious practice (and if so, what kind) is connected to political participation and orientation. Their research finds that there is a connection between participation in one's religious community and political participation. They find that Muslims participate more than Christians. Yet, they also find that economic concerns are a stronger predictor of political behavior than religious identity and religious participation.

Ionana Emy Mateson's research in chapter five looks more closely at the Prosperous Justice Party (PKS) in Indonesia. She asks why, despite repeated scandals over the last five years, support for the party remains high. She offers three answers: the party's social networks, the overlap of the party and the larger network, and the well institutionalized nature of the party has helped it transcend scandals around key party leaders so that the party continues to win more support in elections. Her work demonstrates the saliency of social and religious networks, combined with institutional structures that help mobilize and channel political support. In the Indonesian political landscape, PKS's strategic adaptation has allowed it to endure and to increase its share of votes over time.

In chapter six, Susy Tekunan looks at the role and radicalization of women in Islamic organizations in Indonesia. She asks if radicalization is a strategy for women to stand out and prove themselves in a traditionally male sphere? Women's participation in conservative and radical Islamist organizations is at an all time high in Indonesia. There is a wide spectrum for participation in more hard line organizations: from participation in study groups on college campuses, to fighting for ISIL in Syria, more women are taking part than ever before. Conservative Islamic political parties are also helping to radicalize women. What does this tell us about women, politics, religiosity, and religious mobilization more generally?

Chapter seven on the Philippines looks at the role of evangelical megachurches as a core base of support for Duterte's war on drugs. Cornelio and Marañon's work finds that Evangelical churches' claim to be "apolitical" is really a cover for tacit support of harsh policies. These churches view drug abuse as a spiritual problem, but they find that these theological views ultimately reflect the interests of the class these megachurches represent and they find little sympathy for the poorer communities who have suffered the harshest effects of Duterte's policies.

The concluding chapter comes back to our original questions and offers ways to think about changes taking place across the region.

Bibliography

Almond, Gabriel and Sidney Verba. (1963). *The Civic Culture: Political Attitudes and Democracy in Five Nations*. Princeton, NJ: Princeton University Press, p. 11-15.

BBC, "Indonesia Election: Joko Widodo Re-Elected as President " May 21, 2019. https://www.bbc.com/news/world-asia-48331879

———, "Thai Parliament Elects Ex Military Government Chief Prayuth as PM." June 6, 2019. https://www.bbc.com/news/worldasia48537664?intlink_from_url=https://www.bbc.com/news/topics/c4l37mgp4q4t/thailand-election-2019&link_location=live-reporting-story

Berger, Peter. (1979). *The Heretical Imperative: Contemporary Possibilities of Religious Affirmation*. Garden City, NY: Anchor Press.

Buehler, Micahel, 2008. "The Rise of Shari'a By-Laws in Indonesian Districts: An Indication for Changing Patterns of Power Accumulation and Political Corruption.' *Southeast Asia Research 16(2)* 255-285.

Burroughs, Callum and Yusuf Kahn, "The Bizarre Story of 1MDB" *Business Insider*, August 9, 2019.

Cook, Erin. "Can Malaysia's New Government Deliver on Reform?" *The Diplomat*, March 15, 2019.

Fossati, Diego, Hui Yew-Foong, and Siwage Dharma Negara, 2017. "The Indonesia National Survey Project: Economy, Society and Politics." No. 10 in *Trends in Southeast Asia* (Singapore, ISEAS

Freedman, Amy 2019a, "Religious Minorities in Southeast Asia: The Ahmadiyya and Why Tolerance Matters for Modernity and Democracy." Chapter in *Modernity, Religion and Democracy*, edited by Vidhu Verma for Oxford University Press, 2019.

———, 2019b "Undermining Democracy Elites, Attitudes, Norms and Behaviors in Southeast Asia." *Journal of Indo-Pacific Affairs,* Winter 2019: 36-56.

Freedom House, "Freedom in the world 2019 Cambodia" https://freedomhouse.org/report/freedom-world/2019/cambodia

———, "Freedom in the world 2019 Indonesia" https://freedomhouse.org/report/freedom-world/2019/Indonesia

———, "Freedom in the world 2019 Thailand" https://freedomhouse.org/report/freedom-world/2019/thailand

———, "Freedom in the world 2019 Philippines" https://freedomhouse.org/report/freedom-world/2019/Philippines

———, "Freedom in the world 2019 Malaysia" https://freedomhouse.org/report/freedom-world/2019/malaysia

Hefner, Robert. (2000). *Civil Islam*. Princeton, NJ: Princeton University Press.

ISEAS, Institute of Southeast Asian Studies, Singapore. The Indonesian National Survey Project 2017.

Lasswell, Harold. *Power and Personality*, (NY: W.W. Norton) 1948.

Menchik, Jeremy. Presentation given at NYU, September 27, 2018 on Indonesian elections.

Peck, Grant. "Final Election Results Leave Thailand Divided" *The Diplomat*, May 10, 2019.

Pye, Lucian and Gabriel Almond. (1965). *Political Culture and Political Development*. Princeton, NJ: Princeton University Press.

Styllis, Greg. "Thai Crackdown Targets Buddhist Monks Amid Accusations of Embezzlement and Fraud." *The Washington Post*, June 24, 2018.

Tan Hui Yee (25 February 2016). "Tense times for Thai junta, Buddhist clergy". *The Straits Times*. Singapore Press Holdings

Taylor, Jim (8 June 2018). "What's behind the 'purging' of the Thai sangha?". *New Mandala*. Archived from the original on 2018-06-12

Tongsakulruangruang, Khemthong. "Thailand's Constitution Capitulates to Buddhist Domination." *East Asia Forum*, January 24, 2018.

US Department of State, "Cambodia in 2018 International Religious Freedom Report" https://www.state.gov/wp-content/uploads/2019/05/CAMBODIA-2018-INTERNATIONAL-RELIGIOUS-FREEDOM-REPORT.pdf

Westerman, Ashley, "What the Ouster of the Royal Consort May Say about Where Thailand is Headed." *NPR*, Oct. 25, 2019. https://www.npr.org/2019/10/25/772716404/what-the-ouster-of-the-royal-consort-may-say-about-where-thailand-is-heading

Willis, Adam. "Church vs. State" Virginia Quarterly Review, Summer 2019.

Wongcha-um, by Panu (2018-05-25). "Thailand raids temples, arrest monks in fight to clean up Buddhism". *The Sydney Morning Herald*.

Chapter 2

Culture in Action: The Case of Contemporary Thai Politics

Christopher Ankersen

Cultural images and expectations are being used in Thailand to construct oppressive structures within the political landscape. While some may claim that these structures are merely manifestations or extensions of long-standing cultural norms, I argue that this is a case of culture in action (Swidler 1986). Following Swidler, I argue that, in this case, "culture influences action not by providing the ultimate values towards which action is oriented, but by shaping a repertoire or a 'toolkit' of habits, skills and styles from which people construct strategies of action" (pg. 373). In other words, elites are using culturally salient building blocks in order to fashion seemingly acceptable rules that suit their own particular goals. Culture, in other words, doesn't determine the form of governance, it's merely exploited by it and makes it possible. In so constructing this legitimacy, elites use traditional values as their toolkit. When this is done correctly, it forms a virtuous circle.

In this chapter, I will illustrate how this construction of legitimacy operates in theory, and how it operates in Thailand. I then argue that there are important changes taking place currently. The king is moving from the role of an object of legitimation to a more active role. This move is poised to alter the make-up of Thai political governance.

HOW IT WORKS

As Thomas Piketty has made clear, the process of legitimation is universal:

> Every human society must justify its inequalities: unless reasons for them are found, the whole political and social edifice stands in danger of collapse. Every epoch therefore develops a range of contradictory discourses and ideologies for the purpose of legitimizing the inequality that already exists or that people believe should exist. From these discourses emerge certain economic, social, and political rules, which people then use to make sense of the ambient social structure. (Piketty 2020: 1)

While universal, Piketty acknowledges that these justifications take on different forms, according to the particular cultural and historical conditions
prevalent in a given society. He defines the resulting "set of discourses and
institutional arrangements intended to justify and structure the economic, social, and political inequalities of a given society" as an inequality regime. Just as the "ambient social structures" differ across societies, so can
the ideologies used to explain and rationalize them. Regardless of cultural
variation, though, these ideologies are elite driven, for it is those on the
top of an unequal society who stand to lose the most if inequalities are not
accepted. This is because the alternative—leveling of a society—can only
be accomplished through violence (Scott 2017).

This potential frightens elites, who would have much to lose if the basis
of their command of an unequal share of social goods (wealth and privilege)
were to disappear. In stark terms, possessing legitimacy can mean the difference between being accepted or unacceptable, between remaining on the dais
or being hoisted on the gallows. Political arrangements are deemed legitimate
when "the decisions of the governors are accepted and obeyed because they
are felt to be justified by standards common to both those who command and
those who obey" (Smith 1970). "Legitimacy means that [an actor] can assume,
in their routine operations, that subjects or citizens will comply with ... orders
... on the basis not only of unreflecting habit or fear of punishment, but also of
a willing disposition to obey, motivated by a sense of obligation and of moral
self-respect" (Poggi 2001). Clearly, more than merely a matter of determining
whether or not a particular group will be obeyed, legitimacy should be viewed
as "a belief by virtue of which persons exercising authority are lent prestige"
(Weber 1964, 382). It is this prestige that allows elites, whether in formal pos-
itons of authority or not, to retain their positions, as unequal as they may be.

Legitimacy is not a natural, fixed, or eternal social arrangement. As I
have argued elsewhere, "legitimacy is contingent, culturally constructed,
dynamic and, therefore, indeterminate" (Ankersen 2014, 50). Therefore, for
legitimacy to remain, it must be constantly maintained by the group possessing it. This maintenance can take several forms, often simultaneously. An
inequality regime may attempt to maintain its legitimacy through enforcement of compliance. Brute force enforcement is always a possibility, but can
by itself generate feelings of illegitimacy. "Every [inequality] regime has its
weaknesses. In order to survive, it must permanently redefine itself, often

by way of violent conflict but also by availing itself of shared experience and knowledge" (Piketty 2020, 124). Therefore, alongside measured doses of enforcement, an inequality regime may need to adopt a strategy of adaptation.

A key ingredient in this process is being able to employ social power to either force acceptance or convince the masses that the basis of legitimacy remains valid. Here the work of Michael Mann is instructive. He asserts that "societies are constituted of multiple overlapping and intersecting sociospatial networks of power" (Mann 1986, 1). These networks draw on for four sources of power: political, military, economic, and ideological. These sources "offer alternative organizational means of social control" (Mann 1986, 3). Political power is the ability to make laws and set administrative priorities. Military power involves the use of physical violence to impose one's will. Economic power revolves around the control over resources or processes of value. Finally, ideological power allows its wielder to denote meaning. Inequality regimes are able to tap into these sources of power and use them—in combination—to uphold their positions within a society. It is noteworthy that the relationship between inequality and power is complex: it is used to maintain *and* justify unequal distributions of resources.

Ideally, a social actor would be able to draw on all four sources of social power simultaneously. However, this is not always the case. A social actor might have a great deal of economic power, but lack military power, for instance. Poggi suggests that in cases such as this, we see actors come together in "a process of mutual accommodation" (Poggi 2001, 81). Powerholders attempt to offset any particular shortfalls in power and leverage their particular elements of power in combination with those of others in order to achieve some desired end. For our purposes, this desired end should be seen as the creation and maintenance of a specific inequality regime. In this way, we can see those with surpluses in some forms of social power working with those who have surpluses in other forms. The government and the armed forces, for instance, might be strong in political and military power, but need to work with business elites and the clergy, for example, in order to gain access to economic and ideological power. As Althusser suggests, the formal elements of the state and less formal elements of society work in tandem to ensure the mass's "subjection to the ruling ideology or the mastery of its 'practice'" (Althusser 2001, 89).

While it may be tempting to see the efficacy of any such ideology as being culturally determined, this is not the case. There is no validity to the essentialist argument that, for example, Western or Asian values lead to a particular set of power arrangements. Indeed, it is precisely the opposite case that pertains. Ann Swidler makes it clear that "culture's causal significance [lies] not in defining ends of action, but in providing cultural components that are used to construct strategies of action" (Swidler 1986, 273). And so, as inequality regimes are created, and social power deployed in order to enforce the ideologies that underpin them: "people do not build lines of action from scratch, choosing actions one at a time as efficient means to given ends. Instead, they construct chains of action beginning with at least some pre-fabricated links. Culture influences action through the shape and organization of those links, not by determining the ends to which they are put" (pg. 277).

The process of justifying inequality in a society is a universal one. Without some form of legitimacy, gross differentials in wealth and status will not be tolerated. As such, inequality regimes are formed, in order to both generate ideological explanations and gain acceptance. Doing so requires a degree of social power and while a given group may not have access to all dimensions of this power, they can work together with other power holders. While there are no ideologies that can be universally deployed to confer legitimacy everywhere, culture does not determine what particular ideologies might look like. Instead of a bottom-up causal force, culture should be seen as a repertoire from which social actors (in this case, elites) may select symbols that are likely to resonate in a society, given their familiarity and salience. Let us now turn to see how this is carried out in the case of Thailand.

HOW IT WORKS IN THE THAI CASE

Thailand is not free from inequality. As one scholar notes "Modern Thailand has bountiful resources, hard-working people, a deep and mysterious culture and millions of people living in poverty while a few thousand Thai people continue to live in extremes of wealth" (Rappa 2017, 3). The dimensions of the inequality in Thailand include wealth, land ownership, social status, and political access (Phongpaichit and Baker 2015). In fact, Thailand was assessed to be the fourth most unequal country in the world in 2018, with a GINI coefficient of 90.2 (Credit Suisse 2018, 117).[1] In 2019, while the situation appeared to have improved somewhat to a GINI coefficient of 84.6, it still meant that the top 1% of the population controlled 50.4% of the country's wealth (Credit Suisse 2019,168-69). As such, Thai elites have had ample need to create ideological justifications to legitimize their particular inequality regime.

Whether we use the term network monarchy (McCargo 2005) or perhaps the deep state (Mérieau 2016), we can see that elites in Thailand have expertly exercised Poggi's stratagem of mutual accommodation. Members of the Thai bureaucracy, business community, and armed forces have harnessed their social power in order to maintain their positions within Thai society. However, while they have strong connections to political, economic, and military power, they have lacked ideological power. Therefore, they have turned to an institution in Thai society that ably fills this gap.

The network of elites in Thailand seeking legitimacy have turned to the monarchy as a source of ideological power through "a sophisticated campaign by the military, the monarchy, the bureaucracy, and ethnic Chinese-owned commercial banks, to represent the overall economic development of the country in the guise of the ascetic practice of the *bodhisatta*-king" (Jory 2016, 180). Of course, it is axiomatic that for this to be effective, the institution of the monarchy needs to have its own form of legitimacy in the first place. After all, in material and spiritual senses, the king represents the apex of Thai society, and therefore, is the most unequal figure in it. Therefore, efforts must be then made to make sure that the king remains regarded as legitimate, and indeed as being the font of legitimacy. The Thai throne has attempted to resist Weber's understanding of political evolution by standing astride two pillars. Rather than transitioning from a traditional, divine footing to a modern, legalistic one, the Thai king is both sacrally and secularly relevant. The king maintains an amalgam of Hindu and Buddhist piety, derived from above, while simultaneously embodying popular sovereignty, derived from below.[2] Constitutionally, therefore, Thailand is described as "a democratic regime of government with the King as Head of State" (*Constitution of Thailand* 2017).

---

1. GINI coefficient is defined as "the extent to which the distribution of income among individuals or households within an economy deviates from a perfectly equal distribution. A Gini index of zero represents perfect equality and 100, perfect inequality" ("OECD Glossary of Statistical Terms - Gini Index Definition," n.d.).
2. For an extended discussion, see Connors 2008. For an opposing viewpoint, see Tejapira 2016.

Indeed, as styled in the preamble to the 2017 constitution, rather than being deposed by a coup of modernist reformers, it was the king who "graciously granted the Constitution" of 1932. As democracy has suffered of late in elite Thai political discourse, the emphasis of the king's legitimacy has shifted decidedly to the notion of merit.

In practice, it goes something like this: the king has *dharma* or *barami*; he has legitimacy through a form of sacredness or near holiness.[3] Those who serve and protect the king are able to get, indirectly, a piece of that holiness reflected upon themselves. This has a utility: nobody wants to be seen as a naked capitalist or the leader of a military *junta*. It is much better to be shrouded within the veil of legitimacy. *What I do, I do in the name of, and for the purpose of protecting, the King.* Furthermore, it is also useful for elites to protect their positions by claiming that any opposition to them and their policies represents opposition the King. And within the inequality regime that has been constructed, such opposition is—to put it mildly—problematic. Section 112 of the Thai Criminal Code ("Insulting or Defaming Royal Family") states that anyone who "defames, insults or threatens the King, the Queen, the Heir-apparent or the Regent, shall be punished with imprisonment of three to fifteen years." It would appear, then, that this source of ideological power is rather a good one to have on your side, given its virtual unassailability. Thus, the monarchy forms a cornerstone of the Thai inequality regime.

What I am suggesting here is not particularly new: the idea of gaining indirect or reflected merit is well described by Christina Gray (Gray 1986). However, there have been developments recently that make this different. The current king[4] is "hijacking" the regular process, a process that was, in and of itself, hijacked (Ünaldi 2012).

Under the previous reign (that of King Rama IX), the monarchy went through an evolution of legitimacy. By the end of the Second World War, the monarchy was not regarded particularly highly: it was an interesting traditional hangover but most of its land had been appropriated, most of its political power had been significantly neutered through the nation building process (started by King Rama V), the 1932 constitution, and the political infighting that took place during the Japanese occupation during the Second World War (Baker and Phongpaichit 2005; Handley 2006).

---

3. Indeed, there are those who hold out the king as a *somuttithep* or guardian angel (Gray 1986, 480). For an extended discussion of the concepts of *barami*, see Jory 2016.
4. King Maha Vajiralongkorn, known officially has King Rama X.

However, what the monarchy did possess was popular appeal. This popularity was harnessed by Field Marshall Sarit Thanarat, who was careful to frame his 1957 coup as having "royal support" as a way of shielding himself from accusations of personal ambition (Chaloemtiarana 2007). Moreover, Sarit portrayed his rule as a revolutionary, one founded on "the overthrow of Western democracy and creates a democratic system suitable to the special conditions of Thailand" (Chaloemtiarana 2007). One of these special conditions was the reverence of the monarchy. Indeed, as Chaloemtiarana asserts, "The Sarit coup of 1957 could be seen, in part, as an attempt to stop criticism against the throne" (Chaloemtiarana 2007, 108). It is here that we see the modern emergence of the pattern of reciprocal legitimacy: the elites boost the monarchy and the monarchy provides those elites with a special patina of legitimacy. This was particularly necessary in the case of Sarit because his government "had little historical basis for legitimacy compared with the leaders of the 1932 Revolution, whose claim to power rested on constitutionalism and their role in overthrowing absolute monarchy...Sensing the instability of its own foundation, the Sarit clique turned to the throne for support and legitimacy" (Chaloemtiarana 2007). This reliance on the king for support spurred Sarit to ensure that the monarchy as an institution and King Rama IX as an individual was heightened through a massive publicity campaign that included royal tours, both domestic and foreign. Sarit, it seems, was on to a winner: "As the prestige of the king increased, the government's popularity grew" (Chaloemtiarana 205).

This reflected prestige fit neatly into another ongoing process, that of American support for Thailand's anti-communist posture. King Rama IX's image was bolstered by both Sarit's Ministry of Interior and the United States Information Service as a unifying figure for the nation. The American involvement in this effort continued until 1979 and contributed greatly to both the public image and political utility of the monarchy (Rattanasengchanh 2019). This reanimation of the monarchy was not limited to waving from motorcars on junkets upcountry. Sarit re-introduced veneration rituals that had long disappeared, such as prostration and the annual royal procession down the Chao Praya River in Bangkok. The institution of the monarchy reclaimed a glory that had all but disappeared after the 1932 coup and in many ways had been abolished by royal modernizers themselves (Tejapira 2016).

As the reign of Rama IX went on, and political leaders came and went, the reputation of the king as a source of legitimacy increased. In turn, the monarchy transferred legitimacy to the other members of the elite through gestures such as the conferral of titles or other rituals of patronage.

There is no doubt that during his long reign King Rama IX was "cherished by the Thai people as a benevolent king, a sacred being and a sentient demi-god" (Rappa 2017, 3). This reputation was due in part to the notion that the king was above politics, separate from the sullying noise and compromise of the day to day running of the country. As Hewison makes clear, this was never truly the case: Rama IX was a shrewd political actor (Hewison 1997). His endorsements of the various coups d'état that occurred during his reign were, like the one carried out by Sarit, used as more than endorsements: they were debate enders, shutting down any meaningful public discussion of the legitimacy of military takeover or the subsequent junta put in place. Haberkorn is correct in saying that, whatever else may be true, one impact of the monarchy has been to create and maintain a "limited space for political expression" (Haberkorn 2017, 280).

What I want to highlight here is that for most of his reign, King Rama IX was rarely seen as an active participant in this process. He was always an object of legitimation, of veneration, not often an overt political actor. His occasional public interventions in politics—such as in 1992 when he scolded naughty politicians, or his cryptic speeches on his birthday—were all the more powerful due to their rarity. The king operated behind the scenes, preferring to exercise his influence through powerful public proxies, such as his privy councilor Prem Tinsulanond (McCargo 2005). As one Thai observer puts it "the monarchy is an elephant in the room of Thai politics, thanks not only to suppressive measures but probably due to the royalist ideology that puts the elephant under a cloak" (Winichakul 2014).

One of the most sustained contributions made by King Rama IX to the inequality regime operant in Thailand was his support for the sufficiency economy philosophy (SEP). Often criticized as being intellectually empty, the SEP was created in 1974 but came into prominence in the immediate aftermath of the 1997 Asian financial crisis. It relies on the King's sacred status as a means of letting Thais know that instead of questioning the wealth of others, they should strive to live sufficiently and to accept their position. It is an overt ideological justification for inequality. A 'royally endorsed' summary of the doctrine states that "Sufficiency economy is a philosophy that stresses the middle path as the *overriding principle for appropriate conduct* by the populace at all levels" (Mongsawad 2010, 127, emphasis added). Following coups in 2006 and 2014, the juntas both promoted SEP, hoping to leverage the legitimacy of the king in doing so (Macan-Markar 2007; Ministry of Foreign Affairs 2017). These efforts largely paid off. The government received international praise for SEP, including from the United Nations, as the SEP was linked to an example of "South-South development cooperation" in the furtherance of the Sustainable Development Goals. Within Thailand, as a royal initiative, SEP was protected from criticism. It served as a powerful plank in the platform of the inequality regime in large part because it bore the imprimatur of King Rama IX's personal popularity.

In contrast, the new King, Rama X, does not enjoy the same level of personal adoration as his father. Because he cannot rely on a spotless reputation, he has opted to take control of the legitimation process, relying on the myths surrounding the holiness and sacredness of the institution of the king, in an attempt to protect himself, making him, as the inheritor of King Rama IX's legacy, also beyond reproach or criticism.[5] In so doing, he has shifted from an object of veneration to an agent of his own legitimation, in the sense that he now has personalized rule and taken over some of those elements of social power that the previous king was content to leave with other elements of the wider network monarchy. For example since his father's death he has taken personal control of the Crown Property Bureau (BBC News 2018); taken over personal command of several military units (Reuters 2019); appointed his mistress as 'noble consort', breaking modern convention as well as a 1935 law against polygamy (Sydney Morning Herald 2019); subsequently stripping her of her titles (Economist 2019); and taking a personal, and much publicized, hand in firing several low-ranking palace staff (Reuters 2019b). Even in the political sphere, Rama X has been active. He rejected the version of the constitution presented to him for endorsement (Economist 2017); inserted changes to the long-standing articles on the appointment of a regent (Deutsche Welle 2017); and overhauled the size and membership of the Privy Council (Bangkok Post 2016). All of these unprecedented moves demonstrate Rama X's "growing aggrandizement of political power" (Chachavalpongpun 2018).

5. I will turn to the matter of assessing the effectiveness of this strategy later in this chapter.

Not all of King Rama X's moves have been so overt. Symbols celebrating the 1932 transition to constitutional monarchy have been removed
throughout Thailand. First a plaque commemorating the event disappeared
from the royal plaza in Bangkok (*Khaosod English* 2017). Later statues of
the leaders of the revolution were removed from a military base (*Khaosod
English* 2019).

There is one development that is at first counterintuitive, but is indicative of a wider move. It is the use of lèse majesté laws (Section 112
of the Thai criminal code). During the reign of Rama IX, these laws were
used to stifle criticism, not only of the king and his immediate family, but
the institution of the monarchy and policies associated with it. It was even
used to charge a Thai academic who questioned the veracity of a legend
about a 16th-century warrior king. Owing to the long sentences often im-
posed on those found guilty of an offense, lèse majesté led to a culture of
self-censorship. The law did not have to be wielded by the palace, but was
within the purview of regular prosecutors. Indeed, members of the public
could accuse others of violating Section 112 and the police were obliged to
open an investigation. After the 2014 coup, the use of prosecutions spiked
as means of shutting down dissent and criticism of the junta *qua* royal defenders (Struckfuss as cited in Chachavalpongpun 2020, 138). After assuming the throne, Rama X dismissed several high profile cases (which was not
entirely unprecedented: his father did so on several occasions). What is
significant is that he instructed the Attorney General to desist from these
kinds of prosecutions altogether (Ruffles 2018).

Some observers have wondered if this change of heart is an indication
of benevolence on the part of the new king (Struckfuss as cited in Chachavalpongpun 2020, 140). I offer a different possibility. I argue that the king
is not limiting prosecution out of genuine feelings of amity with his subjects. Rather it is yet another indication of the personalization of royal
power. He is denying the network monarchy the opportunity to wield this
legal sword, ostensibly as a means of protecting his honor. He is reserving
for his personal use the ability to defend himself. Moreover, the disappear-
ance and deaths of some royal critics suggest that benevolence is not the
only possible explanation (Ellis-Petersen 2019).

What is even more interesting is that while prosecutions under Section 112 have indeed been slashed, the government has continued their

quest to quash criticism of the ruling regime. As Sunai Phasuk, a researcher with Human Rights Watch in Thailand puts it, "While there has been a
sharp drop in lese-majeste prosecutions, Thai authorities have switched to
using other laws, such as the Computer-Related Crime Act and sedition law,
to prosecute critics..." (Ruffles 2018; see also TLHR 2019).

It would appear that the king has designs on returning to some form
of absolutism (Chachavalpongpun 2018). Especially given the erasure of
the symbols of the 1932 revolt, King Rama X wants to dismiss any notion
that he is merely a figurehead. This is not to say that the king has depart-
ed from all of the previous conventions. On the eve of the 2019 election,
for instance, he issued a royal announcement, reminding his people that
they should cast their votes for "good people," urging them to "to perform...
[their] duty, for harmony, national security, and the people's happiness, and
to recall the legacy of His Majesty the late King Bhumibol and Her Majesty
Queen Sirikit of King Rama IX, who always have love and concern for the
nation and people" (*Prachatai English* 2019). Innocuous enough, perhaps,
but "[t]he term 'good people' is not neutral in Thai political discourse. Since
well before the coup in 2014, conservatives have used it time and again
against their opponents" (*Prachatai English* 2019; see also Thompson 2020).

In a bold break with past practice, especially noticeable during the final years of his father's long reign, King Rama X has repeatedly exercised
his personal prerogative in a bid to ensure that he controls not only the dis-
pensation of legitimacy, but also amasses other sources of social power as
well. No longer content to share power with the wider network monarchy
in the way that his father did, King Rama X has made concerted efforts to
break away from Poggi's pattern of mutual accommodation. Rather than
being only the holder of ideological power, the monarch has consolidated
his control over economic, military, and political power as well.

SO WHAT?

It is tempting to interpret this move as a signal that since social power
is being consolidated in Thailand, we might expect a more stable, albeit
more arbitrary and less democratic, round of politics (Rappa 2017). However, such an interpretation is likely to turn out to be far too optimistic.
Instead, we can see that the king's attempt to personalize rule is having
precisely the effects that we might expect when viewed through Mann's

social power lens. And these effects are precisely what the other elements of the Thai inequality regime have long dreaded.

Rather than rely on mutual accommodation, the king has taken steps to go it alone, attempting to draw on all sources of social power, cutting out the need for dependency on the elements of the wider network monarchy. Without the reliable participation of the king himself, the network monarchy is left without a key player. The results of this lacuna are now visible and confirm the fears of elites. For example, the military has realized that it does not have the legitimacy it craves. The military seems painfully aware that it is fallible and well within the ambit of public criticism. Three recent events in particular have illustrated this. The worst active shooter incident in Thai history took place in February 2020; the gunmen was an active duty non-commissioned officer from the Thai army. It was later revealed that the soldier stole a weapon from a base armory, as he was upset over a business deal involving his superior officer. When the shooting spree was over, 29 people were dead. The public was shocked. In a speech, the army commander, General Apirat Kongsompong, expressed his condolences to the families of the deceased but attempted to shield the institution from criticism by declaring, "Don't blame the army...The military is a sacred national security organisation" (*Bangkok Post* 2020). The general's comment is entirely consistent with its self-generated and prevailing "ideology [that] locates it (the military) as a servant of monarchy—the most traditional of the Thai elite" (Sripokangkul and Chambers 2017, 2).

Despite considerable theatrics—the general wept as he delivered his address—his assertion fell on deaf ears. Writing shortly after the incident, a prominent columnist began her piece with a stunning sentence: "The Thai army is a closed system governed by feudal authoritarianism which breeds corruption and abuse of power" (Ekachai 2020). In her assault, she did not just single out the army: her contempt for other key institutions, all prominent components of the network monarchy, demonstrated that whatever legitimacy each possessed, it was not universally recognized across Thai society. "Is it a coincidence that these three autocratic organisations [the army, the clergy, and the police] are ridden with corruption, power abuse, and violence? Is this why they are fiercely resistant to external oversight and public calls for reform to protect their power?" (Ekachai 2020).

Indeed, the army continues to be subject to increased public dissatisfaction. The practice of conscription has long been resented by Thais; especially those non-elite Thais who are unable to evade it. In addition to its very existence, criticism has grown over abuses of power levied against conscripts. Many are used as "military maids" performing domestic chores for senior officers, but more alarming are stories of ritualized physical and sexual abuse of recruits. Thais have decided to vote with their bodies: this year the army has expressed dismay over the poor conversion rate, the number of conscripts who "re-up" and choose to remain in the military after their compulsory service (Macan-Markar 2020).

Thailand has (so far) managed the COVID-19 crisis well. Its strong health care sector has enabled the country to avoid catastrophic casualty figures. However, public criticism has been levied on the army nonetheless. For example, "The first major community-based transmission cluster infecting well over 100 people was linked to an Army-owned Thai Boxing ring in Bangkok, sparking questions: why does the Army own a boxing ring, and why was the Army not following the government's own social distancing guidelines?" (Abuza 2020).

The army's shield of legitimacy is failing them. And it is worth noting that even as these assaults mount, the palace has been silent, leaving the military even more exposed and alone.

Similarly, the nominally civilian elected government, led by former general and coup instigator Prayuth Chanocha, is feeling the heat. The king's unwillingness to 'play along' with the usual script was in evidence immediately after the death of King Rama IX (as discussed above). Such recalcitrance has reduced the overall social power available to Prayuth. He attempted to gain his own store of ideological power through the ballot box, but his poor showing in, and the illiberal nature of, the 2019 elections failed to deliver. This dual effect has left him significantly weakened. This makes him less valuable to other elements of the network monarchy. Indeed, showing support for an unpopular figure, already sullied in the eyes of much of the elite and Hi-So "middle class" (Thai parlance for the neo-proprietarian class, a modified take on British 'high society') electorate merely by dint of being a politician, can be a liability to those looking to boost their own image. Veteran observer of Thai military-political relations, Paul Chambers, posits that Prayuth's control over the armed forces is no longer guaranteed (Chambers 2019).

Prayuth's support from the wielders of economic power and co-network members is similarly in jeopardy. The so-called Big Five family-run conglomerates have done well since the 2014 coup and have been important backers of the military and the government. Struggling to sustain the response to COVID-19, Prayuth leant on the country's wealthiest families, publically calling for them to pitch in. This has backfired: it has exposed the government's own weak fiscal position and called attention to the yawning economic inequality in Thailand (Crispin 2019; Abuza 2020).

For many decades, the system of control, a combination of both formal and informal measures enacted by both state and non-state institutions, has worked reasonably well to prop up the inequality regime in Thailand. As Michael Nelson points out "[w]hat we witnessed in the [2016] referendum vote [on the new constitution]...was a conscious consolidation of authoritarian structures, an acceptance by a majority of citizens of their disempowerment, including a substantive reduction of their role as the genuine sovereign of the Thai political order" (Nelson 2016).

It is possible, in hindsight, to see this as the high-water mark for the inequality regime. Despite the existence of ideological cover, coupled with repressive laws and extrajudicial violence, anti-royalism has long existed in Thailand (Anderson 1993; Anonymous 2018). Indeed, we may be seeing an increase in critique of the royal edifice. Ekachai's blistering critique of the army (mentioned above) was barely restrained by the bounds of self-censorship, and it made allusions to the fact that times and people's expectations were changing: "This is the 21st century. Like any organizations stuck in outdated traditions, the military must catch up with the times. Respecting people's voices is a good start" (Ekachai 2020). In a society accustomed to self-censorship and elliptical references where the monarchy is involved, her targeting of "organizations stuck in outdated traditions" is ambiguous enough to carry a strong message. More directly, the king's behavior has been the target of ridicule on social media. After commenting on a scandal involving the inconvenience surrounding the movement of royal motorcade through Bangkok, a 25-year old was arrested under the Computer Crimes Act (*The Bangkok Post* 2019). More recently, King Rama X's absence from Thailand, amplified by stories of his "self-isolating" in a luxury spa in Bavaria with a harem of twenty companions, during the onset of the COVID-19 pandemic, led to over a million instances of #whydoweneedaking (*Reuters* 2020; Ng 2020).

As the patina of legitimacy of the throne continues to flake away, the impact will be felt by the other elements of the network. As Abuza notes, the army is already feeling it: "The defense of the monarchy is not just a constitutional responsibility, but the central justification for the military's incessant meddling in politics. And yet, they are defending a monarch who has spent most of the crisis outside of the country" (Abuza 2020).

WHAT COMES NEXT?

We are witnessing a significant weakening of the mechanism of mutual accommodation that has so well served the Thai inequality regime. We could even be witnessing the beginning of its total collapse.

It is evident that we must revise our appreciation of the network monarchy. We cannot assume that it enjoys harmonious relations between its constituent elements. We must see recent events as "a challenge to the notion of a unitary "network monarchy" hiding behind Thai politics" (A. A. Johnson 2019). Furthermore, we need to ensure that we do not lose sight of the monarch in the monarchy. Perhaps what has been viewed as a functional institutional arrangement needs to be understood as a contingent condominium, possible in large part because of the persona of King Rama IX. To the extent that the legitimacy shared amongst the elites was the produce of a particular set of conditions—some real and some mythic—inherent in one person, perhaps the network monarchy's golden age deserves the label of "Bhumibol Consensus" (Tejapira 2019). The actions of the current king have been insufficient to generate similar levels of legitimacy through devotion. He is now attempting to offset this by his own version of mutual accommodation—the increased personal control over the other sources of social power. But if the king is just a normal power holder and one without the personal appeal or "backwards legitimacy" of his father (Ünaldi 2012), and "[i]f monarchical authority can function in the same way as political authority, there may be no room for power outside the constitution. The military, then, would be set adrift without a source of legitimacy for its actions. Such a situation might mean a world where the military is accountable to Thai civilians for its actions" (Johnson 2019).

We can see clearly that when one variable is removed or drastically altered, the formula of mutual accommodation fails to compute. The centrality of the monarchy as the lynchpin of Thai politics is not natural, not the product of bottom up culture, nor should it be regarded as "a foregone conclusion" (Pecastaing 2019). It is a social construct, the result of sustained effort. Struggling to adjust to the post-Bhumibol reality, we see that the elite network is alive and shifting as it struggles for either self-sufficiency (i.e., access to more, and ideally, all sources of social power) or a new formula for mutual accommodation. Legitimacy is, after all, a social process (Johnson, Dowd, and Ridgeway 2006). It must be broadly accepted in order for it to be effective.

The co-dependency of the network monarchy means that if you cannot supply the others with elements of social power they need, you are at risk of being pushed aside. The co-dependency is such, in the Thai case, that each element is necessary. No one on their own has proven themselves capable—so far—of autonomous standing. In the starkest terms, it is a case of hanging together or hanging separately. As Chambers observes, the network dynamic is such that it is prone to "domino effects": "Prayuth is no paladin of popularity. What is more, history shows that Thailand is coup-prone. If Thailand's regal institution loses patience with him, the army... could easily become restless" (Chambers 2019). Far from being a cozy arrangement, the network monarchy is a cutthroat alliance of self-interest, where the underlying operant norm is scratch my back or get out of the way while I find someone else who can.

As Michael Montesano observes, "Ideology has tried to depoliticize the Thai political sphere, but we may now be seeing an increase in the room allowed for 'normal' political discourse" (Montesano et al. 2019). Within that discourse there will undoubtedly be calls for greater democracy and equality.

Where this will end up is not easy to forecast. We will probably see Prayuth removed from the scene, as he appears to have lost the support of the army, the business elites, the palace, and the people. We may also see increased attempts at overt repression as a stop-gap measure to forestall public dissatisfaction manifesting itself as violence (Kunst et al. 2017). This would be in keeping with the pattern of behavior of the military in Thailand, particularly after the 2014 coup. In either of these scenarios it is highly likely that the king will be involved in the decision making, if only so far as giving quiet assent to any action taken. There is a third possibility though. Political dynamism and a desire for some kind of responsive government may be able to be delayed and even constrained, but it cannot be wished away entirely. We may yet see the people take back the mantel of legitimacy and develop a system that meets their aspirations.

Bibliography

Abuza, Zachary. 2020. "In Thailand, the Men in Green Have the Blues." *BenarNews*, April 24. https://www.benarnews.org/english/commentaries/asean-security-watch/thai-military-04242020150555.html.

Anderson, Benedict. 1993. "Radicalism after Communism in Thailand and Indonesia." *New Left Review*.

Ankersen, Christopher. 2014. "The Evolution of Civil–Military Cooperation in Peace and War." *The Politics of Civil-Military Cooperation: Canada in Bosnia, Kosovo, and Afghanistan*, edited by Christopher Ankersen, 36–50. Rethinking Peace and Conflict Studies. London: Palgrave Macmillan UK. https://doi.org/10.1057/9781137003355_3.

Anonymous. 2018. "Anti-Royalism in Thailand Since 2006: Ideological Shifts and Resistance." *Journal of Contemporary Asia*, February. https://www.tandfonline.com/doi/pdf/10.1080/00472336.2018.1427021?needAccess=true.

The Bangkok Post. 2016. "King Appoints 10 Members to His Privy Council," December 6. https://www.bangkokpost.com/thailand/general/1152824/king-appoints-10-members-to-his-privy-council.

———. 2019. "Man Arrested amid #royalmotorcade Controversy," October 8. https://www.bangkokpost.com/thailand/general/1767574/man-arrested-amid-royalmotorcade-controversy.

———. 2020. "'Don't Blame Army,'" February 12. https://www.bangkokpost.com/thailand/general/1855334/dont-blame-army.

BBC News. 2018. "Thai King Takes Control of Crown Assets," June 16, sec. Asia. https://www.bbc.com/news/world-asia-44507590.

Chachavalpongpun, Pavin. 2018. "Beware the Thailand King's New Power Play." *The Diplomat*, October 12. https://thediplomat.com/2018/10/beware-the-thailand-kings-new-power-play/.

———. 2018. "The Return of Royal Absolutism Under Thailand's King Vajiralongkorn." *Forsea* (blog), December 7. https://forsea.co/the-return-of-royal-absolutism-under-thailands-king-vajiralongkorn/.

———, ed. 2020. Routledge Handbook of Contemporary Thailand. Abingdon, Oxon ; New York: Routledge.

Chaloemtiarana, Thak. 2007. *Thailand: The Politics of Despotic Paternalism*. Studies on Southeast Asia, no. 42. Ithaca, N.Y: Southeast Asia Program Publications.

Chambers, Paul. 2019. "What If Thailand's Junta Can't Control the Military?" *New Mandala* (blog). March 14. https://www.newmandala.org/what-if-thailands-junta-cant-control-the-military/.

Crispin, Shawn W. 2019. "Thailand's 'Five Families' Prop and Imperil Prayut." *Asia Times*, December 13. https://asiatimes.com/2019/12/thailands-five-families-prop-and-imperil-prayut/.

Deutsche Welle. 2017. "Thai Parliament Backs Constitutional Changes Allowing King Easier Travel," January 13. https://www.dw.com/en/thai-parliament-backs-constitutional-changes-allowing-king-easier-travel/a-37121671.

Economist. 2017. "Thailand's New King Rejects the Army's Proposed Constitution," January 24. http://www.economist.com/asia/2017/01/14/thailands-new-king-rejects-the-armys-proposed-constitution.

———. 2019. "King Vajiralongkorn Dismisses His Official Mistress," October 24. http://www.economist.com/asia/2019/10/24/king-vajiralongkorn-dismisses-his-official-mistress.

Ekachai, Sanitsuda. 2020. "Army Not Sacred nor above Criticism." *Bangkok Post*, February 15. https://www.bangkokpost.com/opinion/opinion/1857964/army-not-sacred-nor-above-criticism.

Ellis-Petersen, Hannah. 2019. "Murder on the Mekong: Why Exiled Thai Dissidents Are Abducted and Killed." *The Observer*, March 17, sec. World news. https://www.theguardian.com/world/2019/mar/17/thailand-dissidents-murder-mekong-election.

Gray, Christina. 1986. "Thailand: The Soteriological State in the 1970s, Volume 1." PhD, Chicago: University of Chicago.

Haberkorn, Tyrell. 2017. "The Anniversary of a Massacre and the Death of a Monarch." *The Journal of Asian Studies* 76 (2): 269–81. https://doi.org/10.1017/S0021911817000018.

Handley, Paul M. 2006. *The King Never Smiles: A Biography of Thailand's Bhumibol Adulyadej*. New Haven: Yale University Press.

Hewison, Kevin, ed. 1997. *Political Change in Thailand: Democracy and Participation*. Politics in Asia Series. London ; New York: Routledge.

Johnson, Andrew Alan. 2019. "New Networks in Thai Royal Politics." *New Mandala* (blog). February 12. https://www.newmandala.org/new-networks-in-thai-royal-politics/.

Johnson, Cathryn, Timothy J. Dowd, and Cecilia L. Ridgeway. 2006. "Legitimacy as a Social Process." *Annual Review of Sociology* 32: 53–78. https://www.jstor.org/stable/29737731.

Jory, Patrick. 2016. *Thailand's Theory of Monarchy: The Vessantara Jataka and the Idea of the Perfect Man.* Albany: State University of New York Press.

Khaosod English. 2017. "City Hall Instructed to Remove 11 CCTVs Before 1932 Plaque Taken," April 19. https://www.khaosodenglish.com/politics/2017/04/19/city-hall-instructed-remove-11-cctvs-1932-plaque-taken/.

———. 2019. "Statues of 1932 Revolt Leaders to Be Removed," December 28. https://www.khaosodenglish.com/politics/2019/12/28/statues-of-1932-revolt-leaders-to-be-removed/amp/?_twitter_impression=true.

Kunst, Jonas R., Ronald Fischer, Jim Sidanius, and Lotte Thomsen. 2017. "Preferences for Group Dominance Track and Mediate the Effects of Macro-Level Social Inequality and Violence across Societies." *Proceedings of the National Academy of Sciences*, May. https://doi.org/10.1073/pnas.1616572114.

Macan-Markar, Marwaan. 2007. "Thailand: Junta Revives King's 'Sufficiency Economy' Model | Inter Press Service." January 17. http://www.ipsnews.net/2007/01/thailand-junta-revives-kings-sufficiency-economy-model/.

———. 2020. "Thai Military Battles Loss of Recruits as Abuses Come to Light." *Nikkei Asian Review*, April 24. https://asia.nikkei.com/Politics/Turbulent-Thailand/Thai-military-battles-loss-of-recruits-as-abuses-come-to-light.

Mann, Michael. 1986. *The Sources of Social Power.* Cambridge [Cambridgeshire] ; New York: Cambridge University Press.

McCargo, Duncan. 2005. "Network Monarchy and Legitimacy Crises in Thailand." *The Pacific Review* 18 (4): 499–519. https://doi.org/10.1080/09512740500338937.

Mérieau, Eugénie. 2016. "Thailand's Deep State, Royal Power and the Constitutional Court (1997–2015)." *Journal of Contemporary Asia* 46 (3): 445–66. https://doi.org/10.1080/00472336.2016.1151917.

Ministry of Foreign Affairs. 2017. "Sufficiency Economy Philosophy: Thailand's Path towards Sustainable Development Goals." 2nd edition. Bangkok: Ministry of Foreign Affairs of Thailand.

Mongsawad, Prasopchoke. 2010. "The Philosophy of the Sufficiency Economy: A Contribution to the Theory of Development." *Asia-Pacific Development Journal* 17 (1): 123–43.

Montesano, Michael John, Terence Chong, Mark Heng, and ISEAS-Yusof Ishak Institute, eds. 2019. *After the Coup: The National Council for Peace and Order Era and the Future of Thailand.* Singapore: ISEAS-Yusof Ishak Institute.

Nelson, Michael. 2016. "Authoritarian Constitution-Making in Thailand, 2015-16: Elite (Aphichon) Capture Turns a 'Dual Polity' into a 'System of Elite Rule with Elections,' or a 'Thai-Style Authoritarianism.'" Working Paper 188. Southeast Asia Research Centre Working Papers. Hong Kong: City University of Hong Kong.

Ng, Kate. 2020. "Coronavirus: Thai King Self-Isolates in Alpine Hotel with Harem of 20 Women amid Pandemic." *The Independent,* March 29, 2020. https://www.independent.co.uk/news/world/europe/coronavirus-thailand-king-maha-vajiralongkorn-grand-hotel-sonnebichl-germany-a9431936.html.

"OECD Glossary of Statistical Terms - Gini Index Definition." n.d. Accessed April 25, 2020. https://stats.oecd.org/glossary/detail.asp?ID=4842.

Pasuk Phongpaichit, and Christopher John Baker, eds. 2015. *Unequal Thailand: Aspects of Income, Wealth, and Power.* Singapore: NUS Press.

Pecastaing, Camille. 2019. "The King, the Junta, and the Juggernaut: Thailand and Counter-Democratization." *The American Interest* (blog). March 22. https://www.the-american-interest.com/2019/03/22/the-king-the-junta-and-the-juggernaut-thailand-and-counter-democratization/.

Piketty, Thomas. 2020. *Capital and Ideology.* Translated by Arthur Goldhammer. Cambridge, MA: Harvard University Press.

Poggi, Gianfranco. 2001. *Forms of Power.* Cambridge, MA: Polity Press.

Prachatai English. 2019. "'Support Good People to Rule This Country,' Says King of Thailand on Eve of Election." March 24. https://prachatai.com/english/node/7990.

Rappa, Antonio L. 2017. *The King and the Making of Modern Thailand.* Routledge Contemporary Southeast Asia Series 87. New York: Routledge.

Rattanasengchanh, Phimmasone M. 2019. "Thai Hearts and Minds: The Public Diplomacy and Public Relations Programs of the United States Information Service and Thai Ministry of Interior." Ohio University. https://etd.ohiolink.edu/pg_10?::NO:10:P10_ETD_SUBID:176514.

Reuters. 2019. "Thailand's King Takes Personal Control of Two Key Army Units," October 1. https://www.reuters.com/article/us-thailand-king-idUSKBN1WG4ED.

———. 2020. "Coronavirus Pandemic Prompts Rare Questioning of Thai Monarchy," March 22. https://www.reuters.com/article/us-health-coronavirus-thailand-monarchy-idUSKBN21918F.

Ruffles, Michael. 2018. "Lese-Majeste Is Dead. Long Live Lese-Majeste." *The Sydney Morning Herald.* November 22. https://www.smh.com.au/world/asia/lese-majeste-is-dead-long-live-lese-majeste-20181121-p50hbz.html.

Scott, James C. 2017. "Take Your Pick." *The London Review of Books,* October 19.

Smith, R. W. 1970. "The Concept of Legitimacy." *Theoria: A Journal of Social and Political Theory,* no. 35: 17–29. https://www.jstor.org/stable/41801858.

Sripokangkul, Siwach, and Paul Chambers. 2017. "Returning Soldiers to the Barracks: Military Reform as the Crucial First Step in Democratising Thailand." *Pertanika Journal of Social Sciences & Humanities* 25 (1): 1–20.

Swidler, Ann. 1986. "Culture in Action: Symbols and Strategies." *American Sociological Review* 51 (2): 273–86. https://doi.org/10.2307/2095521.

Sydney Morning Herald. 2019. "Recently Married Thai King Presents New Consort to the World." August 27. https://www.smh.com.au/world/asia/recently-married-thai-king-presents-new-consort-to-the-world-20190827-p52l58.html.

Tejapira, Kasian. 2016. "The Irony of Democratization and the Decline of Royal Hegemony in Thailand." *Southeast Asian Studies* 5 (2): 219–37.

———. 2019. "Thailand's First Elections in the Post-Bhumibol Era." *New Mandala* (blog). January 23, 2019. https://www.newmandala.org/thailands-first-elections-in-the-post-bhumibol-era/.

Thai Lawyers for Human Rights. 2019. "Changes in Thailand's Lèse Majesté Prosecutions in 2018." *Thai Lawyers for Human Rights* (blog). January 15. https://www.tlhr2014.com/?p=10431&lang=en.

Thompson, Mark R. 2020. "The Good Versus the Many 'Good Governance' and Democracy in Thailand and the Philippines." *Governance and Democracy in the Asia-Pacific : Political and Civil Society.* New York: Taylor and Francis.

Ünaldi, Serhat. 2012. "Modern Monarchs and Democracy: Thailand's Bhumibol Adulyadej and Juan Carlos of Spain." *Journal of Current Southeast Asian Affairs* 31 (2): 5–34.

Winichakul, Thongchai. 2014. "The Monarchy and Anti-Monarchy Two Elephants in the Room of Thai Politics and the State of Denial." *"Good Coup" Gone Bad.* ed. Pavin Chachavalpongpun, 79-108. Singapore: ISEAS.

Chapter 3

Bonds of Loyalty & Bonds of Royalty: The Role of Cham Muslims in the New Mandala of Hun Sen's Cambodia

William Noseworthy

INTRODUCTION

Recognition of the repression of local press and political dissent, broad sweeping human rights abuses, and the potential re-transformation of Cambodia into a single-party state reached a new peak in the international press circa the 2018 elections in the mainland Southeast Asian state. As the results were announced, the Cambodian People's Party (*Kanakpak Pracheachon Kâmpuchéa*, CPP) celebrated. They now controlled the legislature, the executive, the judiciary, and virtually every district and provincial level government seat, almost unanimously, and all under Prime Minister Hun Sen. Hun Sen thus remains one of the single longest ruling heads of state in the entire continent of Asia, only to be outdone by Sayyid Ali Hosseini Khamenei, Supreme Leader of the Islamic Republic of Iran. Sullivan (2016) composed an excellent study of factors in Cambodian electoral politics, especially focusing on international complacency and the role of the local ruling elite in establishing networks to support Hun Sen's lengthy rule. Yet, the study was published just before the critical 2017 communal elections and thus before full understanding of the extent of repression over any and all realistic political opposition leading up through the 2018 general elections. Numerous other excellent studies and reports, including Amer (2006) and Hutt (2016), have noted the vital position that discussions of the Vietnamese minority community have played in Cambodian politics. The Cambodia National Rescue Party (CNRP), *the* opposition party in Cambodia politics, for example, became particularly well-known for deploying anti-Vietnamese rhetoric in attempts to gain popularity among nationalist elements of the voting public. Nonetheless, there has not yet been a scholarly study reflecting upon the important role of Cham Muslim communities in contemporary Cambodian electoral politics. Studies on Cham Muslim communities in Cambodia tend to focus on three areas: first, dealing with the memory of the genocide in Cambodia that occurred between 1975 and 1979; second, anthropological studies focused on language, religion, and culture; and third, historical studies focused predominantly on either the arrival of Cham communities in Cambodia, or their gradually transforming notions of religious practice. This is not to say that these studies are not important and should not continue. It is simply to note that the direct links between deeper historical trends and contemporary electoral politics are often glossed over. Additionally, among the most recent and best historical monographs in the field of Cham Studies focused on Cambodian communities, Philipp Bruckmayr adopts an analytical lens that accepts both Malay and Meccan centered discourses, thus de-coupling Cham positionalities from mainland Southeast Asian contexts and linguistic frameworks (Bruckmayr 2019). Nonetheless drawing inspiration from the meticulous studies of Bruckmayr, in this work, I aim to demonstrate how historical conditions have shaped the positions of Cham communities in general conceptions of contemporary Cambodian politics. In this chapter, I draw upon historicized press as well as anthropological accounts, fieldwork in Cham communities between 2012 and 2014, archival documents from the National Archives of Cambodia, and the record of Cham Manuscripts, to argue Hun Sen has effectively established a political network that allows him to stand in the position of *de facto* monarch, mobilizing historical memory and a royally approved network of clerics to secure political power.

In this chapter, I demonstrate the formation of a *new mandala* of pa-tron-client relations for Hun Sen. This *new mandala* allows him to assert himself as a duly elected head of state of a multi-party parliamentary de-mocracy, while simultaneously standing in for the monarch, and transform-ing Cambodia into a single-party state.[1] While this process was enacted by the mobilization of power networks and confirmed, or perhaps better said, "rubber stamped," by electoral results, it was also aided by historically con-tingent factors. First, the current king, Norodom Sihamoni, serves only as monarch because he was approved by a small nine person council in 2004, a council that included Hun Sen (Weggel 2007). Second, the well-recognized figure associated with the monarchy, Norodom Sihanouk—Sihamoni's father —passed away in 2012 (Chen 2012). While Sihanouk formed his own royalist

---

1. Here, I am drawing, naturally, from O.W. Wolter's *mandala* model of socio-political organization for pre-colonial Southeast Asia (Wolters 1999).

political positions—most famously with the Sangkum and FUNCIPEC parties—with his death, the potential of a royalist position in Cambodian electoral politics evaporated. A third, lesser discussed factor, is an illustration of the transformation. The Cham Muslim community historically held a very important symbolic relationship with the Cambodian monarchs (Noseworthy 2017; Pérez-Pereiro 2012). In the contemporary political context, the reformulation of this relationship has allowed the Cambodian head of state to emphasize his claims to a pluralistic liberal democracy, vis-a-vis this symbolic relationship, in addition to asserting the position of "stand in" for the monarchy. This is not to say Cham Muslim leadership and communities do not benefit, necessarily, from having a peaceful, if not amicable, relationship with the Cambodian head of state. Indeed, relationships have been complex in the historical past, with various communities and leaders splitting into pro- and anti- royalist factions, especially in the 19th century (CM 38 [8]; CM 29 [37]; CM 49–52; Weber 2011; Nguyễn Văn Luận 1974; Zain bin Musa 2001). Furthermore, they were disastrously fraught during the genocidal Khmer Rouge's establishment of the Democratic Kampuchea (DK) regime under Pol Pot from 1975–1979 (De Nike et al. 2000, 523–552).[2] During this period the Cham Muslim community was targeted explicitly, with estimates ranging up to 80% of the clerics executed, resulting eventually in the verdict of Case 002 at the Extraordinary Chambers of the Courts of Cambodia (ECCC) (Osman 2006; 2005; 2002; Kiernan 2008, 251-310; Ganesan and Sung 2013, 257-277; Peou 2013). Hence, it is understandable that the overarching push from the most senior leadership in Cham Muslim religious communities has been to maintain extremely friendly relations with Hun Sen, to the point that they have proven willing to participate in events that might otherwise be ruled "propagandistic" in their nature. The key actors in this narrative are Cambodian state officials and their appointed ministers. These individuals might be Cambodian or Cham. In the past, they would have been associated directly with the monarchy, although from the 1990s onward they were associated with more contemporary secular structures, including membership in both the royalist FUNCIPEC party and Hun Sen's CPP (Bruckmary 2006). Such officials include the religious elites of Cham communities, who mediate between the state, on the one hand, and the

---

2. There was an immediate tribunal that charged DK leadership, in absentia, with genocide.

laity on the other. Thus, their relationships are both bottom-down and top-up, especially as religious elites of Cham communities have often operated as members of the state apparatus, solidifying both formal and informal relations with state power. Currently, estimates for the Cham population in Cambodia reach between 600,000 and 800,000—concentrated especially in Battambang, Kampong Cham, and the suburban communities southward of the Tonlé Sap, through Phnom Penh and Kandal, to Sihanoukville – making up anywhere between 3% and 5% of the total population. While the percentage of the total population may be too small to decide an election that is not hotly contested, the traditional place and organization of Cham communities in Cambodian society, as fishing villages, along river banks, as trading centers, and with a relatively centralized religious hierarchy, offers ample opportunities for symbolic brokerage.

The key actor in this chapter from the 19th century onward is the *mufti*, the number one real and symbolic broker of relations for Cham Muslim communities in Cambodia. Subordinate to them, *imam* and *katip* clerics are furthermore local brokers that have been traditionally embedded into the royal administration of the kingdom. The *mufti*, however, when the office has been well-defined and not contested, would be the senior cleric of the Cham Muslim community. During the 19th and 20th centuries, the *mufti* operated with simultaneous approval from the Cambodian monarchy and the French Colonial government. There are numerous, quite complex, ever changing, specific titles for this position. Additionally, we have evidence from periods of Cambodian history, such as the period of Marcel Ner's research in the 1930s, where the office was clearly contested (NAC 745, RSC 8465; NAC 811, RSC 9200; NAC 2968, RSC 25968; NAC 3052, RSC 27641; NAC 3310, RSC 30380; Ner 1941). Nonetheless, the general position of a *mufti*, operating with royal approval, was maintained, and maintained through the transition to post-conflict Cambodia, although the nature of the position did shift over time. The first notable nature of this shift is the physical geographical location of the office of the *mufti*. To establish some context, we should note that when the monarch of Cambodia, King Ibrahim I of Longvek, converted to Islam vis-a-vis a marriage relationship in the 17th century—as the only figure in the history of the Cambodian monarchy to do so—the Cham, Malay, and Cham-Malay communities in Cambodia became ubiquitously known as "*chvea*" in the early modern records. However, any potential expansion of Muslim influence in Cambodian court politics was truncated with Vietnamese intervention, as were any potential lines of succession (Garneir 1871; Mak 1981). Later, in the 19th century, a mystic named Imam San formed a notable relationship with the Cambodian monarch, Ang Duong, which resulted in the special recognition of his community in the vicinity of the capital at Oudong (Noseworthy 2014a; Trankel 2003; Stock 2010). Yet, upon Ang Duong's death in 1860, the monarchy was even further weakened and with the French conquest of Cambodia in 1865, the royal networks were manipulated. King Norodom, Ang Duong's son, opted to move the capital to Phnom Penh in 1866 and while the *Kaum Imam San*,[3] as Imam San's community was called, retained prominence at Oudong, including in relation with the royally approved Buddhist *sangha*, their influence in the new capital was non-existent.

A new administration emerged in the mid-to-late 19th century, one that incorporated the clerics who were already approved as regents (*Oknha*) or provincial authorities (*Preah Balat*) with royal approval. Such positions were predominantly held by non-Muslims, but they were also commonly held by the clerical elite (*qadi*) in the context of Cham Muslim communities. Gradually, the *Kaum Imam San* were subordinated to the new office of a *mufti*, situated at Sangkat Chrouy Changva, a fishing and trading outpost on a peninsula that juts out into the Tonlé Sap and Mekong rivers, just across the Tonlé Sap River from the downtown boulevards that lead to the royal palace, only a short boat ride away on the royal barges or an available fishing vessel. Here, despite the occasional dispute over succession, the *mufti* acted as a mediator between the French state, the Khmer royalty, and Muslim communities for the next 100 years (NAC 3115, RSC 28319; Noseworthy 2017).[4] During the post-colonial epoch, although King Norodom Sihanouk was forced to face an ever-changing political landscape,[5] the office of the *mufti*, in effect, did not change its general location. However, when the Khmer Rouge entered Phnom Penh in 1975, the office was forcibly abandoned (Zain bin Musa 2011; Zain bin Musa 2001). Although the DK regime was deposed with the support of the People's Army of Vietnam (PAVN) and a new People's Republic of Kampuchea (*Sathéaranakrâth Prachemeanit Kâmpuchéa* PRK) was established in 1979, the office of the *mufti* and

3. Kaum is Malay for "group." Contemporary Cham L1 speakers sometimes use the colloquial Chamized word "Kan" as in "Kan Imam San," although the Cham word for group is kawem or kawom.
4. Clear evidence of the subordination appears by the 1930s.
5. An example occurred with Hun Sen, in particular, especially after a wave of Buddhist activism in 1991, which allowed Hun Sen to reconcile with Sihanouk (Juergensmeyer 2008, 146).

Cambodian Muslim communities were not fully restored, even as Hun Sen became the head of state in 1985. Indeed, it was only during the transition-ary period of the State of Cambodia (1989–1991) and the subsequent res-toration of the Kingdom of Cambodia (1991/1993–Present) that the office of the *mufti* has been restored, with the appointment of Sos Kamry as the *Grand Mufti* of post-conflict Cambodia (Radio France 2007). The important implication here is that there could not be a senior cleric in Cambodia *with-out* a royal appointment. Consequentially, the organization of clerics across the country was also not as centralized. By restoring the monarchy, there was the ability to restore the position of the senior cleric. By establishing the office of the senior cleric, there was a head patriarch for the Muslim community in Cambodia. This would then create an intermediary office, the office of the *mufti*, for support funds from Malay, Kuwaiti, Saudi, or oth-er Muslim aid associations to work through. Additionally, appointments to provincial senior clerical posts were established through the office of the *Grand Mufti*. Furthermore, the physical position of the office had changed. Notably, this means the observable "center" of Cham Muslim communities in Cambodia had changed again. Currently, it is located at the sub-urban development of Chrang Chamres, where the three largest and most popular *masjid* are popularly known by their distance from the center of Phnom Penh using road-markers, in Khmer: "KM7 mosqué," "KM8 mosqué," and "KM9 mosqué" (Blengsi 2009). Furthermore, with the shift in the new cen-ter for the majority, under the *Grand Mufti* Sos Kamry, the *Kaum Imam San* group appears to have become more distinct again, when compared to points during the middle of the 20th century, as they had been in earlier decades of the 20th and 19th centuries. Indeed, the leader of their group maintains close ties with representatives of the Cambodian Buddhist sang-ha, albeit from the location of Oudong.

While the Imam San community retains prominence in the vicinity of the old capital at Oudong, especially through allegiances to Theravada Buddhist clergy of the Mohanikay order, they simply do not have the same political positionality of the office of the *Grand Mufti*, which has retained a direct relationship with Hun Sen, from Chrang Chamres, nine kilometers northward of downtown Phnom Penh. Still, the historical evidence suggests formal relations between the Cambodian head of state and senior Cham Muslim clerics are a well-recognized deep structure of symbolic power. The study of the history of this symbolic relationship is critical to understand for those individuals interested in the study of politics and society in Cambodia. While maintaining a symbolic relationship with Cham communities allows Hun Sen to argue that he supports a religiously and ethnically pluralistic society, it also creates a strong aura that he supports the ideals of liberal democracy. Thus, while we may not have access to a satisfactory amount of quantitative data to draw conclusions about the raw electoral implications for Hun Sen's support in Cham communities, and indeed this may not even have a remotely significant impact on his real electoral results, we can draw potential conclusions about how this relationship may shape the public perception of Hun Sen as a figure, to his advantage. In other words, the positionality of leadership in Cham communities under the *Grand Mufti*, with respect to Hun Sen, allows for an affirmation of the creation of a *new mandala* of power politics in Phnom Penh, replicating the deeper structures of circles of kingship (*mandala*) and patron-client relations, which have been so well highlighted in the studies of deep history and 20th century politics throughout Southeast Asian societies (Scott 1972a; Scott 1972b; Eisenstadt and Roniger 1980; Wolters 2008; Acharya 2012, 51-104; Cioroiari 2010, 131-175; Trocki 1998, 7-16). Furthermore, through the appeals to the international community, "the case of the Cham," becomes a strong file in the casebook of evidence that Hun Sen's government can present to international audiences, further solidifying his base in Cambodian politics. For the time being, it would seem that multi-party electoral politics in Cambodia has been replaced with a neo-monarchical structure, with Hun Sen playing the role of monarch, without any of the dangers of being an actual monarch, affirmed by his patron-client relations, and rubber stamped by an electoral process that is nominal at best. To move this analysis further, we would be best to focus on the revival collapse of the political opposition to Hun Sen from 2013 through 2014.

Ebb & Flow: The Failure of the CNRP's Hope for Change

In 2013, Phnom Penh appeared as a society visibly entering a new era of history. Unsure, tenuous, and excited. Youth gathered frequently in the city streets throughout the early months of the year and, gradually, they galvanized distinctly into the support of Sam Rainsy. The previous summer, the Sam Rainsy Party (formerly the Candlelight Party) and the Human Rights Party, led by Kem Sokha, had merged. In April 2013, they registered as a new party: the Cambodia National Rescue Party (CNRP), an opposition

party allied with the Liberal International and the Council of Asian Liber-
als and Democrats (Noren-Nilsson 2017; McCargo 2013). When Sam Rainsy
announced his run in 2013, youth continued to gather in the streets, but increasingly shifted their support toward him. Many were clearly aware of his
background as a Cambodian opposition party leader, in various iterations,
since 1995. However, many were seemingly unaware of the problematic relationship that Rainsy's rhetoric posed for the Vietnamese minority population in Cambodia. If they were aware, they were not bothered by it. Nonetheless, in Phnom Penh, simply hoping for a different voice was enough.
The sentiment was that the ruling CPP and their leader, Hun Sen, would
be defeated. That Hun Sen had been in power, through various political
manifestations, since 1985, certainly did not work in his favor. Additionally,
the CNRP, now headed by Sam Rainsy and Kem Sokha, was a credentialed
opposition. In this vision, the death of the CPP would be a natural one, the
power transition would be peaceful, and the rule of law would be maintained. To add to the promises of maintaining a multiparty democracy, Sam
Rainsy and Kem Sokha added a populist economic platform. They promised
increased pensions, raising the minimum wage, guaranteed prices for farm
produce, expanded free medical care for the poor and needy, equal opportunities for education, equal opportunities for employment, lowering the
cost of fuel, lowering the cost of electricity, and lowering the cost of student
loans by lowering interest rates.

Yet, this left-populist approach was not enough for the CNRP to gain
ground against the CPP, which already had put forward a number of similar platforms. Hence, in an attempt to stir up support among centrists and
nationalists, Sam Rainsy and Kem Sokha were increasingly willing to stoke
anti-Vietnamese sentiments and Cambodian nationalist sentiments. However, the CNRP was also fighting another simple fact: Hun Sen was a member of the Khmer Rouge, but one who had defected, and returned with PAVN
to depose the DK regime, while Sam Rainsy had backed the Khmer Rouge
after they were deposed. The fact that Hun Sen returned with PAVN in 1979
and immediately took a position as the Foreign Minister of the PRK, until
he became Acting Prime Minister in 1984, and formerly assumed the office on January 14, 1985, only to be occasionally challenged since, did seem
to associate him with Vietnamese state power. Domestically, the Supreme
Patriarch of the Cambodian Theravada *sangha*, Tep Vong, has been allied

with Hun Sen since the 1980s and urged internal allegiance within the *sangha* to him (Freeman 2013). Externally, as the Vietnamese military occupation of Cambodia lasted a full decade from 1979 through 1989, it is not surprising that support for the Socialist Republic of Vietnam is an unpopular position in Cambodian politics. However, this criticism of Hun Sen was ineffective. Hun Sen had essentially washed his hands of Vietnamese political allegiances in the early 1990s, during the period of the United Nations Transitional Authority of Cambodia (UNTAC) (Aksu 2003, 179-209). By the time he took power after the coup d'état of 1997, and after the 1998 elections, Hun Sen had reaffirmed his credentials as a staunch nationalist, balancing a relationship between the United States of America (USA) and the People's Republic of China (PRC) on the one hand, along with tepid relations with the Kingdom of Thailand and the SRV on the other (Peou 2013). Furthermore, the position of Theravada monastics changed during these elections. Monks (*bhikkhu*) first had voting rights in 1993. Then monks of both the Mohanikay (royalist) and Dhammayuti (reformist) orders were stripped of their voting rights in 2003 by their senior dignitaries. After Tep Vong was appointed to the head of *both* orders in 2006, votingrights for *bhikkhu* in 2008 were affirmed again.. However, the position of the *sangha* in elections remained unclear, as a result of the semi-frequent rule changes regarding monks and their right to vote, causing internal dissent within the Theravada community and speculation regarding the nature of the stability of politics in Cambodia more broadly (Freeman 2013). This sentiment was shared by others in Cambodian society as well. In May 2013, there was widespread speculation about the stance that Hun Sen would take in the elections. *Would he rely upon the military, in another partial coup d'état, as he had done in 1996 if he were to lose? Was it really worth it to destabilize the government? Were the reminders of the civil war, genocide, and tanks rolling down the streets of Phnom Penh anything more than scare tactics?*

By the end of May 2013, allegations that the elections were already bought and paid for were widespread. Yet, the idea that votes should be bought was well accepted. The dispute was more *how* they were being bought and why the CPP was the only purchaser allowed at the *psar* (market). The Cambodian economy was consistently on the rocks. Furthermore, since the elections of American President Barack Obama (2008 and 2012), the CPP was under increasing scrutiny from the United Nations Human Rights

Council (UNRC) over allegations of widespread abuses in Cambodia. As the Obama Administration entered their second term, still championing the rhetoric of the "Pivot to Asia," American leadership pushed increased compliance with UNHRC standards as an issue of import. Pressure on the CPP was building. All through July, youth, students, young adults, and activists, young and old, gathered across Cambodia's central provinces in support of the CNRP. But on July 29, the pressure burst. The CPP experienced their most dramatic losses of parliamentary seats in 15 years in power. Yet, they retained the majority. Ever frustrated, rather than celebrating their gains and regrouping, the populist elements of the CNRP burst into the streets, accusing the CPP of electoral fraud. Human Rights Watch (HRW) appeared to confirm these allegations through a report that they released. Allegations of fraudulent processes from Sam Rainsy continued, especially targeting Vietnamese immigrant communities in Cambodia. Catalyzed by the lack of due representation, in their view, pro-CNRP protesters took to the streets. Yet, the energy had begun to transform them, galvanizing support among numerous anti-CPP critics. The protest movement was no longer simply a question of the campaign platform of the CNRP.

After the elections of 2013, the anti-CPP protesting opposition in Cambodia was dramatically more numerous, more diverse, and therefore, more disparate. Political corruption, illegal logging, abuses of laborers and the press, flagrant human rights violations, and even assassinations of activists were all causes cited by anti-CPP protesters, sometimes in smaller individual protests and other times as part of larger platforms in various combinations calling for reform. An enormous number of protesters were workers in the garment industry, an industry that is still 90% female, and while involving numerous multinational corporations, such as Adidas, Gap, and Nike, has infamously under paid its workers, especially in Cambodia. These workers' strikes and protests were very much part of a larger wave of class and gender conscious protests across the Southeast Asian mainland circa 2013, which targeted the garment industry as a matter of intent and focus. At the same time, in Cambodia, economic protests were often merged with political dissent of the post-election protests. Tension rose. In September, a man was shot trying to pass police barricades on his daily commute home after work. Although he was not a protester, the protests quickly latched upon him as a martyr figure. The same day, 20,000 gathered in Freedom Park (Hodal 2013). By October, Theravada monks regularly joined the protests, although those who did were mostly mid-level and junior *bhikkhu*. Officially, Cambodia has had a unified *sangha* since 2006. However, it was clear that the senior monastics, along with those most affiliated with the royalist Mohanikay schools, still supported the CPP and would not attend. Nonetheless, younger protesting *bhikkhu* marched 200 strong to the Royal Palace and petitioned King Norodom Sihamouni to delay the opening of the parliament and assisted in the organization of protests, establishing a network of 1,000 in Phnom Penh alone and 4,000 across the country (Freeman 2013; Nghiem 2013). In November, another individual was killed by police—and nine were injured—in a crackdown on a garment worker protest 40,000 strong (Lipes 2013). Strikes spread again. Militarized police fought to disperse them. By January, the police had killed another four individuals and injured many more when they opened fire on a crowd in Phnom Penh (Narin and Chun 2014).

As I was living in Phnom Penh between 2013 and 2014, September 2013 marked a clear turning point. Messages from Cambodians-abroad keeping track of the news in the United States, France, and Australia became more frequent. "*This is Cambodia. You do not know when tanks will roll down the streets!*" exclaimed one, out of concern. Although I recall discussing with others how this was a bit overdramatic, it clearly did not seem so for a society with a genocide (1970s) and subsequent coup d'état (1990s) in its collective memory. Fortunately, tanks did not come in 2013. Nonetheless, the foment of popular protest continued to broil. Residents of the city simply adopted their routines to move around police barricades. However, basic amenities briefly became more expensive in neighborhoods partitioned off by barricades and protests. The pressure continued to build. The King Norodom Sihamouni did not respond to the request from Cambodian monks and the parliament opened. The CNRP held a counter-opening ceremony in Siem Reap, nearby Angkor Wat, to symbolically continue their protest but the pressure was already easing. By 2014, the wave had crested and reality sunk in for the pro-CNRP contingent. The high-water mark of the popular movement was already clear. It had been a massive CNRP pre-election gathering in Freedom Park in 2013. Speakers emphasized the promise of change, healthcare for all poor people in Cambodia, and living wages. Cambodian Rock & Roll ripped across the square. Monks and laity alike crowded near the stage to watch the scene, while some relatively more senior monks even spoke in support of the CNRP. Afterward, the aura of optimism dissipated into a haze of desperation in the lead-up to the elections. Then the elections broke into protests as the rhetoric highlighted that the needs of Cambodian workers were not addressed. Pictures of younger smiling monks at the heads of protests still occasionally appeared in the press. However, the protesters and the members of the *sangha* who joined them were becoming increasingly embroiled with nationalist anti-Vietnamese sentiment. The CNRP leader, Sam Rainsy, had a questionable record regarding his past anti-Vietnamese rhetoric, including siding with the former leadership of the DK Regime in 1982, simply because they were anti-Vietnamese,[6] and just before the election he re-ignited anti-Vietnamese sentiment to stoke nationalist fervor (Sokha 2013; Hutt 2016). The stance opened up a left-flank for the CPP to flaunt comparatively liberal value statements, promising legal residency to an immigrant Vietnamese population of at least 160,000 individuals, forcing Sam Rainsy to offer a similar platform to deflate CPP support, although he quickly reneged on the claims (Hutt 2016). While the damage was done to the CNRP campaign and the Vietnamese community in Cambodia, the *Phnom Penh Post* did issue reports that anti-Vietnamese sentiment had declined in the post-election climate by September 2014, although it was still widespread (Wight 2014). However, in contrast with the role of pro- or anti- Vietnamese sentiment played in Cambodian electoral politics, the role of the Cham Muslim community has been less well discussed in scholarly publications.

Hun Sen, Cham Communities & Contemporary Elections

While the 2013 elections were essentially a two-party contest between the CPP and the CNRP, after the collapse of the CNRP, the 2017 Communal Elections were open to many more parties, at least nominally. Nominally, because, of the 11,572 councilor positions, royalist FUNCIPEC managed just 28 seats. The center-right Khmer National United Party — having split from FUNCIPEC in 2016—secured just 24. New left-wing opposition parties appeared promising at first, but gained just 10 seats altogether. The Grass roots Democratic Party (center-left, f. 2015) took just five, the League for

---

6. It is worth noting that the American government also backed the Khmer Rouge during this period, for essentially the same reason.

Democracy Party (LDP, center-left) gained four, and the Beehive Social Democratic Party (center-left, f. 2015) won just one. Furthermore, the CNRP was formally dissolved on November 16, 2017. Consequentially, by the 2018 national elections, the CPP was the only party with real political power. The CPP won all available parliamentary and senate seats in 2018. Hun Sen won yet another term as Prime Minister. The Great Supreme Patriarch of the Cambodian Theravada *sangha*, Tep Vong, played an important role in these elections, remaining loyal to the allegiance that he has had since the 1980s. He stressed a nationalized understanding of the suffering of the *sangha* under the DK Regime, specified that understanding to the right of Buddhists to practice religion freely after Hun Sen came to power, and emphasized Hun Sen's ability to maintain stability. Since the Great Supreme Patriarch holds power over the *sangha* and monks could now vote, this created a formalized client network of support for Hun Sen within the *sangha*. In 2017, Tep Vong, nonetheless went so far as to claim the victory was "predetermined," even while emphasizing the sangha should formalize approval with votes (Koemsoeun and Nachemson 2017). The role of the Grand Mufti, Sos Kamry, in these elections was directly parallel. Nonetheless, widespread critical analyses have charged the CPP leadership with creating a single-party authoritarian state.

I would contend the relationship between Hun Sen and Cham communities has remained symbolically important from 2013 through the present. In part, the role of Cham Muslims in Cambodian society is that of a widely recognized, highly visible, religious and ethnic minority. The quite improved recognition of the plight of Cham Muslims under the DK Regime in the international community allows Hun Sen to draw further rhetorical contrast. Although younger members of Cham communities mirrored the population as a whole in their willingness to consider the CNRP a potential alternative. Older members of the communities were generally more adamant with regard to Hun Sen's position as "victor" in his quest to remove the genocidal Khmer Rouge from power. The conviction of Nuon Chea (then 92) and Khieu Samphan (then 87) under Case 002 of the ECCC for crimes related to genocide, specific to crimes committed against Cham communities, was a factor that furthermore worked in Hun Sen's favor (BBC 2018). Hun Sen's defection from the Khmer Rouge is often portrayed as heroic and coupled with his support of the ECCC. It is used to argue he has a record of supporting the Cham community as a whole, despite well-established criticisms of the court (Peou 2013).

Hun Sen's background affords him additional connections with Cham communities. He is from Kampong Cham, a province that has had a significant Cham Muslim population since at least the 17th century, known even to the Eastern Cham community in Vietnam as *Nâgar Chiam Kur*, or "the lands of Cambodia-Cham." Riverbank fishing and trading communities were important during the 19th century and early 20th century for their variously pro- and anti-royalist sentiments. As a mid-point in an overland trade route across the southern uplands and foothills of the Annamite Chain, through what is now Lam Đồng province in Vietnam, to Cham communities along the coasts in what are now Ninh Thuận and Bình Thuận provinces, Kampong Cham attracted a flourishing community (Noseworthy 2017). As part of the Khmer Rouge cadres, Hun Sen was a commander in Kampong Cham, where the significant Cham Muslim community remained opposed, in their majority opinion, to the project of the KR cadres. Furthermore, when the guerilla movement took the streets of Phnom Penh in April of 1975, there was a distinct campaign to eliminate Islamic practices and eradicate the Cham language, along with patterns of ethno-linguistically motivated executions and forced migration. It was a campaign of extermination of Cham ethnicity in no other terms (Le Coz 2014). Yet, when Hun Sen defected and returned, a revered leader from the Muslim community, Mat Ly, was at his side. The presumed loyalty to the CPP among Cambodia's Cham Muslim community is not so much a matter of justification in normative political terms, beyond the charge of "maintaining stability." While some members of the Cham Muslim community became pro-royalist FUNCIPEC activists, many more joined the CPP, even holding positions relatively high-up in the party organization (Bruckmayr 2006).

Hun Sen himself has not been silent about his relationship with Cham Muslim community leaders, even when relationships were quite strained. One example of such tensions comes ostensibly from the realities of development economics. Cham communities have historically been located nearby riverbanks (*kampong*) where fishing is fruitful, yet outside urban centers where rice can be farmed, and in such areas where *masjid* can be built on flat land. The semi-urban pattern of peripheral settlement makes Cham lands in contemporary Cambodia attractive to developers from Cambodia, Thailand, the SRV, and the PRC. Coerced purchases, cooptation, and outright land-grabs have became increasingly common in Cambodia from the 1990s through the 2010s. Land conflicts often have broader repercussions, as well. A debate over border posts erupted in 2010 between local Cambodian officials and representatives of the SRV (Phnom Penh Post 2010a; 2010b; 2011). This helps explain why Sam Rainsy took a stronger anti-Vietnamese stance, rhetorically, in his political speeches. Activist Chhut Vuthy and a 14-year-old child were shot in conflicts resulting from land grabs in 2012, an assassination that gained the attention of UNHRC. Tensions resulting from the lands of Cham communities have not been so publicly discussed or criticized. Regardless, it is notable that the community where the *Grand Mufti* resides, Chrang Chamres, fits the model of "prime land" for developers. A 2013 report highlighted that the community of 3,000 was ripe for prospecting developers. Wealthy families, with position and larger plots, were given the impression they could expect compensation. Poorer families were concerned. They expected nothing (L.H. 2013). Perhaps shockingly to outside readers, there has been no strong evidence of attempts to organize alternative means of protesting against land grabs as of this writing. Instead, what petitions there are seem to be entirely filed through official channels and brokered networks, although it should be noted that these are networks that the clerics subordinate to the *Grand Mufti*, and thus loyal CPP party members have ultimate control over.

In 2013, the traditional loyalty to Hun Sen as head of state in Kampong Cham, Chrang Chamres, and Chruoy Changvar was tested. An Imam of the KM9 *masjid* in Chrang Chamres discussed a potential land-grab, addressing concerns. He stated, nothing was "*...clear about the compensation...What is clear is that they will develop the road and take the land. It's all the residents— we all have to go, and I will move too, and we may get nothing*" (L.H. 2013). Hun Sen did not address the dispute and responded with a plea to popular appeal. In May 2013, he planned to recount the virtues of the Cham Muslim population. However, his final public statement only settled on one virtue, followed by a stream of leaps, prejudices, and logical fallacies. He began with a clear statement: Cham Muslims did not drink alcohol. Therefore, he argued, they were less likely to get HIV/AIDS (Sokheng 2013). He may have intended to give a simultaneous statement criticizing male drinking culture in Cambodia. Thus, he believed, "drunk Khmer men," spent more time at brothels. There, his argument contended, they were more likely to contract—note "contract" as opposed to "spread" —HIV/AIDS. In his stigmatization of HIV/AIDS patients, along with his misogynist assumptions regarding female sex-workers as primary carriers of the disease, Hun Sen also only managed to praise the Cham Muslim community through a form of racist love for the behavior of abstaining from alcohol. Following upon his flubbed appeal, Hun Sen attempted another. Also in May 2013, Hun Sen celebrated Cambodia's "Freedom of Religion" at a Qur'anic recitation in Chatomuk Conference Hall. He stated "Cambodia's Muslims" should feel "lucky" because "other countries" did not allow such open practice of Islam. Hun Sen did not state which "other countries" he meant, of course, because in 2013, perhaps the only well-known ASEAN country that was not so open was Myanmar, the government of which has subsequently been accused of the crime of genocide for its treatment of the minority Muslim Rohingya population, which was increasingly reported upon by 2013. To be frank, it does not seem likely that this was a veiled threat, so much as yet another flubbed appeal. All the same, "better than genocide," even rhetorically, of course is a horrendously low bar. Yet, if there was to be a bar that resonated with the Cham Muslim population, that would be one that would guarantee that Muslim leaders were paying attention.

Even if Hun Sen's statement was taken as an oblique reference to the SRV and Thailand, both of which were countries that were hosting regularly quite open Qur'anic recitations in 2013, but had less formal state recognition of their Cham Muslim communities, the claim was still obtuse. Asserting that the community should feel grateful for everything that the government did to celebrate them, while simultaneously coopting their land, read as absurd. Cham Muslim communities, nonetheless, have indeed held a complicated place in their long history in Cambodia, with the majority being generally pro-royalist, based on the evidence historians have mounted to date. There are certainly other figures who have invoked this relationship, but it is notable that Hun Sen also did so, while he proceeded to double-down on his previous appeals, stating "...*the Cambodian King always allowed Cambodian Muslims to pray in the Royal Palace, such as for his birthday*" (Sokheng 2013). He went on to flaunt his $5,000 contribution to Qur'anic recitations each year, positioning himself in the role of the monarch, as patron of the Cham Muslim community. In reply, the Grand Mufti Sos Kamry announced the Cham community would support Hun Sen in the coming July 2013 election, *quid pro quo*. Of course, the *Grand Mufti* could not deliver 100% of the vote in Cham communities, or in Muslim communities more broadly. What of those members from the Kaum Imam San group? What of those individuals who simply dissented from the rulings of their senior clerics over matters of ideology or promises of new platforms? Regardless, to ignore the political weight of the senior cleric calling for his *ummah* to support Hun Sen, would be missing a giant's thumb placed on the scales, as it were. Based upon oral accounts, only a handful of younger adults and students dissented, though they did not all flock to the CNRP (Sokheng 2013). Regardless, following upon his victory, Hun Sen pledged funds to support an annual Ramadan feast, while Zul Ziply (46, Russei Keo) noted that it was Hun Sen's first time attending a Ramadan feast (*Eid al-Fitr*) (Sovuthy 2014). In other words, while the Cham community did receive some out front recognition from the head of state, along with very real material support, the real tangible results for the community are nominal, whereas the benefits for the *Grand Mufti* as the broker of this relationship were also intangible, but likely much greater.

Very much like the 2013 elections, in the 2017 and 2018 elections, political appeals were made to the Cham Muslim community in Cambodia. In 2017, Hun Sen nominally congratulated communities who completed the fast with a post on his Facebook account, even as, or perhaps, "especially as," individuals noted that support for the CPP was waning in the *ummah* in March 2017 (Paviour and Odom 2017). After Sam Rainsy resigned, the new CNRP leader, Kem Sokha, attempted to capitalize on disenchantment. He promised to be a defender of human rights, a lover of freedom, and to end discrimination against Cham Muslims, particularly those who were supporters of the opposition party (Hawkins and Sony 2017). Ahmad Yahya, Secretary of State of Social Affairs and a prominent member of the community, along with *Grand Mufti* Sos Kamry, did not offer comment. However, CPP spokesman, Sok Eysan, fired back at the claims, asking *"If there is discrimination, could Cham Muslims have joined him?"* (Sokhean 2017). In other words, Sok Eysan's argument was that because there was no discrimination in the case of *some* members of the Cham Muslim community, there was no discrimination experienced by the entire community. *Could Muslims have been encouraged to join Kem Sokha as a means to reach out and suggest there was no controversy? Could others be more critical of the CPP outside of CPP strongholds, but not have the access to networks to voice their concerns?*

Could others have positions where they do not support the CPP, but also do not support the CNRP? These questions are difficult to answer based upon the currently available evidence. Proving active discrimination is exceedingly difficult because of the extreme risk that it could entail for those who offer their personal experiences as testimony. It took years to convince members of the Cham community to testify at the ECCC. Considering the socio-historical context, scholars, students, and members of the press should consider the above questions, even if they come to accept certain arguments that the CPP offers as official stance. Internationally, for example, leading up to the 2018 election, *Al-Jazeera* published a story updating the international community on the climate of the 2018 elections. The report highlighted intimidation of voters by CPP officials, including statements claiming that boycotting the election was illegal. However, the report did not reveal any specific information on Cham Muslim communities, save a photo of a truck, with a couple of young men and several young women in a *hijab* – themed with CPP banners and colors – waving CPP and Cambodian national flags, smiling (Thompson 2018). *What is a picture worth?* The photo was distinctly reminiscent of several myself and others took, leading up to the 2013 elections. Perhaps understanding more details regarding the fabric of Cham Muslim communities in Chrang Chamres helps to explain the image.

Ngak Biruw-Rai: Modernizing Chrang Chamres

Before 1975, as previously noted, the Islamic community in 20th century Cambodia was centered at Chruoy Changvar, just across the Tonlé Sap River from Phnom Penh. During the Cambodian Genocide under the Democratic Kampuchea (DK) regime, from 1975–1979, the community was de-centered. Gradually, through the 1990s, *Grand Mufti* Oknha Kammarudin bin Yusof (generally: "Sos Kamry" or alt.: "Sos Kamri") emerged as the senior patriarch, in a strong allegiance with the Cambodian government generally, and the CPP especially. Sos Kamry is most associated with the leadership of *Masjid Nurrunaim* and *Masjid Jama'a bin Yasir* in Chrang Chamres, now practically a suburb of Phnom Penh. Known alternatively as "Chrang Chamreas" or "Chrang Chamreh" in French colonial documents, this community was formerly subordinate to the senior clerics of Chruoy Changvar, although it had emerged as an important tertiary center as early as the 1930s. Along the riverside, moving northward from Phnom Penh, the kilometers are marked by roadstones, "KM7," "KM8"—*Masjid Nurrunaim—*

and "KM9"—*Masjid bin Yasir*. Although the mosques are known colloquially by their kilometer markers in English, French, and Khmer, they are also known by the same terms in Cham, a sign of their recognition across communities. Furthermore, even if several provinces away, it is not uncommon for members of the Cham community to simply refer to "KM8" or "KM9" without even mentioning Chrang Chamres. The pattern of colloquialization has also been adopted in press accounts, while Sos Kamry is generally referred to by his informal Khmer language name and English approximations of his Khmer language titles. Nonetheless, by avoiding the reference to his full title as "*Grand Mufti* Oknha...," these discussions often miss an extra opportunity to highlight the connection of the senior cleric to the *ummah* in Cambodia to the royalty. An Oknha is a royal regent. A royal regent appointed by the monarch. The Oknha, thus, are not ethnically exclusive positions. Indeed, Cham Muslims have held prominent positions in the Kingdom of Cambodia since at least as early as the 19th century, if not steadily since the 17th century. Sos Kamry, through his title of Oknha, carries with him the seal of approval of the office of the monarchy. Through stated support for the CPP and indeed, his active membership within the organization, his approval shifts that positionality, as if an individual approved by a past monarch has granted his support for the next monarch. Indeed, Sos Kamry's endorsement of Hun Sen highlights the positionality of the head of the CPP as a stand-in for the office of the royalty.

While Oknha Kammarudin bin Yusof was already a senior cleric in Cambodia when he was appointed to the position of *Grand Mufti* in 1996, his new position secured him a place within the political arena of post-Conflict Cambodia. After the gradual dissolution of the United Nations Transitional Authority of Cambodia (UNTAC), this was important as the political arena was quite uncertain. With the 1997 coup d'état and the 1998 elector victory of the CPP, however, it was clear that Hun Sen would remain the central figure in Cambodian politics for the coming years and it was indeed Hun Sen who extended the *Grand Mufti*'s appointment to a lifetime appointment in 2000. Commonly, in the early 21st century, there were claims circulated that Oknha Reachea Thippedei Res Lah (alt.: Oknha Raja Thippedy Res Los) was the only previous predecessor of the *Grand Mufti* (Blengsli 2009; Stock 2010; Collins 2009). The claim features several critical points. First, it highlights that even though the *Grand Mufti* is clearly a *new* position, the cleric himself is connected to a recognized intellectual lineage. Second, it illustrates that the office of the *Grand Mufti* is a more developed position than even the previous Oknha Reachea Thippedei Res Lah's position was, while asserting that for those who wish to support the rebuilding of the *um-mah* in post-genocide Cambodia, that the *Grand Mufti* is a proper authority. Third, it consolidates the power of clerics who also hold positions as royal regents (*Oknha*) under the authority of the *Grand Mufti*. In reality, the office is simply a continuation of 19th and 20th century legal practices, and thus, the assertion that Res Lah, who was appointed by Norodom in 1960 at Chruoy Changvar, is the only predecessor to the *Grand Mufti* is clearly highly erroneous. The senior cleric of Cambodia, especially as a position with royally granted approval, has a long history (Zain bin Musa 2011; 2008, 60-64; 2004, 51; Stock 2012, 141-60). This does not diminish the position that Sos Kamry has, or the general sense that he is indeed in a "new position," with only one well-recognized predecessor in post-colonial Cambodia. Indeed, if there were multiple senior clerics, conflicts of understanding would naturally arise, and the disagreements could lead to serious divisions in the Muslim community, as they did during the 1930s. At the same time, the nature of the appointment, with Sos Kamry as "*Grand Mufti* for life," a new title, a new position, a new location, and a new *masjid*, is an important illustration of the means that Hun Sen began to use to assert himself as central to Cambodian politics, even taking on the role of monarch, by appointing the senior cleric. The appointment relies upon Sos Kamry and others re-centering the Muslim community at Chrang Chamres.

Jama'ah al-Chrang Chamreh: The Congregation of Chrang Chamres

During my early fieldwork in 2013, I observed that the Muslim community of Chrang Chamres was a bustling, diverse mix of backgrounds, including Malay, Cham, Khmer, Vietnamese, Chinese, South Asian, and others. While the South Asians in the community were less numerous, there were also a few Arabs, Europeans, and Americans who could occasionally be found visiting the communities. This included, for example, an American convert, an Arab-European NGO worker, and several South Asian individuals working in educational capacities. In total, the community was an estimated 3,000 plus individuals, all attending a collection of a handful of *masjid* and numerous prayer halls. In Khmer and Cham language, the Malay term *surao* was often adopted to describe these prayer halls, although some congregants and signage made use of the Arabic, *musallah*. Just on the south end of the community, roughly in the vicinity of the center of the Russey Keo settlement, the *Masjid Nurul-Ihsan* stands at KM 7. While this construction is older, dating back to the late 1970s or early 1980s, it is notable in that it still attracts a large number of practitioners during Friday prayers (Cham: *Hârei jamaat*). In part, daily prayers were less well attended at the masjid because of the availability of two nearby prayer halls, which were simply more convenient locations. The first was the *Surao Da'ee* from the roadside, although after proceeding down a weave of alleys on the same side of the road as the KM 7 mosque, tucked amidst a collection of wooden shops and corrugated rooves; another rather more active prayer hall, in 2013 and 2014 was visited by all locals, especially shop-keeping families (*Musalla Nurud-Da'ee*). Nearby, on the right-hand side of the road, presuming one is proceeding north, another sign pointed toward the *Musalla al-Mubarak*. The latter *musalla* was clearly a newer construction and virtually on the banks of the Tonlé Sap River. It was frequented predominantly by fishing families who spoke a mix of Cham and Malay, as well as, quite notably, members of the *Tablighi Jamaat* reformist group. Unlike in earlier historical epochs, it was not possible to discern if there was a particular orientation of the prayer halls based upon their usage of the Malay term *surao* or the Arabic term *musalla*, although those using the Arabic term did tend to be relatively newer constructions and seem to have been better supported by the community. Nonetheless, the *Tablighi Jamaat*, being a group that travelled more frequently than local Cham Muslims, made appearances at these smaller halls in rotation, according to their own accounts, in an attempt to perform "outreach" as they described it.

While the *Tablighi Jamaat* arrived as a clear movement in Cambodia in the middle of the 1990s, it is notable that the majority of members of the organization locally were younger individuals who had studied in Malaysia, as well as their predominantly male kin and clan networks who had joined them, especially in the case of those that I met at the *Musalla al-Mubarak* (see also Guérin 2004; Collins 1996). By contrast with the Russey Keo community, the next major masjid in the neighborhood, *Masjid Nurunnaim*, also known as "KM8," was comparatively more diverse in its attendees, although there was also a nearby prayer hall, the *Musalla al-Hidayah Phum Tuol*, which was clearly a very new construction for the local community. With a two-story-tall bright pink structure, adorned by white and blue highlights, and four three-story tall minarets, the architecture and coloration of the *Masjid Nurunnaim* speaks of both South Asian and Malaysian influences. The structure is reminiscent of contemporary re-interpretations of Moghul masjids and was quite unlike almost every other masjid in the country, although the central dome and much of the architecture, including the particulars of blue checkered patterns outlined in white, were quite similar to the *Masjid Sultan Salahuddin Abdul Aziz* in Kuala Lumpur, Malaysia. Typical of more recent Buddhist wat in Cambodia, but less common among masjid, the names of donors were inscribed on elements of the interior walls, where vast ceilings covered a unique reading room and rather extensive library, filled with Arabic and Malay *du'a* prayer manuals, *hadith* collections, and a number of notable *kitab* commentaries on the Qur'an. Materials in the library were predominantly in Arabic, Malay, and Cambodia, with a substantial number of works in French and English as well. Lectures from the senior *imam* at the mosque included a relative mix of mostly Arabic and Malay, followed by Cham, with some occasional phrases in Khmer.

Continuing northward along National Route 5, just north of the *Masjid* Nurunnaim, there were numerous prayer halls in 2013 and 2014 for the Chrang Chamres community, with at least five that had been opened since the 1990s. The first two, *Musulla Rahim*, tucked slightly away from the road, and *Musulla Ni'mah*, a bit closer to the road, had clear signs from the main thoroughfare, meaning that they could be utilized by travelers along the route. Consequentially, they were quite well attended. Approaching the large, clearly visible KM9 masjid, a sign for the *Surao al-Amin* included Arabic signage as well (*Musulla al-Amin*). However, this prayer-hall was tucked very close to the riverbank and was mostly frequented only by locals. Looking across the waters of the Tonlé Sap, the *Masjid al-Mukarram* was clearly visible on the opposite bank of the river, although, even though this mosque was just a short boat-ride away, a number of individuals in the area stated plainly they had never been to it. Still, like the above-mentioned *Musalla al-Mubarak*, *Musulla al-Amin* was a prayer hall that was frequented by both Malay and Cham members of the *Tablighi Jamaat* group. Just northward of this location, on National Route 5, there was an alley on the left side of the road, which led quite far away from the main thoroughfares to *Musulla Nurul-Huda*, a prayer hall predominantly for local residents. Returning out to National Route 5 and just northward again, another prayer hall, *Musulla al-Akbar* was notable. This was previously the site of a *masjid* by the same name. However, the prayer hall and parking lot here were reconstructed when the project to build the new, grandiose, *Masjid Jama'a Ammar bin Yasir* (KM9) began. The site of the KM9 mosque itself is pristine, situated at the center of a large brick courtyard, sprinkled with lamps to light the scene in the evening. The courtyard unfolds before an immense white building, accented by light-green minarets and an emerald roof upon the central dome.[7] Numerous visitors to this area have mistakenly associated the architecture of the *masjid* as a sign of Saudi Arabian influence in Cambodia, although, admittedly, the influence likely stems from financial and educational support from Emirati-based (United Arab Emirates) organizations. Indeed, the attached *madrasah* is widely known by its complete name, the "Phnom Penh-Dubai Islamic School." Furthermore, the associated funding support of the broader community are widely associated with Emirati and Kuwaiti organizations. This is not to say that these organizations have any form of direct influence on the Cambodian government, but rather to say that it is likely that the office of the *Grand Mufti* was able to attract further recognition abroad specifically because of his position within the structure of the Cambodian government. He was then able to direct those funds toward specific projects within the Chrang Chamres community. It is noteworthy that although the official office of the *Grand Mufti* is down the road from the KM9 masjid, just between the *Musulla Ni'mah* and the *Musulla al-Amin*, on the left hand side of National Route 5, among the general public the bin Yusof (Sos Kamry) himself is widely associated with the KM9 masjid.

Conclusions:

The Cham Muslim community at Chrang Chamres is well over a century old, with records of the community dating to the French colonial period and before. Yet, it became the center of Islam in Cambodia only in the 2000s Previously, the Muslim community in Cambodia had been centered at the peninsular community of Chruoy Changvar, and perhaps even at Oudong before that. Yet, the positionality of Chruoy Changvar was advantageous for its centrality, along the Tonlé Sap and Mekong rivers, just across from the royal palace. However, during the Democratic Kampuchea regime, this community, like all Muslim communities in Cambodia, was devastated. In post-conflict Cambodia, the relationship with the Cambodian royalty was

7. See photo in Noseworthy (2014b).

restructured. Hun Sen took on the role of the monarch (in forging ties with the Muslim community), although not the title, appointing Kammurudin bin Yusof to his position for life. In 2001, bin Yusof specifically reaffirmed his relationship with Hun Sen and took lengths to offer overtures to the United States, speaking explicitly against acts of terrorism as an unnecessary form of violence (Sokheng 2001). After the 2003 Denpensar, Bali bombing, the community faced further criticisms. The Saudi-affiliated Umm al-Qura group's central educational institution was closed, due to affiliations with members of the Jama'ah Islamiyyah (JI) organization, which had claimed responsibility for the bombing. Hun Sen's government expelled tens of individuals tied to JI. Kuwaiti and Emirati organizations were viewed more favorably within the country after 2003, although American reporting from Cambodia conflated the groups. The U.S. Department of Treasury, for example, misreported the raid on the 2003 Umm al-Qura school as a raid on the Kuwaiti Revival of Islamic Heritage Society (RIHS). Later there was an arrest of a JI member to the west of Phnom Penh, at an RIHS affiliated school (Chakrya and Stranglo 2010). Furthermore, American official organizations prevented any U.S. citizens from engaging in any support of RIHS affiliated organizations, including two orphanages in Cambodia that had been supported with RIHS funds. This position has been criticized as a misunderstanding by members of the Cambodian Muslim community, who categorically deny that there is an association between RIHS funds and threats to security. Nevertheless, these circumstances help to explain the relative lack of criticism for the CPP among important Islamic intellectuals through context, as well as the broad encouragement of Cambodian Muslims to join the CPP after 2008. Furthermore, in the wake of the Arab Spring (2011), Hun Sen has since consistently warned Cambodian Muslim leaders to be wary of change, while encouraging them to celebrate the stability of their relationship with his government. While his political rhetoric emphasizes the essential "Khmerness"—rather than "Cambodian," "Cham" or "Malay" aspects —of the Muslim community, it echoes the nationalizing rhetoric of "Khmer Islam" that Norodom Sihanouk introduced in the 1950s and 1960s. Hence, although Sam Rainsy made efforts to reach out to Chrang Chamres in 2008 and the CNRP argued that only they advocated for slow, incremental change, for respect for democracy *and* for freedom of religion, through 2015, they could not muster substantial political support in the community

(Reaksmey 2015). Indeed, the loyalty of the senior leadership of the Cham Muslim community and the symbolic loyalty of the community to Hun Sen as a whole, was reaffirmed in elections in 2014, 2017, and 2018 (Meyn 2017). Moving forward, it appears that these spokes of the *new mandala* will hold, confirming a pattern that exists in other cases in Cambodian electoral politics more broadly.

Bibliography

Cham Manuscripts by Code:
CM 38 (8), CM 29 (37), CM 49, CM 50, CM 51, CM 52

National Archives of Cambodia (NAC):
NAC Box 745, RSC File 8465. Classification R. 29. (1934) Fermeture des écoles Malaisies clandestines situées à Phnom Penh [Closure of Clandestine Malay Schools located in Phnom Penh]
NAC Box 811, RSC File 9200. (1905–11). Tribunal correctionnel de Battambang: affaire judiciaire de vol commis par trois Malais [Criminal Court of Battambang: A Criminal Case of Theft Committed by Three Malays]
NAC Box 2968, RSC File 25968. Classification: F99. (1918–19). Résidence de Kompong Chhnang. AS de la nomination des chefs pour les mosquées Cham [Residence of Kampong Chnnang: On the Subject of the Appointment of Heads of Cham Mosques]
NAC Box 3052, RSC File 27641. Classification: C.012. OR no. 74 (September 10, 1929). Relevant de ses fonctions d'Oknha Reachea Pheak Koey, Montrey Changvang Nong Chef de mosquée Cham du khum de Khleang Sbek nord, Khand de Ponhea Lu, Kandal [Royal Ordanance no. 74 (September 10, 1929). [Falling under the functions of the Oknha Reachea Pheak Koey, Montrey Changvang Nong, head of the Cham Mosque, khum Kleang Sbek north, khand Ponhea Lu, Kandal];

NAC Box 3115, RSC File 28319. Classification: F.99. 1/OR No. 54 du 22 Avril
1936 nommant le sieur Ahmad Hadji Isam El comme chef de mosque
d'Ek a Chruoi Changvar (ville de Phnom Penh). 2/OR No. 67 du 29 avril
1936 chargeant le sur nomme des fonctions de chef par interim des
Cham Malais du royaume.

NAC Box 3310, RSC File 30380. Classification: F. 99. AM. N. 53 (April 17,
1934). Nommant les sieurs Hj.-Salai-Man et Hj.-Sam-Sou respective-
ment chef (Préa mékémaven 6 pâns de dignité) et sous-chef de mosquée
cham de Naparat-Botoum-Bochantréa de Vat Dangker (Battambang)
[Ministerial Order no. 53 April 17, 1934: Appointing Mr. Hj. Salai Man
and Mr. Hj. Sam Sou, respectively, to the Chief (Preah Mekemavan with
6 stripes of dignity) and Senior Assistant of the Cham Mosque in Na-
parat Botoum Bochantreah of Wat Dangker (Battambang)]

Journalistic & Scholarly Sources:

Acharya, Amitav. 2012. *The Making of Southeast Asia: International Relations
of a Region.* Ithaca, NY: Cornell University Press.

Aksu, Eşref. 2003. *The United Nations, Intra-State Peacekeeping and Normative Change.* Manchester, United Kingdom: Manchester University
Press.

Amer, Ramses. 2006. "Cambodia's Ethnic Vietnamese: Minority Rights and
Domestic Politics." *Asian Journal of Social Science* 34 (3): 388–409.

BBC. 2018. "Khmer Rouge Leaders Found Guilty of Cambodia Genocide," *BBC
News,* November 16. https://www.bbc.com/news/world-asia-46217896.

Blengsli, Bjorn Atle. 2009. "Muslim Metamorphosis: Islamic Education and
Politics in Contemporary Cambodia." In *Making Modern Muslims: The
politics of Islamic Education in Southeast Asia,* ed. Robert W. Hefner,
172–204. Honolulu, HI: University of Hawai'i Press.

Bruckmayr, Philipp. 2006. "The Cham Muslims of Cambodia: From Forgot-
ten Minority to Focal Point of Islamic Internationalism." *The American
Journal of Islamic Social Sciences* 23 (3): 1–23.

———. 2019. *Cambodia's Muslims and the Malay World: Malay Language,
Jawi Script, and Islamic Factionalism from the 19th Century to the Present.*
Leiden, The Netherlands: Brill Press.

Chakrya, Khouth Sophak and Sebastian Stranglo. 2010. "NGO holds alleged
link to terrorism." *The Phnom Penh Post,* February 25, 2015. http://www.
phnompenhpost.com/national/ngo-holds-alleged-link-terrorism/.

Chen, Dene-Hern. 2012. "Condolences for King Sihanouk Arrive From Home and Abroad." *The Cambodia Daily*, October 16. https://english. cambodiadaily.com/sihanouk/condolences-for-king-sihanouk-arrive-from-home-and-abroad-3930/.

Cioroiari, Jonh. 2010. *The Limits of Alignment: Southeast Asia and the Great Powers since 1975.* Washington, DC: Georgetown University Press.

Collins, William. 1996. "The Chams of Cambodia." In *Interdisciplinary Research on Ethnic Groups in Cambodia*, Final Draft Reports, 1–107. Phnom Penh, Cambodia: Center for Advanced Studies (CAS).

–––. 2009. "The Muslims of Cambodia." In *Ethnic Groups in Cambodia*, ed. Hean Sokhom, 2–110. Phnom Penh, Cambodia: CAS.

De Nike, Howard J, John Quigley, Kenneth J. Robinson, Helen Jarvis, Nereida Cross. 2000. *Genocide in Cambodia: Documents from the Trial of Pol Pot and Ieng Sary.* Philadelphia: University of Pennsylvania Press.

Eisenstadt, S.N. & Louis Roniger. 1980. "Patron-Client Relations as a Model of Structuring Social Exchange." *Comparative Studies in Society and History* 22 (1): 42–77.

Freeman, Joe. 2013. "In Cambodia, monks get political after unpopular elections." *Public Radio International* (PRI), October 8. https://www.pri.org/stories/2013-10-08/cambodia-monks-get-political-after-unpopular-elections.

Ganesan, N. and Sung Chull Kim. 2013. *State Violence in East Asia.* Lexington, KY: University of Kentucky Press.

Garneir, Francis. 1871. *Chronqiues Royale du Cambodige.* Paris, France: Imprimerie Nationale.

Guérin, Mathieu. 2004. "Les Cams et Leurs 'veranda sur la Mecque' : L'Influence des les Malais de Patani et du Kelantan sur les Cams du Cambodge." *Aséanie* 14: 29–67.

Hawkins, Hannah and Ouch Sony. 2017. "Cham Muslims Celebrate End of Ramadan Fasting Month." *Cambodia Daily*, June 26. https://www.cambodiadaily.com/news/cham-muslims-celebrate-end-of-ramadan-fasting-month-131764/.

Hodal, Kate. 2013. "Cambodian Election Protests grip Phnom Penh." *The Guardian,* September 16. https://www.theguardian.com/world/2013/sep/16/cambodia-election-protests-phnom-penh.

Hutt, David. 2016. "The Truth about anti-Vietnam Sentiment in Cambodia." *The Diplomat*, October 20. https://thediplomat.com/2016/10/the-truth-about-anti-vietnam-sentiment-in-cambodia/.

Juergensmeyer, Mark. 2008. *Religious Challenges to the Secular State, From Christian Militias to al-Qaeda.* Berkeley, CA: University of California Press.

Kiernan, Ben. 2008. *The Pol Pot Regime: Race, Power, and Genocide in Cambodia under the Khmer Rouge*, 1975–1979. New Haven, Connecticut: Yale University Press.

Koemsoeun, Soth and Andrew Nachemson. 2017. "CPP-linked monastic leader tells Cambodia's monks to vote for ruling party." *The Phnom Penh Post*, December 13. https://www.phnompenhpost.com/national-politics/cpp-linked-monastic-leader-tells-cambodias-monks-vote-ruling-party.

L.H. 2013. "Cambodia's Cham: A Road Runs through Them." *The Economist*, January 23. http://www.economist.com/blogs/banyan/2013/01/cambodia%E2%80%99s-cham.

Le Coz, Clothilde. 2014. "The Question of Genocide and Cambodia's Muslims." *Al-Jazeera*, November 19, 2015. http://www.al-jazeera.com/news/2015/11/question-genocide-cambodia-muslims-151110072431950.html.

Lipes, Joshua. 2013. "Woman Shot Dead by Cambodian Police in Protest Clampdown." *Radio Free Asia*, November 12. http://www.rfa.org/english/news/cambodia/clash-11122013172259.html.

Mak, Phoeun. 1981. *Chroniques Royales du Cambodge (Collection de textes et documents sur l'Indochine).* Paris, France: EFEO.

Meyn, Colin. 2017. "The Price of Loyalty." *Globe: Lines of Thought Across Asia.* May 9. https://southeastasiaglobe.com/cambodia-patronage/.

McCargo, Duncan. 2013. "Cambodia in 2013: (No) Country for Old Men?" *Asian Survey* 54 (1): 71–77.

Narin, Sun and Chun Han Wong. 2014. "Four Dead in Cambodia Garment Strike." *The Wall Street Journal*, January 3. https://www.wsj.com/articles/cambodian-police-fire-on-striking-workers-witnesses-say-1388727756.

Ner, Marcel. 1941. "Les Musulmans de l'Indochine Française." *BEFEO*, XXXXI: 151–202.

Nghiem, Ashleigh. 2013. "Monks appeal to Cambodia king over contested election." *BBC News*, September 20. https://www.bbc.com/news/av/world-asia-24170428/monks-appeal-to-cambodia-king-over-contested-election.

Nguyễn Văn Luận. 1974. *Người Chăm Hồi Giáo Miên Tây – Nam – Phần Việt Nam*. Tử Sách Biên Khảo. Bộ Văn-Hóa Giáo-Dục và Thanh Niên.

Noren-Nilsson, Astrid. 2017. "Elections and Emerging Citizenship in Cambodia." *In Citizenship & Democratization in Southeast Asia*, eds. Ward Berenschot, Henk Schulte Nordholt, and Laurens Bakker, 68–95. Leiden, The Netherlands: Brill Press.

Noseworthy, William. 2014a. "Mamun and the 'Kaum Imam San' of Cambodia." *The Newsletter* (IIAS) 69: 9–10.

———. 2014b. "Bophana Audio Visual Archives, Phnom Penh." *Dissertation Reviews*, April 10, 2014. http://dissertationreviews.org/archives/8167.

———. 2017. "*Khik Agama Cam*: Caring for Cham Religions in Mainland Southeast Asia, 1651–1969." Ph.D. dissertation in History. University of Wisconsin-Madison.

Osman, Ysa. 2002. *Oukoubah: Justice for the Cham Muslims under the Democratic Kampuchea Regime*. Phnom Penh, Cambodia: Documentation Center of Cambodia.

———. 2005. "The Cham prisoners in the Khmer Rouge's secret prison." *Jembat: Malaysian Journal of History, Politics and Strategic Studies* 32: 100–133.

———. 2006. *The Cham Rebellion: Survivors' Stories from the Villages*. Phnom Penh, Cambodia: Documentation Center of Cambodia.

Paviour, Ben and Sek Odom. 2017. "In Phnom Penh, Cham Quietly Drift Away from Ruling Party." *Cambodia Daily*, March 22. https://www.cambodiadaily.com/news/in-phnom-penh-cham-quietly-drift-away-from-ruling-party-126861/.

Peou, Sorpong. 2013. "Mass Atrocities in Cambodia under the Khmer Rouge Reign of Terror." In *State Violence in East Asia*, eds. N. Ganesan and Sung Chull Kim, 129–58. Lexington, KY: University of Kentucky Press.

Pérez-Pereiro, Alberto. 2012. "Historical Imagination Diasporic Identity and Islamicity among the Chams of Cambodia." Ph.D. dissertation in Anthropology, Arizona State University.

Phnom Penh Post. 2011. "Is the Sam Rainsy Party's Candle Burning Out?" March 9.

Phnom Penh Post. 2010a. "Border Scuffle." December, 14.

Phnom Penh Post. 2010b. "Border Mapping Moves Ahead." December 9.

Radio France Series. 2007. "Entre Karma et Justice [Between Karma and Justice]. Cambodge, le pays des tigres disparus. [Cambodia, the country of the tigres that have vanished]." Bophana Audio Visual Resource Center. Phnom Penh, Cambodia.

Reaksmey, Hul. 2015. "Hun Sen Advises Muslims to be Wary of Political Change." *Voice of America*, October 14. https://www.voacambodia.com/a/hun-sen-advises-muslims-to-be-wary-of-political-change/3005518.html.

Scott, James. 1972a. "Patron-Client Politics and Political Change in Southeast Asia." *The American Political Science Review* 66(1): 91–113.

———. 1972b. "The Erosion of Patron-Client Bonds and Social Change in Rural Southeast Asia." *The Journal of Asian Studies* 32(1): 5–37.

Sokha, Cheang. 2013. "Return sparks CNRP." *The Phnom Penh Post*, July 21. https://www.phnompenhpost.com/national/return-sparks-cnrp.

Sokhean, Ben. 2017. "Kem Sokha Promises Political Tolerance to Cham Muslims." *Cambodia Daily*, June 22. https://www.cambodiadaily.com/news/kem-sokha-promises-political-tolerance-to-cham-muslims-131604/.

Sokheng, Vong. 2001. "Cham Muslims accept US stand." *The Phnom Penh Post*, October 12. http://www.phnompenhpost.com/national/cham-muslims-accept-us-stand/.

———. 2013. "Muslims 'Lucky to Live in Cambodia,' PM Says." *The Phnom Penh Post*, May 6. http://www.phnompenhpost.com/national/muslims-%E2%80%98lucky-live-cambodia%E2%80%99-pm-says/.

Sovuthy, Khy. 2014. "Hun Sen Denies, 'Muslim Extremists,' Pledges Ramadan Funds." *Cambodia Daily*, July 19. https://www.cambodiadaily.com/news/hun-sen-denies-muslim-extremists-pledges-ramadan-funds-64498/.

Stock, Emiko. 2010. "Les Communautes Musulmanes du Cambodge: Un Apercu." In *Atlas Minorites Musulmanes en Asie*, ed. M. Gilquin, 183–216. Bangkok, Thailand: IRASEC/ Paris, France: CNRS.

———. 2012. "Au delà des ethnonymes: A propos de quelque exonyms et endonymes chez les musulmans du Cambodge [Beyond Ethnonyms: Notes on some Exonyms and Endonyms used among Muslims in Cambodia]." *Moussons* 20: 141–60. Aix-en-Provence, France: IRSEA.

Sullivan, Michael L. 2016. *Cambodia Votes: Democracy, Authority and International Support for Elections, 1993–2013.* Copenhagen, Denmark: NIAS Press.

Thompson, Nathan A. 2018. "Fear in the Rice Fields–Cambodia's Controversial Election." *Al-Jazeera*, July 28. https://www.aljazeera.com/news/2018/07/fear-rice-fields-cambodia-controversial-election-180726195219559.html.

Trankel, Ing-Britt. 2003. "Songs of Our Spirits: Possession and Historical Imagination among the Cham in Cambodia." *Asian Ethnicity* 4(1): 31–46.

Trocki, Carl. 1998. *Gangsters, Democracy, and the State in Southeast Asia.* Ithaca, NY: Cornell University Press.

Weber, Nicholas. 2011. "Securing and Developing the Southwestern Region: The Role of the Cham and Malay Colonies in Vietnam (18th and 19th Centuries)." *Journal of Economic and Social History of the Orient* 54: 739–72.

Weggel, Oskar. 2007. "Cambodia in 2006: Self-Promotion and Self-Deception." *Asia Survey* 47(1): 141–47.

Wight, Emily. 2014. "Out of 20 of my Friends, 17 Hate the Vietnamese." *The Phnom Penh Post*, September 6. https://www.phnompenhpost.com/post-weekend/out-20-my-friends-17-hate-vietnamese.

Wolters, O.W. 1999. *History, Culture and Region in Southeast Asian Perspectives.* Ithaca, NY: Cornell University.

———. 2008. "Southeast Asia as a Southeast Asian Field of Study." In *Early Southeast Asia: Selected Essays*, ed. O.W. Wolters, 39–56. Ithaca, NY: Cornell University Press.

Zain bin Musa, Muhammed. 2001. "Malay and Cham Relations with the Kingdom of Cambodia during and after the French Protectorate Period (1863–2000)." *Journal of the Malaysian Branch of the Royal Asiatic Society* 74(2): 1–21.

———. 2004. "Islam as Understood and Practiced by the Muslims in Indochina." *Islamiyyat* 25(1): 51.

———. 2008. "Dynamics of Faith: Imam Musa in the Revival of Islamic Teaching in Cambodia." In I*slam at the Margins: The Muslims of Indochina*, eds. Omar Faouk and Horiyuki Yamamoto, 60–64. Kyoto, Japan: Center for Integrated Area Studies, Kyoto University.

———. 2011. "History of Education among the Cambodian Cham Muslims." *Jebat: Malaysian Journal of History, Politics & Strategic Studies* 38(1): 89–92.

Chapter 4

From Pulpit to Protest: Religious Practice and Political Participation in Indonesia

Danielle N. Lussier, M. Najib Azca,
Hakimul Ikhwan, and Wahyu Kustiningsih

Introduction

In 2019, Indonesian President Joko "Jokowi" Widodo won reelection to a second term of office, supported by the secular Indonesian Democratic Party of Struggle (PDI-P). In an obvious attempt to lure religious voters away from opponent Prabowo Subianto, who had received the backing of several Islamist political parties, Jokowi selected conservative Islamic cleric, Ma'ruf Amin, as his running mate. As Chairman of the Indonesian Council of Ulama, Amin had signed a number of conservative *fatwa*, including a controversial 2005 opinion that had declared liberalism, pluralism, and secularism to be against Islam, and another in 2016 stating that Jakarta Governor Basuki Tjahaja Purnama (known commonly as Ahok)—Jokowi's former deputy governor who is Christian—was guilty of blasphemy. An effective electoral strategy, Jokowi's political marriage of convenience highlights the heightened politicization of religion observed in Indonesia in recent years.

Political headlines in both the Indonesian and international press suggest that religion has become an increasingly important fault line in Indonesia, yet we have limited empirical knowledge about the drivers of religion's politicization. The world's largest Muslim-majority democracy, Indonesia has never claimed to be a secular state, although tolerance toward religious minorities has long been part of the dominant civic culture. One of the most curious and contradictory developments of Indonesian democracy over the past twenty years has been the simultaneous freeing up of the media and rules for speech and association with increased religious policing of that speech. In Indonesia, free speech is protected, along with freedom of assembly and press freedoms, yet, there is increasing pressure to curtail speech and behavior that seems to challenge or offend conservative religious doctrines and beliefs. For example, it was in the context of a campaign speech in September 2016 when Ahok made his infamous reference to a verse in the Qur'an that ultimately led to charges of blasphemy, mass mobilization against the once popular governor, and his serving almost two years in prison. The mobilization that helped unseat and imprison Ahok was largely believed to have emanated through mosque networks, with conservative religious leaders agitating for political change (Institute for Policy Analysis of Conflict 2018). Yet, other evidence suggests that it could be high stakes electoral competition that exploits religious difference for political advantage. For example, Buehler (2016) finds that shari'a by-laws passed by local governments are not a result of pressure from religious quarters, but rather a product of secular political forces that are trying to outbid their Islamic partisan rivals. Is religious difference driving political mobilization, or is the competitive nature of democratic politics seeking out religious fault lines as a terrain for political conquest?

This chapter approaches the dynamic of increased politicization of religion in Indonesia by focusing a lens on the micro-level behaviors of the average worshipper. Existing scholarship on the linkage between religious practice and political participation in Indonesia offers only the most limited insight into the relationship, which has been examined primarily through the lens of group actors and political elites. We have limited empirical knowledge about how the average Indonesian citizen—particularly the average citizen who is religiously engaged—fits into this broader dynamic. The goal of this chapter is to examine in closer detail the connection between religious practice and political participation among non-elite actors, namely Indonesian Muslims and Christians worshipping in similar local and community contexts. Such individuals comprise the average voters in elections, as well as the broader mass public who are affected by public policy and whose participation matters in meaningful ways when thinking about the role of elections in determining access and distribution of political power.

In particular, we engage two broad questions. First, are religious engagement and political participation correlated in Indonesia? In other words, do individuals who are more active in religious life participate in politics in ways that are different from those who are less religiously engaged? If so, how? Second, do Indonesian Muslims and Christians differ in the respective roles that houses of worship play in their political lives? We explore these questions through analysis of an original survey of worshippers at four mosques and four churches in the city of Yogyakarta, Indonesia. Our analysis unfolds in four parts. After situating our study within the broader literature on religion and politics in Indonesia, we explain our case selection and survey design. We then provide an overview of the descriptive measures of religious engagement and political participation revealed in the survey. Following the descriptive analysis, we conduct a series of logistic regression analyses that test whether religious engagement is a meaningful predictor of political engagement. As the forthcoming analysis reveals, religious engagement can be a path to political participation, but such a path is not direct, determinative, or universal.

Religion and Political Participation in Indonesia

As the world's largest Muslim-majority democracy, the intersection of religion and politics in Indonesia has received extensive scholarly attention. The role of Islamic organizations in Indonesia's political development, from the revolutionary to the post-Suharto *reformasi* eras, in particular, has been researched by scholars in all social science disciplines (see Hefner 2000, Buehler 2016, Azra and Hudson 2008, Menchik 2016, Kunkler and Stepan 2013, Mujani 2003). Indonesia is home to the world's largest mass Muslim organization, the traditionalist Nahdlatul Ulama (NU), as well as the modernist Muhammadiyah, and these organizations are frequently a topic of scholarly investigation, particularly given the assumption that membership in one organization or the other is politically consequential for individual political loyalties.

Yet, in spite of the significance of Muslim social organizations in the landscape of Indonesian public life, studies examining the precise role of religion on individual-level political participation are limited. Although Muslim mass organizations play a visible and far-reaching role in the Indonesian public sphere, it is important not to conflate their members—who self-select into the activities of such organizations—with the average Indonesian Muslim or the average member of the Indonesian electorate. Indonesian Muslims and Indonesian voters comprise much larger and more diverse populations than the individuals who participate in Muslim mass organizations or are active in Islamic political movements and parties. It is precisely this overlooked population of average Indonesian citizens that is the focus of our work.

Two recent books by groups of veteran scholars and analysts of Indonesian public opinion have started to fill an important empirical gap on the topic of religion and politics among the average Indonesian citizen. In *Piety and*

Public Opinion (2018), Pepinsky, Liddle, and Mujani focus on the opinions and behaviors of ordinary Muslims, as opposed to self-selecting activists, to better understand the relationship between religious devotion, religious practice, and public life. While the bulk of the empirical analysis in their book is concerned with attitudes and opinions, one chapter examines Islam and party politics. In an extension of their earlier work on the same topic (Pepinsky, Liddle, and Mujani 2012), they find that Islamic party platforms essentially serve as a heuristic to Muslim voters, but provide a political advantage only when respondents are uncertain about political parties' economic platforms. Their data suggests that pious voters never select Islamic parties over secular parties when economic platforms are known and understood, implying that political mobilization along religious lines is conditional on other factors.

Voting Behavior in Indonesia since Democratization (2018) by Mujani, Liddle, and Kuskridho is the most comprehensive study of individual-level political participation in Indonesia published to date. Drawing on extensive national-level public opinion surveys that span the period from 1999 through 2014, the authors argue that patterns in Indonesian voting behavior are most clearly explained by a rational cost-benefit calculation rooted in expectations about the role of the state in shaping economic outcomes. The authors test a number of other theoretical models of voting behavior, including sociological explanations rooted in class, religious, and ethnic identities, as well as psychological explanations driven by ideological attachments and partisanship, but find that these factors are rather weak predictors of Indonesians' vote choice. While Mujani, Liddle, and Kuskridho (2018) find weak evidence that religious identification motivates Indonesian political participation, their work highlights another path through which religion intersects with the political lives of the average Indonesian. As in *Piety and Public Opinion* discussed above, Mujani, Liddle, and Kuskridho (2018) develop a measure of religiosity among survey respondents, noting considerable variation across Indonesian Muslims in the extent to which they carry out obligatory and recommended religious practices. When considering their measure of piety against both frequency of voting and involvement in campaign participation prior to voting, they find that, "pious Muslims who regularly carry out the obligations of their religion tend to be more politically active" (Mujani, Liddle, and Kuskridho 2018, 79).

In explaining this relationship, Mujani, Liddle, and Kuskridho invoke the civic voluntarism model of political participation introduced by Verba, Schlozman, and Brady (1995) in their study of American politics. The civic voluntarism model emphasizes the individual-level resources that are accrued when people become involved in the activities of their religious communities, independent of their personal sense of religiosity. In applying this concept to the Indonesian context, Mujani, Liddle, and Kuskridho explain how Indonesians' involvement in their religious communities via a range of activities that are more social in nature than praying and fasting alone at home "opens a space for involvement in the larger nonreligious community" (Mujani, Liddle, and Kuskridho 2018, 81), primarily by habituating them to participating in broader social networks that ultimately engender political mobilization. Lussier (2016) similarly employs the civic voluntarism model to explain a relationship between religious practice, norms of civic and social activity, and higher levels of non-voting political participation in Indonesia.

Whether or not a similar pattern adheres among Indonesian Christians, however, is less clear. As Mujani, Liddle, and Kuskridho point out, the overall small percentage of non-Muslims captured in nationally-representative samples of Indonesian voters makes the likelihood of finding statistically-significant relationships based on religious differences highly unlikely, even if they may exist in practice. Yet, the authors note, there is a robust and extensive literature linking religiosity and religious practice to political participation in predominantly Christian countries. Much of this scholarship has focused on the role of parishes and church congregations as mobilizers of political action, emphasizing a positive association between religious engagement and political participation (Greenberg 2000; Johnston and Figa 1988; McDaniel 2008). Building on Verba, Schlozman, and Brady's civic voluntarism model, several other studies have specifically examined the role of churches as providing skill-development opportunities for worshippers (Brown and Brown 2003; Djupe and Gilbert 2006; Jones-Correa and Leal 2001). Yet, others have noted that high levels of religious involvement among evangelical Christians, for example, can reduce connections to broader social networks, potentially leading to a withdrawal from civic engagement (Campbell 2004). Research focusing on the relationship between religion and politics at the level of the individual worshipper or voter among Indonesian non-Muslims, however, remains in the scholarly frontier.

The forthcoming analysis builds on these broad strands of literature by comparing data from an original survey that allows for a more direct comparison between Muslims and Christians. Earlier findings from related projects suggest that the intersection of religion and politics in Indonesia might differ based on religious denomination. Using participant observation data, Lussier (2019) finds that Indonesian Christians are exposed to more opportunities to develop participatory civic skills through their churches than Indonesian Muslims are in their mosques. Similarly, Ahnaf and Lussier (2019) have found that Indonesian Christians and Muslims also receive different political messages in sermons at their houses of worship, although most messages are both tolerant and indirect. These two studies, Mujani, Liddle, and Kuskridho (2018), and the broader literature on religion and politics in churches all draw attention to the social or communal aspect of religious life, which is more specific than religious identification, yet is also distinct from one's attitudinal or spiritual attachment to the tenets of a specific religious doctrine. Bearing in mind this connection in emphasis, there are two concepts we introduce in this chapter that require clarification before embarking on empirical analysis.

First, we examine individual Muslims and Christians who are nested within specific houses of worship. We define "house of worship" as a permanent physical space where individuals of the same religious denomination come together with the primary purpose of fulfilling devotional duties related to their religious practice. This physical space has a consistent group of individuals who worship in it, as well as religious leaders who tend to it. Thus, mosques, parishes, churches, temples, and synagogues are all examples of "houses of worship," even though the significance of worship space may vary across different religious denominations.

The second concept requiring clarification is "religious engagement," by which we mean participation in worship or social activities organized in a house of worship or in the surrounding community, intended for members of the house of worship. Our understanding of "religious engagement," is broader than simply fulfilling devotional duties associated with specific religious obligations, such as praying *sholat* five times daily for Muslims or attending weekly Sunday services for Christians. Rather, we consider the full range of activities that bring individuals together in the worship space or in community with fellow worshippers from the same house of worship. While the bulk of activities considered under the concept of religious engagement are connected to worship or prayer, many others are more social or administrative in character. As such, our understanding of religious engagement is broader than the concepts of piety or religiosity. Moreover, we make no *a priori* assumptions about the intentions of individuals participating in activities relating to a house of worship. Rather, we expect that individuals are motivated to engage in religious life for a variety of reasons, ranging from piety, a desire for social or communal engagement, or societal expectation or obligation. We are less interested in identifying why people choose to engage in activities at houses of worship than in understanding how their religious engagement corresponds with their political participation.

We now turn to a discussion of our cases and the survey design.

Case Selection: Yogyakarta, Indonesia

The Indonesian Constitution adopted in 1945 recognizes Pancasila as the state ideology. Article 29 of the Constitution makes two brief statements about religion: 1) The state shall be based on One and Only God (*Kutuhanan Yang Masa Esa*); and 2) The state guarantees all inhabitants the freedom to choose different religions and to worship according to their own religious beliefs (1945).[1] Over time, Indonesia's Ministry of Religious Affairs came to interpret Article 29 in such a way as to acknowledge six official religions: Islam, Catholicism, Christianity (meaning Protestantism), Hinduism, Buddhism, and Confucianism. According to the 2010 census, 87.2 % of Indonesians identified as Muslim, 6.9% as Protestant, 2.9% as Catholic, and less than 2% each of the remaining three religions. In spite of the fact that Indonesia is the largest Muslim-majority country in the world, the numbers of non-Muslims present are not inconsequential. In terms of absolute numbers, according to the 2010 census, more than 23 million Catholics and Protestants lived in Indonesia, which is greater than the entire population of the Netherlands.

Indonesia's religious diversity is reflected geographically, as well. While Islam is the majority religion in all but five of Indonesia's 34 provinces, most contain substantial Christian minorities. Religious expression in Indonesia is further shaped by differences in ethnicity and language, all of

---

1. Authors' translation from the original Indonesian.

which influence the local context in which religion is practiced, giving rise to a heterogeneous religious landscape. It is impossible to capture the full range of possible variation along these parameters within a single study. For this reason, we chose a comparative case study approach, examining houses of worship within a single city, Yogyakarta, Indonesia. By holding the local political context constant, we are confident that any variation observed across groups of individuals is due to differences in houses of worship only.

While recognizing that no single city can provide the breadth of variation in religious experiences witnessed across Indonesia, Yogyakarta shares several characteristics that enhance its value as a typical or representative case for examining the relationship between religious engagement and political participation. First, its religious composition is similar to the national-level breakdown, with a slightly higher percentage of Christians. According to 2013 statistics published by the regional Ministry of Religious Affairs, the city's population is 82.4% Muslim, 10.6% Catholic, and 6.5% Protestant. Second, as an educational center in Indonesia, Yogyakarta has attracted substantial numbers of Indonesians from across the archipelago, imbuing this traditional Javanese city with considerable ethnic and religious pluralism. Lastly, the city's history of religious tolerance has generally facilitated the open practice of religion across a broad range of denominations.

Religious pluralism is present in both Islamic and Christian practices. While Muhammadiyah, which was founded in the city in 1912, has a strong, visible presence in the city, it does not monopolize the religious landscape. Rather, many mosques comprise a mix of traditions, including the modernism of Muhammadiyah, the traditionalist practices of NU, and Salafist customs adopted from the Middle East. According to the regional Ministry of Religious Affairs, 45 Protestant congregations are present in Yogyakarta, representing 24 different denominations, the largest of which is the Christian Church of Java (*Gereja Kristen Jawa*, henceforth GKJ). The city has seven Catholic parishes. Collectively, these characteristics provide a valuable vantage point for describing relationships between religious engagement and political practice among average worshippers that can hold some meaning for broader trends in Indonesia.

Survey of Worship Communities

In July–August 2017, we conducted an original survey of worshippers across eight different houses of worship in Yogyakarta. We first selected houses of worship with the goal of capturing a range of different worship experiences among both Muslims and Christians. The four mosques chosen for the study include a medium-sized mosque with a mix of both modernist and traditionalist elements (Mosque 1); a fairly large, modernist mosque with a strong Muhammadiyah tradition (Mosque 2); a small, neighborhood mosque also displaying a mix of traditions (Mosque 3); and a mosque with close connections to NU (Mosque 4). The four churches include two Catholic parishes located in different parts of the city, a mainline GKJ church (Protestant Church 1), and an evangelical Pentecostal Church (Protestant Church 2). Once houses of worship were selected, we worked together with officials in the mosques and churches to develop a random sample of worshippers from each house of worship. Details about the houses of worship and their representation within our survey are in Table 1.[2] All survey interviews were conducted face-to-face by an interview team that shared the religious background and gender of the respondent.

Our survey comprised a broad range of questions, including demographic characteristics, participation in organizational life, social networks, political participation, and an extensive battery of questions about the

---

2. Prior to developing our survey sample, we first conducted a power analysis to determine the optimal sample size for each house of worship based on its approximate number of worshippers. We determined targets for each house of worship and developed a sampling strategy appropriate for each house of worship to reach the desired sample size. The specific sampling strategy varied by house of worship depending on how the information about worshippers was conveyed to us. For mosques, we were given names of households in densely populated neighborhoods. We used a randomized walking pattern to select households and a further randomization to select a member of the family. For Protestant Church 2, we received specific names of worshippers and selected a random sample from this list. For the other three churches, we first selected neighborhood districts as organized by the church and then randomly selected households from these districts, with a further randomization to select a member of the family. While we succeeded in reaching our targets for most of the houses of worship, our sample sizes were smaller than desired for Mosque 2, Mosque 4, and Catholic Parish 2. For each house of worship, we sought to oversample individuals who were active in taking on voluntary organizational responsibilities in the community, usually by selecting a random sample from names identified to us as active volunteers.

Table 1: *Survery of Worship Communities*

House of Worship	Approimate Number of Worshippers (Survey Sample Size)	% of respondents who have less than complete junior high school	% of respondents with post-secondary education	% of respondents in vulnerable SES category
Mosque 1	800 (*N* = 79)	15.2 (*N* = 12)	45.6 (*N* = 36)	12.7 (*N* = 10)
Mosque 2	1,400 (*N* = 129)	8.5 (*N* = 11)	37.2 (*N* = 48)	19.4 (*N* = 25)
Mosque 3	150 (*N* = 121)	3.4 (*N* = 2)	25.4 (*N* = 15)	25.4 (*N* = 15)
Mosque 4	300 (*N* = 59)	15.7 (*N* = 19)	30.6 (*N* = 37)	14.9 (*N* = 18)
Catholic Parish 1	7,400 (*N* = 136)	16.2 (*N* = 22)	30.2 (*N* = 41)	25.7 (*N* = 35)
Catholic Parish 2	10,000 (*N* = 72)	6.9 (*N* = 5)	18.1 (*N* = 13)	22.2 (*N* = 16)
Protestant Church 1	3,000 (*N* = 110)	11.8 (*N* = 13)	29.1 (*N* = 32)	17.3 (*N* = 19)
Protestant Church 2	1,700 (*N* = 122)	7.4 (*N* = 9)	46.7 (*N* = 57)	9.8 (*N* = 12)

Note. Muslims: N = 388; Christians: N = 440

frequency with which individual respondents engaged in activities at their houses of worship. These latter questions were designed such that Muslims, Catholics, and Protestants answered questions that were tailored to their religious experiences, but with question wording designed to facilitate comparison across traditions.

In terms of demographics, our overall survey sample ranged in age from 18 to 89, with a median age of 50. Among our overall respondents, 66.2% are married, 47.6% percent are heads of their household, and another 21.4% are part of a couple that is the head of the household. The overwhelming majority of respondents—88.2%—identify as ethnic Javanese, and most (65.5%) reported using a mix of Indonesian and Javanese languages for daily communication. Of the remainder, 22.3% use Javanese, 11.7% use Indonesian, and four respondents mix Indonesian with a language from outside of the region.

Determining individual respondents' socioeconomic status is much more complicated due to the cross-cutting nature of multiple factors that contribute to status, including level of education, occupation, and the wealth and consumption of individuals and their family members. Singular indicators for measures of socioeconomic status, such as education level or income, are insufficient measures in a country like Indonesia due to the complexity of social relationships that emerge to redistribute wealth and provide for family needs across members of the same extended family or community. While a multigenerational family in a single household, for example, might have higher levels of wealth based on assets and consumption, individual members of that family might have low levels of education and rely primarily on the status of one or two members for their material needs. Alternately, there are households in which the overall level of education might be higher and family members might be closer in their individual-level status, but a measure of income and assets would place them in a lower socioeconomic bracket. Moreover, the frequent use of live-in domestic labor in upper middle class families, as well as the common practice in urban communities of middle class families fostering the children of poorer rural relations, results in situations in which individuals who are of a lower socioeconomic status are residents of wealthier households.

Because the unit of analysis for our survey was individual respondent and not household, we do not have sufficient information to develop a comprehensive measure of household wealth. As proxies, however, we have developed three measures for individuals in the survey, which we can also examine collectively at the level of the house of worship to better understand the socioeconomic status of each community. First, we have measures of the highest level of education completed, which we have recoded into four categories: incomplete junior high education or lower; junior high education; high school education; and post-secondary education. Within these categories, 11.2% of respondents in our sample had less than a complete junior high school education; 11.6% had completed junior high school; 43.2% had completed senior high school; and 33.7% had post-secondary education. These reported levels of educational attainment suggest that our sample has a considerably higher level of education than the average for Indonesia, as a whole, and for Yogyakarta, in particular.[3] Given our

3. According to the Indonesian Bureau of Statistics, in 2017 the comparable levels of educational attainment for urban areas in Indonesia were: 34.6% with less than a complete junior high school education; 21.4% with a complete junior high education; 32.2% with a complete high school education, and 11.8% with a post-secondary degree (Badan Pusat Statistik 2017, 71). This same report provides information on the average number of years spent in school, broken down by province (158). For Yogyakarta, the average is 9.6 years, which, though a full year more than the Indonesian average of 8.5, still evens out to the average resident having an incomplete high school education.

sampling procedure, which relied on randomization of known worshippers, we suspect that the educational skew present in our sample is a result of two factors: 1) more highly educated worshippers may be over represented in the official registries of houses of worship, and 2) interview refusal rates may have been higher among less educated respondents in our sample.

In addition to education level, we have two further indicators that can help us to approximate socioeconomic status. The first is quality of the respondent's housing, which is a measure based on observational charac- teristics noted by the interviewers when the survey was completed in the respondent's dwelling. Interviewers noted whether the dwelling type was permanent or semi-permanent, as well as the materials of the dwelling's floor, walls, and ceiling. Using this information, we developed a housing in- dex and then further categorized respondents into three categories of low, middle, and upper for housing quality. As a final proxy of socioeconomic status, we created a category of social vulnerability and coded respondents into this category if they met any of the following characteristics: they are the head of household and report a monthly income of less than 600,000 rupiah; there are more than three families living in the respondent's dwell- ing; and the respondent is the head of the household, is not working, and is the only adult in a household with children under the age of 18.

In order to compare the socioeconomic levels of the worship commu- nities under investigation, we examined these different indicators pooled at the level of the specific house of worship which respondents attend, the details of which are included in Table 1.[4] This information confirms our own observations from visiting these houses of worship and conducting interviews in the communities—they contain considerable socioeconom- ic diversity within the same community, and our proxy indicators are not necessarily strongly correlated. For example, all communities show that the percentage of respondents in a vulnerable socioeconomic category is greater than the percentage living in the lowest quality housing, suggest- ing that housing alone is an insufficient indicator of status. Two commu- nities stand out as poles on either end of the range of socioeconomic indi- cators. At one end, Catholic Parish 1 has both the highest concentration of respondents with less than a junior high school education, as well as the

---

4. In the interest of space, we omit the information on housing quality. We found this the least reliable measure and the one for which data were most limited.

highest percentage of individuals in a vulnerable socioeconomic category. At the other end, Protestant Church 2 has both the highest percentage of respondents with post-secondary education, as well as lowest percentage of respondents in a vulnerable socioeconomic category. Yet, across the entire survey, 45 respondents with post-secondary education meet one of the criterion to be categorized as socioeconomically vulnerable, with 11 of them located in Catholic Parish 1. The remaining houses of worship, however, all cluster in the middle. Some, such as Mosque 1, have high numbers of both highly educated and lower educated worshippers. These dynamics suggest that all of the communities contain a broad cross-section of society and cannot be easily ranked in terms of wealth or status. To the extent that we observe meaningful differences across worship communities, such differences are not likely due exclusively to variation in concentrations of wealth, education, or poverty.

Descriptive Trends:
Religious Engagement and Political Participation

As a first point of analysis, we looked at the frequency of religious engagement in houses of worship, based on responses to a number of different questions. Muslims were asked about the frequency with which they perform daily prayers at the mosque; participate in Qur'anic study groups (*pengajian*) at the mosque, participate in Qur'anic study groups at the houses of individuals from the mosque; and participate in other types of activities, such as Qur'anic recitation, meetings, or other activities at the mosque. Protestants and Catholics were asked about the frequency with which they attend Sunday worship services (or Mass); attend daily worship services (or daily Mass); attend prayer services, Bible study, Vespers, or Rosary; participate in social or preparatory activities at church, including rehearsals; participate in neighborhood activities organized by their church congregation; and visit the church to pray in solitude. Responses to all of these questions were recoded into a four-part ordinal measure of religious engagement in which a respondent is categorized into a group depending on whether they engage 1) more than once per week; 2) several times per month; 3) several times per year; or 4) rarely/never. Table 2 shows the frequency of respondents that fall into each category. Preliminary analysis of survey questions showed relatively limited differences across mosques, as well as between Catholics and Protestants.

Therefore, to simplify our analysis, our remaining descriptive tables pool all Muslims into one category and combines Catholics and Protestants into one "Christian" category.

Table 2: *Frequency of Religious Engagement in Houses of Worship*

Frequency of Religious Engagement at Houses of Worship	Muslims (%)			Christians (%)		
	Total	Men	Women	Total	Men	Women
More than once per week	66.8 (N = 259)	81.1 (N = 167)	50.6 (N = 92)	49.1 (N = 216)	42.3 (N = 88)	55.2 (N = 128)
Several times per month	15.0 (N = 58)	9.7 (N = 20)	20.9 (N = 38)	48.2 (N = 212)	53.9 (N = 112)	43.1 (N = 100)
Several times per year	7.0 (N = 27)	2.4 (N = 5)	12.1 (N = 22)	1.4 (N = 6)	1.9 (N = 4)	0.9 (N = 2)
Rarely/Never	11.3 (N = 44)	6.8 (N = 14)	16.5 (N = 30)	1.4 (N = 6)	1.9 (N = 4)	0.9 (N = 2)

As Table 2 reveals, 66.8% of Muslim respondents engage in religious activities in their mosque more than once per week, which is more than 17 percentage points higher than the percentage of Christians who engage with the same frequency. If we examine the top two categories of frequency of engagement, however, we see that more than 95% of Christians in the survey engage at least several times per month. In contrast, more than 18% of Muslims in the survey engage with their mosque only several times per year or less frequently. This overall difference in engagement level might be partly explained by differences in survey sampling strategy. Since mosque worshippers generally live in walking proximity to their house of worship, our sampling strategy likely included individuals who identify as Muslim but are not religiously engaged. In contrast, individuals who identify as Christian but are not engaged in religious life might not appear on the roster of church members from which we drew our sample.

At first glance, one might reasonably expect that the higher percentage of Muslims than Christians concentrated in the top category of religious engagement is reflective of differences in worship obligations between Muslims in Christians, with Islam emphasizing daily prayer and Christians weekly communal service obligations. While it is true that all of our Muslim respondents who report frequenting the mosque several times per week pray there regularly, almost all participate in activities other than obligatory prayer as well. For example, 77.4% of Muslim respondents who report participating in worship activities in mosques several times per week attend Qur'anic study at least once per month. In fact, only 12 respondents in the sample report coming several times a week to pray at the mosque but otherwise engaging in other activities less often than once per month.

In addition to measuring the frequency of attending activities at houses of worship, we also measured religious engagement in two other ways. First, we asked respondents, on average, how many hours they spent on activities at their houses of worship in the previous week. Muslim respondents averaged 4.1 hours per week, while Christians averaged 1.2 hours, a statistically-significant difference. If we remove individuals who did not spend any time at their houses of worship the previous week in order to compare only those who invested some time, Christians average 2.6 hours and Muslims average 5.8 hours, also a statistically-significant difference. These findings suggest that, on the whole, Muslims spend more time on a weekly basis on activities in their houses of worship than do Christians. Second, we asked respondents if they had ever served in a leadership capacity in their house of worship, such as chairing a committee or serving in a specific volunteer capacity upon which others in the worship community depended, such as assisting in leading worship. Within our sample, 56.7% of Muslim respondents and 49.6% of Christians have performed leadership roles, suggesting high levels of religious engagement across both denominational groups, but slightly higher engagement among Muslims.

Levels of religious engagement also vary by gender. As the data in Table 2 show, a gender gap of 30 percentage points separates Muslim men and women in the highest level of religious engagement. Nevertheless, the majority of Muslim women attend activities at their mosque more than once per week, and less than one-third report engagement levels of only several times per year or less. In contrast, Christian women show higher levels of overall engagement than Christian men. A gender gap of nearly 13 percentage points in the highest level of religious engagement exists between Christian men and women. When we consider the two highest levels of religious engagement, however, the gender differences among Christians generally disappear. What is, perhaps, the more interesting comparison is the differences in religious engagement by gender across religious denomination. The percentages of Muslim and Christian women who engage in religious activities more than once per week differ by less than five percentage points, suggesting that broader social factors that shape the frequency with which women are able to engage in religious activities affect both Muslim and Christian women in similar ways. In contrast, the percentage of Muslim men who engage in religious activities more than once per week is nearly double that of Christian men.

Table 3: *Frequency of Religious Engagement in Houses of Worship by Socioeconomic Status*

Frequency of religious engagement at houses of worship	Muslims (%)		Christians (%)	
	Post-secondary	Vulnerable SES	Post-secondary	Vulnerable SES
More than once per week	75.0 (N = 102)	60.0 (N = 27)	47.6 (N = 68)	65.0 (N = 39)
Several times per month	16.9 (N = 21)	13.3 (N = 6)	51.8 (N = 74)	31.7 (N = 19)
Several times per year	1.5 (N = 2)	8.9 (N = 4)	0.7 (N = 1)	1.7 (N = 1)
Rarely/Never	6.6 (N = 9)	17.8 (N = 8)	0 (N = 0)	1.7 (N = 1)

Does level of religious engagement vary according to socioeconomic indicators? We examined this question by looking at engagement levels across different strata. Table 3 displays frequency statistics for two poles in our status indicators: individuals with post-secondary education and individuals categorized as being in a vulnerable socioeconomic category who have less than a post-secondary education. These data reveal that individuals at both ends of the socioeconomic spectrum engage frequently in religious life. Among Muslim respondents, 75% of individuals with post-secondary education engage more than once per week, as do 60% of socioeconomically vulnerable individuals. Among Christians, the majority of individuals in a vulnerable socioeconomic category engage in religious activities more than once per week, revealing a participation rate that is 17 percentage points higher than Christians with post-secondary education. When we combine the top two levels of religious engagement, we see a stronger, positive association between socioeconomic status and participation, with 92% of Muslims and 99% of Christians with post-secondary education engaging at least several times per month. The participatory gap between vulnerable Muslims and Christians is greater when the top two categories are examined together, with 73% of vulnerable Muslims participating at least several times per month, compared to 96% of Christians. Nevertheless, the data reveal high levels of religious engagement across a broad cross-section of Muslim and Christian society in Yogyakarta.

We now turn to looking at political participation. In this analysis we are employing Joan Nelson's (1979, 8) definition of political participation as "action by private citizens intended to influence the actions or the composition of national or local governments." In applying Nelson's conceptualization of political participation, we are drawing a clear line between political participation and broader forms of civil society engagement, such as belonging to mass organizations or engaging in broader civic initiatives not directly connected to a specific public policy or government official, including public awareness campaigns connected to social issues like environmental degradation, public health, etc. For example, membership in one of Indonesia's mass Muslim organizations, Muhammadiyah or NU, is not considered a form of political participation. However, engaging in an act of protest against a government policy organized by one of these organizations is political participation. Similarly, membership in a political party is alone not an example of political participation, but campaigning for a candidate running for election is.

Our survey instrument asked about a broad range of political activities, including voting, participating in activities related to electoral campaigns, contacting public officials for constituent services or to make a complaint, and engaging in acts of contentious politics. In sum, we asked about respondents' overall record of voting in the past 15 years, whether they had voted in a mayoral election held several months prior to our survey, and the frequency of their participation in nine forms of non-voting participation over the past four years. All respondents report voting at high levels: 86.8% of Christians and 80.9% of Muslims claim to have voted in all elections over the past 15 years, and 92.8%

of Christians and 90.7% of Muslims report voting in the 2017 mayoral election.[5] When examining the frequency of religious engagement with voting frequency, we found that, on the whole, a higher percentage of Muslims who vote less frequently attend religious activities more than once per week than do Muslims who are regular voters. The reverse dynamic is visible among Christians. However, when the top two categories of religious engagement are considered together, the differences between more or less frequent voters within the same religious denomination disappear.

Greater variation in political participation is revealed when we examine the nine questions focused on non-voting political participation. For each question, respondents were asked the frequency with which they undertook the specific act over the past four years, and were given the response options, "never," "one time," "several times," and "often." Generally speaking, participation levels showed high levels of consistency for acts within the same category of political activity for both campaign activity and contacting, as measured by Cronbach's alpha. Therefore, we recoded responses in these categories to combine responses across different acts to develop a general measure of frequency for campaign participation and for contacting. Due to low levels of inter-item covariance across questions pertaining to contentious politics, we do not aggregate responses to those questions.[6] Lastly, we combined responses across the nine questions to develop a general, ordinal measure of non-voting political participation. Individuals who report never engaging in any non-voting political participation over the past four years are coded as "never;" individuals report engaging in any act "one time," are coded as "one time;" individuals who reported engaging in more than one act "one time" or one act "several times" are coded as "several times;" and individuals who reported engaging in two or more acts "several times" or any act "often" are coded as "often." The frequency of political participation across these different categories is reported in Table 4.

5. While social desirability bias likely contributed to individuals self-reporting higher levels of voting than their behavior indicates, Indonesia, in general, has high levels of voting. The IFES Election Guide for Indonesia reports an average turnout of 75.3% between 2004 and 2014 (www.electionguide.org), and multiple media sources reported turnout between 80% and 81% for the 2019 national elections. Mujani, Liddle, and Kuskridho (2018) document an overall decline in voter turnout from 1999 to 2014.
6. Table 4 does not include a row for participating in strikes since only a total of four respondents in the entire sample, one Muslim and three Christians, reported participating in strikes.

Table 4: *Frequency of Non-Voting Political Participation*

Frequency of participation	Often (%)		Several times (%)		One time (%)		Never (%)	
	Muslim	Christian	Muslim	Christian	Muslim	Christian	Muslim	Christian
Campaign Activity	7.7 (N = 30)	6.6 (N = 29)	6.4 (N = 25)	3.9 (N = 17)	8.0 (N = 31)	11.2 (N = 49)	77.8 (N = 302)	78.4 (N = 344)
Contacting public officials	2.1 (N = 8)	1.1 (N = 5)	12.6 (N = 49)	6.4 (N = 28)	4.9 (N = 19)	7.1 (N = 31)	80.4 (N = 312)	85.4 (N = 375)
Signing Petitions	1.8 (N = 7)	1.6 (N = 7)	5.2 (N = 20)	4.6 (N = 20)	2.6 (N = 10)	4.3 (N = 19)	90.5 (N = 351)	89.5 (N = 393)
Demonstration	2.6 (N = 10)	0 (N = 0)	1.8 (N = 7)	0.7 (N = 3)	2.6 (N = 10)	2.5 (N = 11)	93.0 (N = 361)	89.5 (N = 393)
All Non-Voting Participation	15.5 (N = 60)	13.2 (N = 51)	13.2 (N = 51)	9.6 (N = 42)	9.6 (N = 37)	13.0 (N = 57)	61.8 (N = 239)	64.2 (N = 282)

Several trends in Table 4 merit discussion. First, overall rates of non-voting political participation across both Muslims and Christians are much lower than voting. Nevertheless, more than 35% of Christians and 38% of Muslims participated in at least one non-voting political act over the past four years. Second, on the whole, frequency of participation appears to be quite similar between Muslims and Christians. For both groups, campaign activity is the subset of participation with the highest level of frequency, with slightly over 20% of both Muslims and Christians reporting some engagement with electoral campaigns. Similarly, for both groups, acts of contentious politics were the least frequent form of engagement, particularly demonstrations. Nevertheless, within this category of activity, Muslims were more likely than Christians to participate in demonstrations and report engaging in this activity more than once.

In summarizing the descriptive trends uncovered in our survey, the majority of Muslims in our sample engage in religious activities more than once per week and nearly half of the Christians in our sample engage at a similarly high level. The data show a fairly substantial gap in religious engagement between Muslim and Christian men, with Muslim men engaging at higher rates, while the differences between Muslim and Christian women are fairly minimal. Additionally, we found that both Muslims and Christians at opposite ends of the socioeconomic spectrum engage in religious life at high levels. When looking at the relationship between religious engagement and political participation, we see that both Christians and Muslims vote at high rates and voting frequency does not appear to be strongly associated with the level of religious engagement. Non-voting political participation is a more complex phenomena. Looking exclusively at levels of participation, there are no striking differences between Muslims and Christians. In order to examine whether religious engagement shapes non-voting political participation, however, we will need to turn to more complex statistical models.

Testing the Independent Effect of Religious Engagement on Political Participation

The indicators of religious engagement and political participation examined in the previous section were measured as ordinal response categories, which was a logical choice for presenting descriptive statistics of frequency of behavior. In moving from descriptive reporting to regression models, however, we simplify some measures to better reflect the nature of our data's distribution. Since the majority of respondents report never participating in non-voting acts, the most meaningful variation to explain is the difference between those who have never participated and those who have. The statistical model that best reflects this structure is a binary model in which we recode responses to the participation questions so that individuals who have engaged in some form of non-voting political participation are coded as "1" and individuals who have never engaged in any such activities are coded as "0." We created similar binary variables for each of the sub-categories of non-voting participation included in Table 4, all of which are analyzed using logistic regression.

The primary independent variable we seek to test in these models is frequency of religious engagement. For simplicity and ease of interpretation, we recoded the frequency variable presented in Tables 3-6 into a binary variable that collapsed "several times a month" and "more than once per week" into one category and "several times per year" and "rarely/never" into another category. These two categories can be understood as individuals who frequently engage in religious life and those who do not. We also add a dummy variable coded as "1" for respondents who have served in a position of leadership at their house of worship and "0" for those who have not. As we expected, individuals who report leadership roles engage in religious activities at much higher levels than those who do not (for both Muslims and Christians), leading these two independent variables to be positively correlated. In order to capture the independent effects of these specific independent variables, we include three demographic controls: education, vulnerable SES status, and gender. Lastly, because this survey is based on random samples of specific houses of worship, we include dummy variables for each house of worship in order to control for factors specific to the house of worship that are not captured by respondents' individual-level characteristics. We analyzed the Muslim and Christian samples separately, using Mosque 3 as the base category for the Muslim sample and Protestant Church 2 as the base category for the Christian sample.[7]

Figure 1 displays the results of the logistic regressions for our dependent variables. Each panel of the figure represents one regression model, with the coefficients and their confidence intervals plotted as odds ratios. If a variable's confidence interval crosses the centerline of the graph panel, we can say with confidence that this variable did not have a statistically significant impact on the form of political participation under investigation. Confidence intervals that are to the right of the centerline have a statistically-significant, positive relationship to political participation, while confidence intervals that are to the left of the centerline have a statistically-significant, negative relationship to political participation. Each row in the figure corresponds to a different dependent variable, with the panels in the left-hand column presenting the results from the Muslim sample ($N=388$) and the right-hand column presenting results from the Christian sample ($N=439$).[8]

---

7. All regression models were estimated using standard errors clustered at the house of worship.

8. For panel A, $N=387$ and for panel H, $N=438$. For the regression in panel H, we found that vulnerable SES status was perfectly collinear with the dependent variable for one house of worship. As the variable was not statistically significant in either the Christian or Muslim sample, we dropped it from the models included in G and H in order to estimate comparable models using the largest possible sample size.

Figure 1: *Logistics Regression Plots for Non-Violating Political Participation*

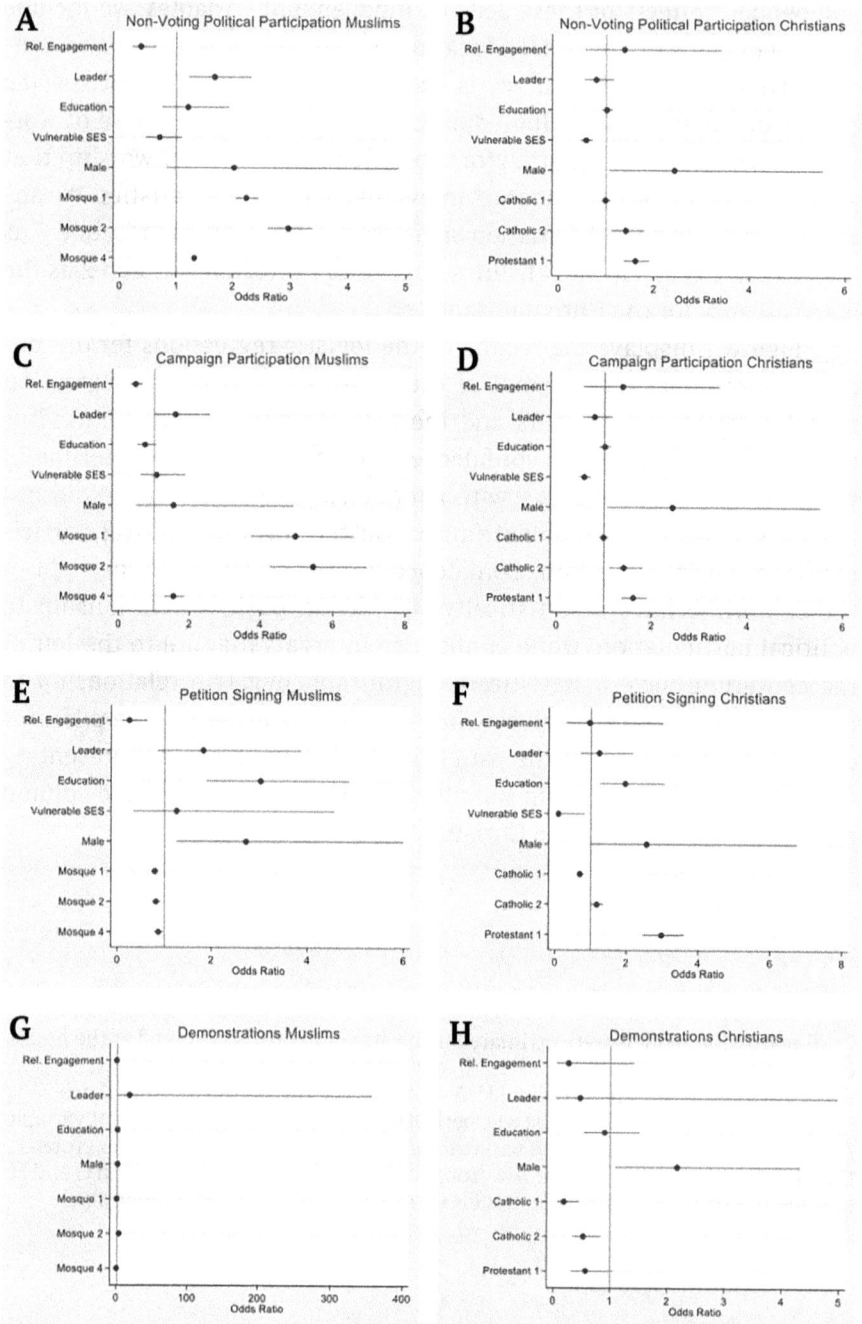

On the whole, the data presented in Figure 1 reveal that, even when socioeconomic and demographic characteristics are taken into consideration, religious engagement and leadership in religious life appear to have a statistically significant relationship on some forms of political participation for Muslims. They do not, however, have a statistically significant impact on political participation among Christians for any of the dependent variables under examination. The impact of religious engagement and leadership in houses of worship on Muslim participation varies across categories of political action. For the most general dependent variable displayed in the first row—participation in any form of non-voting political act—Muslims who are more religiously engaged are less likely to participate than those who are less engaged. However, individuals who have served in leadership roles in their mosques are more likely to participate in politics. It is valuable to note that these two independent variables are statistically significant, while the control variables for socioeconomic status and sex are not, suggesting that religious engagement is a stronger predictor of non-voting political participation than are socioeconomic and demographic factors—a finding consistent with Mujani, Liddle, and Kuskridho's (2018) study of voting behavior. This same overall dynamic is present in models of the other dependent variables for the Muslim sample, although the relationships are not always statistically significant.[9] More specifically, we have evidence of a statistically-significant relationship for the impact of both religious engagement and leadership on campaign activity, for the effect of religious engagement on petition-signing, and for the influence of leadership on demonstrating.

The models presented in Figure 1 offer compelling evidence that Muslims who are more involved in carrying out the leadership work of their mosque are more likely to be active in non-voting political participation, while Muslims who are more religiously engaged, but do not take on leadership roles, are less likely to be politically active. Moreover, leadership experience in mosque life appears to be a stronger predictor of non-voting political activities than are education level, socioeconomic status, and sex. For Christians, however, demographic variables were stronger correlates of non-voting political participation than were levels of religious engagement

9. No statistically significant relationships occur between the religious engagement and leadership variables and contacting public officials, so we omit graphs of these regressions in the interest of space.

or leadership experience. On the whole, Christian men were more likely to participate in non-voting political activities than Christian women, and individuals in a vulnerable SES category were less likely to be politically active. With the exception of signing petitions, for which education is a positive and statistically-significant predictor for both Muslims and Christians, education level did not correlate with political participation.

Lastly, the results in Figure 1 reveal that the dummy variables for individual houses of worship were frequently statistically significant for both mosques and churches. At the most basic level, the statistical significance of these dummy variables tell us that belonging to one or another house of worship appears to have a statistically-significant impact on whether an individual participates in political life, independent of the individual-level characteristics included in the models. Such statistically-significant differences could be a consequence of specific neighborhood or community-level attributes we cannot account for here, including the overall level of political mobilization in a given neighborhood where a mosque or church might be located, as well as some specific feature about the intersection of religious and political life in individual communities. For example, if a member of a house of worship had put themselves forward for a local or regional election, perhaps members of that religious community might have become more involved in campaign participation to support their co-worshipper. Alternately, if a specific local issue was deeply relevant to the neighborhood in which a house of worship is located, perhaps worshippers there became more involved in contacting, petitioning, or demonstrating. Exploring the dynamics behind these specific control variables are beyond the scope of the present analysis, but they strongly suggest that neighborhood-level and community-level factors that extend beyond individual-level socio-economic and religious resources play a role in mediating the relationship between religious life and political participation.

In order to develop a clearer understanding of the strength of the relationship between religious engagement and political participation among the Muslims in our sample, we calculated several predicted probabilities based on the logistic regression models estimated in panels A and C of Figure 1, varying hypothetical levels of religious engagement and leadership, as well as sex and education level. As the results across both dependent variables revealed similar trends, we limited our analysis to the model in panel A, for which the predicted probabilities are displayed in Table 5. Each row in the table contains the predicted probabilities for a different mosque included in the sample, while each column represents a different combination of religious engagement, leadership experience, education level, and sex. Thus, looking at predicted probabilities within the same row allows one to consider the breadth of relationships between different individual-level variables that obtain within a single house of worship, while looking at predicted probabilities within the same column sheds light on predicted political participation across individuals with similar characteristics in different worship contexts. For each mosque, the highest and lowest predicted probability of participation is marked in bold.

Generally speaking, the predicted probability of political participation is higher in Mosques 1 and 2 than in Mosques 3 and 4, but in all mosques the combination of variables that leads to the highest predicted probability of participation is infrequent religious engagement and lack of leadership in religious activities among men with post-secondary education. For example, in Mosque 2, a man with higher education who is an infrequent participant in religious life at his mosque has a predicted probability of 0.74 of participating in non-voting political activities. In other words, he has a three-out-four chance of engaging in political activities other than voting. Curiously, the combination of variables that fosters the second highest predicted probability, however, is for men with higher education who have both high levels of religious engagement and leadership in their mosques. As a point of comparison, the predicted probability of participation for this set of characteristics in Mosque 2 is 0.64. Yet, for both men and women, the relationship to religious engagement that results in the lowest predicted probability of political participation is for individuals who engage in religious activities frequently, but do not take on leadership responsibilities. This trend holds regardless of education level, suggesting that there is something particular about leadership roles rather than engagement in religious life more generally, that fosters political participation.

As Table 5 shows, the predicted probabilities for non-voting political participation are lower for women than for men. Across all four mosques, even when we compare women and men with similar levels of religious engagement and leadership experience, men with incomplete junior high education still have higher predicted probabilities for political participation

Table 5: Predicted Probabilities for Non Voting Political Participation

Education	Male						Female					
	Religious Engagement Low/ No Leadership		Religious Engagement High/ No Leadership		Religious Engagement High/ Leadership Experience		Religious Engagement Low/ No Leadership		Religious Engagement High/ No Leadership		Religious Engagement High/ Leadership Experience	
	High	Low	High	Low	High	Low	High	Low	High	Low	High	Low
Mosque 1	**0.68**	0.54	0.44	0.31	0.57	0.43	0.51	0.37	0.28	**0.18**	0.40	0.27
Mosque 2	**0.74**	0.61	0.51	0.37	0.64	0.50	0.58	0.44	0.34	**0.23**	0.47	0.33
Mosque 3	**0.48**	0.35	0.26	0.17	0.37	0.25	0.32	0.21	0.15	**0.09**	0.23	0.14
Mosque 4	**0.55**	0.41	0.32	0.21	0.44	0.31	0.38	0.26	0.19	**0.12**	0.28	0.18

than women with higher education. Among the 24 predicted probabilities of non-voting political participation for women calculated in Table 5, only two are above 0.50—the threshold that suggests individuals are more likely than not to participate—both for highly educated women who are not religiously engaged. In other words, irrespective of level of education and place of worship, women are simply less likely to become involved in non-voting political participation.

Conclusion

The preceding analysis, which focused on the religious engagement and political participation of the average worshipper in mosques and churches in Yogyakarta, Indonesia, a fairly typical Javanese city, suggests that the relationship between religion and politics in Indonesia is more complex than what is portrayed in media headlines. At the outset, we sought to answer two questions: 1) Are religious engagement and political participation correlated in Indonesia? And 2) Do Indonesian Muslims and Christians differ in the respective roles that houses of worship play in their political lives? Our analysis finds that the answers to these questions are interrelated, with religious engagement having a differential impact on Indonesian Muslims and Christians. Our measures of religious engagement reveal similar levels of activity between Muslims and Christians, with majorities of both groups engaging in activities at their houses of worship several times per month, and substantial numbers of both Muslims and Christians reporting leadership experience within in their houses of worship. Similarly, both Muslims and Christians vote at very high rates and a sizeable minority of both groups report engaging in at least one form of non-voting political participation in the last four years.

Nevertheless, our multiple regression models reveal some meaningful differences in the relationship between religious engagement and political participation between Muslims and Christians. The logistic regression models estimated on our Christian sample found no evidence of a statistically-significant correlation between frequency of religious engagement or leadership experience in houses of worship and non-voting political participation. In contrast, we found that these variables were statistically-significant predictors of some forms of non-voting political participation among Muslims. More specifically, when a statistically-significant relationship between religious engagement and political participation is present, the correlation is negative: those more active in religious life were less likely to be engaged in political activity than those who spent less time engaged with their mosques. Yet, in contrast, previous service in a leadership role in one's mosque is a statistically-significant, positive predictor of political participation. Nevertheless, as the predicted probabilities in Table 5 reveal, even the positive boost for political activity provided by leadership experience in one's house of worship yields a lower predicted probability of political activism for respondents with this experience than for those individuals who were less engaged in religious life. It is also important to note that indicators for socioeconomic status and sex, which are commonly believed to be among the strongest predictors of political participation, were rarely statistically-significant predictors of political activism among our Muslim respondents. Similarly, where one worships frequently had a statistically-significant impact on political activity. All of these trends point to the idea that, for Muslims, where one worships and how engaged they are in their worship community, can be politically consequential, either in fostering or dampening their level of political involvement. This finding merits closer scrutiny in future research, as individual worship communities likely play a crucial mediating role in determining under what circumstances religious engagement proves consequential for political outcomes. Survey data alone cannot reveal what religious messages respondents are hearing in their houses of worship and how those messages are understood and transmitted.

The findings presented in this chapter have several implications for the broader dynamic of religion and politics in Indonesia. First, they sound a cautionary note against assuming a direct line between religious engagement and religiously-based political activism. While there may be specific examples of mosque-level political mobilization that helped populate street protests and voting against Ahok in 2016-2017, mosques do not appear to serve as a universal mobilizer of Muslim political activity in Indonesia. Rather, our survey offers some evidence suggesting that individuals who spend more time in their worship communities are less likely to be politically engaged than those with more limited religious engagement. This observation echoes a finding from scholarship of evangelical Christian churches in western countries that shows a tendency for evangelical Christians to be so deeply involved in their religious communities that they are less likely to contribute time to non-religious civic causes (Campbell 2004). Second, these findings suggest that we must continue to scrutinize which aspects of religious life foster Islamist political participation in Indonesia. If engagement in worship communities is not necessarily driving political activism in the name of Islam, what is? What are the mechanisms by which individuals are mobilizing around religious identities or in the name of religious causes to engage in politics? Our finding that Muslims who take on leadership responsibilities within their mosques are more likely to engage in non-voting forms of political participation than others suggests that future research might productively explore the potential role played by elites in crafting religiously-based appeals and communicating them to receptive audiences. At a minimum, the findings from our analysis of multiple houses of worship within the same city suggest that there is considerable variation and nuance within Islam and a direct line between religiosity and political activism should not be assumed. More concretely, this study suggests that there is weak evidence that the religiosity of the masses is driving the politicization of religion in Indonesia.

Authors' Note

The original survey analyzed in this chapter was funded by a Global Religion Research Initiative International Collaboration Grant. The authors are grateful for the extensive work of a number of individuals who helped make this survey possible. Mustaghfiroh Rahayu and Kuskridho Ambardi made valuable contributions to question wording and sampling strategy; Gregorius Ragil Wibawanto, Fachry Aidulsyah, and Odam Asdi Artosa directed field operations and oversaw data collection; Citra Maudy Mahanani, Jalu Tathit, Amelinda Pandu K., Liana Dewi, Bilal As'Adhanayadi, Vidyanto Purusadhi, Sokemd Arjunaroi M., and Muharrioh conducted interviews; and Monita Nur Fitriani and Ayu Chandra Fitri provided critical administrative support.

Bibliography

Ahnaf, Mohammed Iqbal, and Danielle N. Lussier. 2019. "Religious Leaders and Elections in the Polarizing Context of Indonesia." *Humaniora* 31(3):227-37.

Azra, Azyumardi, and Wayne Hudson, eds. 2008. *Islam Beyond Conflict: Indonesian Islam and Western Political Theory*. Burlington, VT: Ashgate.

Badan Pusat Statistik. 2017. Portret Pendidikan Indonesia: *Statistik Pendidikan 2017*. Jakarta: Badan Pusat Statistik.

Brown, R. Khari, and Ronald E. Brown. 2003. "Faith and Works: Church-Based Social Capital Resources and African American Political Activism." *Social Forces* 82(2):617-41.

Buehler, Michael. 2016. *The Politics of Shari'a Law*. Cambridge, UK: Cambridge University Press.

Campbell, David E. 2004. "Acts of Faith: Churches and Political Engagement." *Political Behavior* 26(2):155-80.

Djupe, Paul A., and Christopher P. Gilbert. 2006. "The Resourceful Believer: Generating Civic Skills in Church." Journal of Politics 68(1):116-27.

Greenberg, Anna. 2000. "The Church and the Revitalization of Politics and Community." *Political Science Quarterly* 115(3):377-94.

Hefner, Robert W. 2000. *Civil Islam : Muslims and Democratization in Indonesia, Princeton Studies in Muslim Politics*. Princeton, NJ: Princeton University Press.

Institute for Policy Analysis of Conflict. 2018. *After Ahok: The Islamist Agenda in Indonesia*. Jakarta: Institute for Policy Analysis of Conflict.

Johnston, Hank, and Jozef Figa. 1988. "The Church and Political Opposition: Comparative Perspectives on Mobilization against Authoritarian Regimes." *Journal for the Scientific Study of Religion* 27(1):32-47.

Jones-Correa, Michael A., and David L. Leal. 2001. "Political Participation: Does Religion Matter?" *Political Research Quarterly* 54(4):751-70.

Kunkler, Mirjam, and Alfred Stepan, eds. 2013. *Democracy and Islam in Indonesia*. New York: Columbia University Press.

Lussier, Danielle N. 2016. *Constraining Elites in Russia and Indonesia: Political Participation and Regime Survival*. New York: Cambridge University Press.

———. 2019. "Mosques, Churches, and Civic Skill Opportunities in Indonesia." *Journal for the Scientific Study of Religion* 58(2):415-38.

McDaniel, Eric L. 2008. *Politics in the Pews: The Political Mobilization of Black Churches*. Ann Arbor: University of Michigan Press.

Menchik, Jeremy. 2016. *Islam and Democracy in Indonesia: Tolerance without Liberalism*. New York: Cambridge University Press.

Mujani, Saiful. 2003. "Religious Democrats: Democratic Culture and Muslim Political Participation in Post-Suharto Indonesia." PhD Doctoral Dissertation, Political Science, Ohio State University.

Mujani, Saiful, R. William Liddle, and Kuskridho Ambardi. 2018. *Voting Behavior in Indoneisa since Democratization: Critical Democrats*. Cambridge: Cambridge University Press.

Nelson, Joan M. 1979. *Access to Power: Politics and the Urban Poor in Developing Nations*. Princeton, NJ: Princeton University Press.

Pepinsky, Thomas B., R. William Liddle, and Saiful Mujani. 2012. "Testing Islam's Political Advantage: Evidence from Indonesia." *American Journal of Political Science* 56(3): 584-600.

———. 2018. *Piety and Public Opinion: Understanding Indonesian Islam*. Oxford: Oxford University Press.

Undang-Undang Dasar Negara Republik Indonesia Tahun. 1945. https://www.docdroid.net/dQNO8VE/uud-1945-sebelum-amandemen.pdf.

Verba, Sidney, Kay Lehman Schlozman, and Henry E. Brady. 1995. *Voice and Equality: Civic Voluntarism in American Politics*. Cambridge, MA: Harvard University Press.

Chapter 5

Piety, Loyalty, and Adaptability: PKS and the Negotiation of Religious Identity

Ioana Emy Matesan

Over the past two decades, there has been a growing scholarly interest in the rise and success of Islamist political parties. Ironically, many of these studies have focused on parties operating in non-democratic settings. This has limited the range of issues explored to questions about determinants of electoral support and debates over whether political inclusion moderates the ideology and behavior of Islamist groups. As the largest Muslim-majority country, Indonesia provides the opportunity to analyze the evolution of Islamist parties in a democratic country, and better understand what affects party adaptation, resilience, and campaign strategies.

Islamist parties tend to run on platforms that emphasize clean politics and morality. In Indonesia, since 2004 the Justice and Prosperity Party (PKS) has been attempting to expand its electoral support base by shifting from a focus on shari'a (Islamic law statues) during its previous instantiation as the Justice Party (PK), to the slogan of "clean and caring," and presenting itself as a reform oriented party rather than an Islamist party. In a context in which patronage and money politics remained prevalent even after the fall of Suharto (Hadiz 2004), and there was a widespread perception that all levels of government had corruption (McCoy 2019, 151), the PKS focus on clean politics paid off. By 2009, PKS became Indonesia's fourth largest party, joining the ruling coalition.

Over the past decade, however, the party has faced a series of scandals involving corruption, bribery, and pornography. The party has also seen divisions between purists and pragmatists, and infighting among the leadership. Consequently, many Indonesian pollsters, journalists, and analysts expected that such divisions and scandals would tarnish the party's image and significantly damage its performance both in the 2014 and the 2019 legislative elections. PKS defied these expectations. After a slight dip in votes in 2014, the party was able to gain a record of 8.2% of the vote in 2019. This electoral gain placed PKS above the PAN party, which is affiliated with Muhammadiyah, the second largest Muslim organization in

Indonesia. PKS increased its vote share by almost 2 percent between 2014 and 2019, whereas the other Islamist parties, PPP and PBB, both witness a decrease in votes.

Even though PKS's success contradicted the expectations of many analysts of Indonesian politics, the issue has not received much attention. For scholars of political Islam, PKS's resilience should be puzzling, since there is significant evidence that to the extent that Islamist parties have a political advantage, it is because of their reputation as competent, trustworthy, and pure (Cammett and Luong 2014). The broader literature on political parties and on niche parties also suggests that character-based valence attributes such as competence, integrity, and unity to affect party image, public opinion, and ultimately, electoral support (Mondak 1995; Clark 2014; Clark 2009). Political scandals and party divisions can also cause parties to lose vote share (Clark 2009). How can we understand PKS's resilience? What has enabled the party to survive internal differences and political scandals of their own? Why do pious members remain loyal to the party in spite of scandals?

I argue that PKS has been able to maintain a relatively stable base of political support because of a combination of 1) party institutionalization, 2) strategic adaptation to the political environment, and 3) an ideological framework that identifies party loyalty as an aspect of the commitment to the religious mission. Such an understanding of party loyalty among the cadres offers a deeper understanding of how the Muslim Brotherhood legacy continues to shape PKS today, and it brings religious values and organizational culture into the analysis of party institutionalization and resource mobilization. Such a perspective can help us better understand how PKS differs from other parties in Indonesia, and why it is able to adapt electorally without alienating the pious core.

The analysis of PKS suggests that the link between religion and politics in Indonesia is both a bottom-up and a top-down process. Religious values affect political mobilization and political behavior. We cannot fully understand PKS resilience without taking seriously the religious commitments and values of its cadres. PKS activists meet weekly to read and memorize the Qur'an, they donate their time and money to the party, they participate regularly in communal activities, and they undergo extensive training in order to advance within the cadre's hierarchy.

At the same time, we would be remiss not to recognize the strategic behavior of the party. PKS not only appeals to its cadres, it also appeals to swing voters. Which voter base it targets during specific elections, and how it frames its political message depends on the political context. As the conservative religious movement in Indonesia has become more prominent in recent years, PKS has started appealing to these conservative voters. In turn, this has reinforced the strength and visibility of conservative religious frames, bringing identity issues once again into national electoral campaigns. Understanding the devotion of the PKS cadres and the pragmatism of the party leaders helps us understand why the party is a potentially powerful ally for populist leaders, and why religious issues continue to remain a powerful mobilizing frame for the near future.

The Origin of PKS

In the context of Indonesian politics, the Justice and Prosperity party (PKS) is the only party that is widely accepted as being a da'wa party inspired by the Muslim Brotherhood model. The party has its roots in the non-political religious tarbiyah student movement of the 1980s. During the 1970s the Indonesian Islamic Preaching Council (DDII), under the leadership of former Masyumi chairman Muhammad Natsir, promoted Islamization on campuses and encouraged students to study in the Middle East. There, many Indonesians came in contact with the Muslim Brotherhood, and returned to Indonesia seeking to emulate the Brotherhood model of non-violent activism, and translating the works of Hassan al-Banna and Sayyid Qutb (Jung 2009, 200). Some suggest that Natsir sent Abu Ridho (one of the founders of tarbiyah) to Saudi Arabia specifically to study the Muslim Brotherhood's curriculum.[1] When these scholars came back, they started interacting with students at mosques around universities, and they organized Islamic trainings at the Bandung Institute for Technology, and subsequently at other prestigious universities.[2]

Thanks to these initiatives, Indonesia witnessed a growth of religious study groups on campuses during the 1980s. These groups consolidated into the tarbiyah student movement, which was structured around

---

1. Interview with Wahyu Bhekti Prasojo, district level coordinator of PKS scout group, June 22, 2013, Depok, Indonesia.
2. Interview with Hermawan Eriadi, November 8, 2012, Jakarta, Indonesia.

the model of "family" cells (*usroh*) that the Brotherhood had spearheaded. Because of the repressive political context under Suharto,[3] the movement was secretive, and exclusively focused on da'wa and grassroots activism. Even though it considered Islamic parties as a necessary means to bring gradual changes in the state (Machmudi 2008, 44), the movement remained purposefully non-political, primarily because it wanted to avoid both repression and co-optation by the regime.[4]

Tarbiyah promoted the notion of comprehensive Islam, and gradual non-violent Islamization that proceeds from the individual to the society and ultimately the state. This process involved cultivating the "perfect character," as well as developing a rigorous membership and training program. Members had to show personal commitment to be accepted into the movement, and they had to display qualities such as uncontaminated faith, correct worship, prefect morals, strong and healthy body, punctuality, and good management (Machmudi 2008, 63).

As the Islamic student movement grew stronger, it began to formally organize its activities through the University Institute for Islamic Propagation (LDK). During the 1990s, tarbiyah members controlled almost all student governments at the major universities (Munhanif 2010, 371). By 1998, tarbiyah activists also founded the Indonesian Muslim Student Action Union (KAMMI), which brought together the nation-wide da'wa groups in an Islamist student movement (Munhanif 2010, 372; Machmudi 2008, 44).

After the fall of Suharto, the new political openings prompted the student movement to consider whether it should enter formal politics. Tarbiyah held a poll on campuses asking its senior members whether the movement should establish a party, a non-governmental organization, or remain unchanged as a student movement.[5] Over sixty percent of respondents favored forming a political party, so PK (the Justice Party) was established in 1998.[6] PK was conceived as a da'wa party based on an Islamic ideology, and seen as a tool for da'wa and for building an Islamic state (Jung 2009, 204).

After the establishment of PK, all tarbiyah members automatically became party members. The regular meetings and rigorous trainings of the

3. The Campus Normalization Act of 1978, for instance, specifically banned political activities by students.
4. Interview with Wahyu Bhekti Prasojo, district level coordinator of PKS scout group, June 22, 2013, Depok, Indonesia.
5. Interview with Hermawan Eriadi, November 8, 2012, Jakarta, Indonesia.
6. Anonymous interview with PKS leader, November 6, 2012, Jakarta, Indonesia.

movement became the basis for the party caderization. The religious and social aspect of the movement did not change, but rather PK was considered both a movement and a party. All religious training and activities were taken over by the party, and the leaders of the tarbiyah movement were included in the main decision-making body of the party, the Majelis Syuro or Consultative Council (Machmudi 2008, 72).

During the 1999 general legislative elections, PK only gained 1.4% of the vote. The first president of PK, Nur Mahmudi Ismail, was appointed as Minister of Agriculture and Forestry, but not having met the electoral threshold of 2 percent, PK was forced to form a new political party, the Justice and Prosperity Party (PKS). The poor electoral performance of 1999 made it clear that for the 2004 elections PKS had to move beyond its tarbiyah core membership and attract new voters. PKS therefore dropped its call for shari'a, and it re-branded itself as a party fighting corruption and working for clean governance.

Under this new platform, PKS was able to win 7.34% of the vote in the 2004 legislative elections, and 7.88% in the 2009 elections (Tanuwidjaja 2010, 34). Whereas the party became more successful electorally as a centrist party embodying Islamic values instead of calling for shari'a, accommodating centrist voters led to tensions within the party. Some senior leaders wanted to focus on da'wa, whereas others wanted to focus on politics.[7] The centrist religious stance was considered by some as a departure from the original tenets of the tarbiyah movement and its Islamist goals (Collins 2003, 16). By 2012, the joke among political analysts was that the PKS was split into two wings: the justice wing and the prosperity wing. Many considered the party to have transformed into a purely pragmatic political actor that played the political game like any other party.[8]

This skepticism was reinforced by the growing allegations of corruptions against party leaders. For instance, PKS founder and former head of the Shari'a Commission, Yusup Supendi, filed a lawsuit against the party, charging that 94% of the 1999 campaign funds came from illegal donations from Middle Eastern benefactors. He accused party leaders of embezzling nearly 1.5 million dollars, and he argued that three senior party leaders entered polygamous marriages without the permission of the party's Shari'a

7. Anonymous interview, November 6, 2012, Jakarta, Indonesia.
8. Interview with Ulil Abshar Abdalla, June 12, 2013, Jakarta, Indonesia; and with Yon Machmudi, June 14, 2013, Depok, Indonesia.

Council (Woodward et al. 2012, 188). After this scandal in December 2013, former PKS president Luthfi Hasan Ishaq was sentenced to 16 years in prison for money laundering and corruption in an attempt to change beef-import quotas (Jakarta Post 2013). Subsequently, a PKS legislator was also caught watching pornographic videos during a parliamentary session. As Woodward et al (2012, 188) point out, such scandals made PKS "the laughing stock of the Jakarta elite," and raised doubts about the party's ability to remain cohesive and to maintain its image as a clean, professional, and religious party. In addition to these scandals, divisions among the leadership culminated in the official dismissal of Fahri Hamzah, one of the most senior leaders of the party (Hakim 2016).

Some argue that these internal divisions and the corruption cases brought against party members explain why the party did not manage to gain more electoral support in 2009 in spite of its strong mobilization capacity (Tanuwidjaja 2010, 33). When considering PKS's performance over the past decade, however, the party has managed to gain significant support, while other religious parties have lost support (Priamarizki and Dinarto 2019). Speaking with PKS cadres in Depok, West Java, in 2012, 2013 and again in 2018, I was impressed by their unwavering commitment to the party. These were not disgruntled rank and file members who did not see a better alternative; they were enthusiastic missionaries of the party.

How has PKS managed to maintain a relatively stable level of loyalty and electoral support over the last decade in spite of the leadership fragmentation and political scandals? What explains this resilience in the face of scandals and leadership divisions, especially when the support of other Islamist parties like PPP and PBB has declined since 2004? If we accept Tanuwidjaja's argument that religious arguments have penetrated the dominant nationalist and Pancasila based political parties, and that Islamic parties are "no longer the lone channel for Islamic aspirations," PKS's stable support becomes even more puzzling (Tanuwidjaja 2010, 29). The next section provides an overview of existing explanations of PKS support, before advancing an alternative framework for understanding party resilience.

Political Participation, Moderation and Resilience

PKS has received significant attention from scholars after emerging as an important player in the 2009 elections. In the context of Indonesian political parties, even in 2009 the success of PKS was puzzling.

Religious parties fared poorly in elections, and the most prominent parties were largely seen as weakly institutionalized and clientelistic. PKS, on the other hand, displayed an impressive capacity for mobilization, despite lacking money, prominent personalities, and associations with Western or traditional powers (Hamayotsu 2011b, 972-73).

Examining the relatively strong support for Islamist parties in the 2014 Indonesian legislative elections, Arifianto suggests that the electoral success can be attributed to the ability of party leaders to retain the support of the most loyal and highly motivated cadres (Arifianto 2014, 9). They were able to do so by promoting a grand narrative that presented corruption scandals as a conspiracy to undermine the party, and by focusing on charitable initiatives to help the poor and victims of natural disasters, which strengthened the bond between cadres and the party (Arifianto 2014, 9).

Arifianto's argument is an important part of the story, and it is one that fits well with the broader social movement theory literature on Islamist groups, which emphasizes the importance of framing and mobilization in accounting for the growing support of Islamist movements (Wiktorowicz 2004). Yet this does not fully capture why the cadres buy into the grand narrative of conspiracy, as framed by the PKS chairman. In my interviews with PKS activists, most accepted that the scandals may be true, but this did not shake their faith in the party, or their commitment to the ideology. To better understand why such a frame can become salient, or why the cadres continue to display loyalty to the organization, it is important to understand the nuances of the ideology and organizational culture that make such commitments possible.

Other scholars emphasize the importance of PKS charitable initiatives (Chernov Hwang 2014, 66). PKS gained public support through the provision of social services and through coalitions with local NGOs, which enabled it to solidify party-mass relations and to broaden its spatial penetration (Hamayotsu 2011b). Baswedan also points out that PKS has benefitted from the emphasis on public services, and service provisions during natural disasters or religious conflicts, or assistance offered to farmers in selling their underpriced crops (Baswedan 2004, 688). Through these services, PKS claims to be pursuing preaching through action (*dakwa bi al-hal*), and the party can generate sympathy from the public, because it implements religious teachings and embodies religious values (Hasyim 2005, 157–58).

What sets PKS apart from other parties is also a "political machinery so well-oiled that it can mobilize members quickly and thus require no jump start at election time" (Baswedan 2004, 689). The party and the social movement are inseparable, and PKS maintains year-round activities for its regular members, which establishes party discipline. Regular meetings geared towards the advancement of religious understanding foster continuous engagement with the party (Baswedan 2004, 688). The centralized structure of PKS also enables the party to unite followers (Jung 2009).

Some argue that PKS has been particularly effective because it is the only movement party in Indonesia (Chernov Hwang 2014, 69). Yet, the Egyptian Brotherhood is also a movement party. This proved effective for mobilization during the first elections after the Arab Spring, but once in power, the Brotherhood was not able to overcome the tension between the movement and the party. To be sure, the nature of the political transition in Egypt, and the lack of strong parties, placed the Brotherhood in a very different circumstance from what PKS ever had to face. Nonetheless, the contextual differences aside, the overlap between party and movement in the case of the Brotherhood led to an identity crisis that made the group even more prone to mistakes during the transition period. As a member of the Muslim Brotherhood political committee confessed in an interview, the question of the proper relationship between the movement and the party was "still a dilemma for the Muslim Brotherhood" in 2012, and "a major internal problem facing the Muslim Brotherhood in the near future."[9] A former Muslim Brotherhood politician suggests that the group lost support in 2013 at least in part because there is an inherent contradiction between being a social movement that seeks to better society, and being a political party that has to compete against parts of the same society in elections. This was at least in part why many people started questioning the credibility of the Brotherhood, perceiving it as using its social services to achieve gains in politics.[10]

These insights from Muslim Brotherhood officials suggest that the overlap between a movement and a party is a double-edged sword that can both benefit and challenge Islamist groups. PKS has been able to negotiate

9. Author interview with Muslim Brotherhood political advisor and member of the political committee, July 5, 2012, Cairo.
10. Interview with Amr Darrag, former Freedom and Justice Party member and Minister of Planning and International Cooperation, December 20, 2018, Istanbul.

the tension between the zeal of the movement and the need for pragmatism experienced by the party. The religiously devout members are an important source of mobilization for the party, and the party is widely regarded as serving the overarching goals of the movement, even though there is a shared understanding that Pancasila defines the rules of the political game at the national level.

These organizational features offer important insights into why PKS has been able to mobilize support, but they do not fully explain why and how the party has been able to maintain this bridge with the social movement, and why both pragmatists and the religiously devout have sustained the party cohesion and discipline. One potential answer is that PKS is actively pursuing two parallel discourses aimed at two separate audiences. For instance, some argue that at the 2011 PKS convention, public sessions emphasized openness and embraced local culture, whereas the closed sessions placed much greater emphasis on core Islamist values (Woodward et al. 2012). Another answer is offered by Hamayotsu, who argues that PSK remains strong, relevant, and cohesive because it has the qualities of a well-institutionalized party: merit-based recruitment and promotion, priority on collective interests, regular succession and regeneration of leadership, and a strong ideological foundation (Hamayotsu 2011a).

Hamayotsu suggests that these organizational characteristics have enabled PKS to moderate ideologically and remain politically relevant. This stands in contrast to Dhume's much more cynical perspective, which lumps PKS and extremist groups in the same boat, and sees PKS as the greatest threat to democracy and pluralism because of its conservative ideology and its ability to mobilize cadres (Dhume 2005). Other ideational approaches, however, attribute the success of the party to its unique religious approach, and the ability to strike a balance between accommodationism and purificationist reformism, and to display flexibility in responding to religious and political questions (Machmudi 2008). Along similar lines, Hilmy classifies PKS as "meliorist" Islamists, characterized by both pragmatism and principled commitments, whose very acceptance of democracy is pragmatic rather than theological (Hilmy 2010). The issue of shari'a implementation is similarly negotiable—whereas the pious members agree on its importance, they also regard it as an issue that the rest of the society has to agree on, but at the same time they have their own internal code of conduct as to how piety should be implemented in their daily lives (Hilmy 2010, 231).

Understanding these aspects of the religious underpinnings of PKS can offer an important glimpse into why the religiously devoted followers might not have been alienated by the pragmatism of the political elites within the party. Yet without a consideration of the organizational characteristics, we miss an important piece of the puzzle. In this chapter, I build on these seemingly divergent arguments and offer a synthesis that proposes that both organizational characteristics and religious interpretations are important, and that ideological factors are constitutive of organizational attributes.

Principled Pragmatism: Institutionalization, Religious Values and Strategic Adaptation

PKS has remained resilient in the face of scandals and leadership divisions because it has been able to maintain the loyalty of its pious cadres, while also astutely adapting its appeal to swing voters. The institutionalization of the party goes a long way in explaining why the pious core has remained loyal to the party. However, institutionalization is not only about organizational structures and party mechanisms; it is also about organizational culture. Rather than considering religious values and resource mobilization as alternative explanations, an appreciation of the Muslim Brotherhood ideology can help us better understand how certain religious values and attributes of organizational culture can facilitate the institutionalization of PKS, and explain the continued loyalty of the cadres.

Inspired by the Muslim Brotherhood, PKS has developed a complex but efficient organizational structure that engages its members throughout the year and establishes a strong link between the party and the community. Unlike most other Indonesian parties, PKS does not rely on the appeal of charismatic figures. Instead, the party has developed efficient mechanisms of internal adjudication, promotion, and decision-making, which the cadres trust even when scandals break out.

Part of this trust and loyalty is not just about the structures that are in place, but also about the organizational culture and the religious values that define PKS cadres. Two aspects stand out. First, the cadres are deeply committed to da'wa. As the only real da'wa party in Indonesia, PKS continues to maintain the support and loyalty of its most pious members. Second, PKS has imported from the Muslim Brotherhood an organizational culture defined by extreme loyalty as an indicator of commitment to the religious mission. From this perspective, then, scandals and leadership divisions are not enough to drive the pious members away. When faced with a crisis, defending the organization and remaining loyal to the party becomes an ideological imperative.

Beyond relying on its pious cadres, however, PKS has also expanded its support from swing voters by aptly adapting to the political context. This has involved two main strategies. The first strategy was to expand the party appeal into rural areas, where national scandals that would affect the party were less salient. The second approach has been to capitalize on the conservative momentum surrounding the opposition to the Jakarta Governor Ahok, and on the growing disillusionment with President Jokowi.

The next sections will develop this argument in greater depth, building on the rich secondary literature, and drawing on interviews I conducted with PKS cadres and leaders in 2012, 2013, and 2018, as well as on electoral data from the Indonesian Electoral Commission. My insights on the organizational culture of the Muslim Brotherhood are based on interviews I have conducted with members of the Egyptian Muslim Brotherhood in 2012, 2018, and January 2020. The next three sections expand on the argument and show how institutionalization, ideology, and strategic considerations interact and explain the resilience of PKS in Indonesia.

Institutionalization and Caderization

Two defining features of PKS are its caderization and its institutionalization, with the former characteristic significantly strengthening the latter. Some estimate that in 2014 PKS had around 800,000 cadres, and that presently this number is probably closer to one million.[11] While these one million members do not account for the majority of votes, having one million missionaries visiting neighborhoods throughout the archipelago and presenting the party program represents an incredible mobilization potential during elections.

In PKS, caderization is more stable than in any other party in Indonesia, and it is not centered around charismatic figures.[12] The process is structured around intensive training and a hierarchy comprised of six levels (Muhtadi 2008, 127–28). Beginner cadres are typically registered at the

11. Interview with expert on PKS, June 8, 2018, Depok, Indonesia.
12. Interview with Bakir Ihsan, Professor of Political Science, Islamic State University Jakarta, June 4, 2018, Ciputat, Indonesia.

sub-district level and they are required to attend regular meetings. If they are recommended by their instructors for the second level, cadres are registered at the district levels, and in addition to attending meetings and participating in PKS activities, they are required to take courses in the social and political sciences. At the third level, cadres undergo more advanced and rigorous training, and by the fourth level, they are recorded in the provincial level branches. Cadres who have reached the fifth and sixth levels can hold strategic positions in the national leadership of PKS and can vote in the party's Majelis Syuro, the main assembly that selects the PKS executives (Muhtadi 2008, 129).

PKS offers a lot of opportunities for professional development. It is telling in this regard that in the summer of 2013, presumably in response to growing accusations of corruption in the media as well as an early preparation for the 2014 elections, PKS distributed an internal document entitled "Cadre Leadership Development." One can interpret this document on one hand as an attempt to reinforce this trust in the system and in the leadership, and on the other hand as a genuine attempt to improve the skills and professionalization of the cadre and leaders at all levels of the party. The book-length document details the party's strategies for leadership development and assessment and astutely integrates this emphasis on leadership within the mission and vision of PKS. The document clearly links capacity building and institution building to its ability to realize the goals of the da'wa and grounds its strategies for leadership development in both religious thought and in leadership theories drawn from psychologists like Maslow, Steve Zaccaro, and businessman Stephen Covey. This versatility underlines the fact that PKS caderization has a powerful aspect of professional development. The party's ability to maintain its overall internal professionalism, encourage the skills development of its members, and continue its system of merit-based recruitment and promotion can be appealing to the political pragmatists within its ranks, independently of their religious commitment to the Islamic mission.

Party caderization is also linked to party institutionalization. In his path-breaking discussion of political institutions, Huntington argued that the level of institutionalization is defined by the level of adaptability (measured by age and functional adaptability), complexity, autonomy, and coherence of organization and procedures (Huntington 2006, 15-20). By these criteria, PKS is fairly institutionalized. In terms of adaptability, the party is not very old, but it has seen peaceful leadership successions, and functional adaptability to the extent that it has appealed to different constituencies over time, and been part of both the governing coalition and the opposition. The organization also has a complex structure, much of which is due to the legacy of the Muslim Brotherhood influence. Whereas the original student movement mobilized in small cells, the party has a clear formal structure that includes a president, an executive committee, a consultative council, as well as different administrative divisions (Hasan 2009, 8). The party has also created a hierarchical national task force that involves members in the provision of social services at the grassroots, extending services to the district level in the fields of education, health, society and economy, culture, and student training (Hamayotsu 2011b, 982).

In terms of organizational coherence, the party can also be seen as largely institutionalized. As Hamayotsu points out, the party has well-established mechanisms for merit-based recruitment and promotion, it emphasizes collective decision-making and interests, it has a strong collective identity, and it has well-established procedures for the succession and regeneration of leadership (Hamayotsu 2011a). Cadres are organized into group at the district levels, and evaluated by senior members in weekly meetings. Furthermore, the party has a judicial committee and a disciplinary body that takes the appropriate disciplinary measures if members break party rules (Hamayotsu 2011a, 149).

What is particularly relevant for the discussion on the potentially detrimental effects of scandals is the fact that party members trust the existing adjudication mechanisms within the party. As several members have emphasized in conversations both in 2013 and in 2018, they recognize that individuals may be flawed, but they trust the party, and they trust that if somebody was truly corrupt the party would take the required disciplinary action.

At the top of the party hierarchy is the shura council (Majelis Syuro), which consists of 100 representatives chosen to represent members in various provinces (Jung 2009, 216). This council selects PKS executives, deliberates party strategy and party positions on political issues, and it determines the party policy. Underneath this council are an advisory council (MPP, Majelist Pertimbangan Partai), a central executive board (DPP,

Dewan Pimpinan Pusat), and a Shari'a Council (DSP, Dewan Syariyah Pusat) (Muhtadi 2008, 110–11). The Shari'a Council decisions must be obeyed and are unquestionable.[13] The chair of the Majelis Syuro, along with the PKS President, General Secretary, treasurer, and the chairs of the advisory board and Shari'a Council form a central board, which discusses party strategy and policy (*The Jakarta Post* 2011).

The central board also appoints a disciplinary court.[14] Thus, when asked why there isn't greater disillusionment with PKS in response to corruption accusations, a member stated in 2013 that "we trust our leader; we have the same vision; and we trust the system."[15] Another cadre made a similar argument in the summer of 2018, pointing out that unlike other parties, PKS leaders come from the Majelis Syuro, which pick the president. "Our leader is given by the system," he remarked, noting that PKS officials "lead based on core values, not by charisma or capabilities; we'll follow if they follow our core values, that's it."[16] The same member later repeated the same emphasis on values when stating "as long as they [the leaders] maintain our core values, we will obey; if they cross our core values, we should remind our leader, and if they correct the agenda fine; if not we will have another Majelis Syuro to replace the leader."[17]

Such comments underline that in order to fully understand party institutionalization and party loyalty among the members, we need to recognize the importance of religious values. Taking religious values seriously can also help us better understand why in a context where PKS is the only da'wa party in Indonesia, support for the party is perceived by the most pious members as support for the religious mission itself. As Syafiq Hasyim noted, "humans can be wrong, right, beneficial to the party, etc, but the party is always true and almost sacred."[18]

If PKS is first and foremost a da'wa party, this raises questions about the level of autonomy of the party, which Huntington considers an element of institutionalization. A truly autonomous organization should not be simply an instrument of certain social groups. For PKS, however,

13. Interview with Wahyu Bhekti Prasojo, district level coordinator of PKS scout group, June 22, 2013, Depok, Indonesia.
14. Ibid.
15. Ibid.
16. Interview with social cadre of PKS, June 21st, 2018, Depok, Indonesia.
17. Ibid.
18. Interview with Syafiq Hasyim, Professor in the Faculty of Social and Political Sciences, Islamic State University Jakarta, June 4, 2018, Ciputat, Indonesia.

the relationship between the party and movement remains contested. Organizationally, PKS enjoys an effective division of labor between the da'wa activities at the grassroots level, and the political activities of its party members, and between its national political campaigns and the local level activities. As Chernov Hwang notes, the party adopts a dual strategy: On one hand, cadres enter political institutions and the bureaucracy in order to translate Islamic concepts and values into policies; on the other hand, da'wa cadres work through grassroots organizations to help the Muslim community (Chernov Hwang 2014, 62–65). Cadres are supposed to embody the exemplary Muslim in order to show that shari'a can be applied in an inclusive manner. A PKS member confessed that his vision is for tarbiyah people to become in charge of law enforcement, courts, and other important areas, because they have the right Islamic values, and this would bring about a "smooth revolution."[19]

PKS conceives of da'wa as involving both horizontal and vertical mobilization. Horizontally, PKS cadres disseminate Islamic teachings at the grassroots level, provide health and social services to the poor, and actively participate in civil society and public and private enterprises. Vertically, PKS cadres seek to enter strategic positions in all key institutions and develop a presence in legislative, judicial, and executive bodies (Hasyim 2005, 162-63).

Since the law on mass organizations was amended in 2017 to ban groups that are opposed to Pancasila (Amnesty International 2017; Hariyadi 2017), the government has been much stricter about prohibiting the mixing of religion and politics. On paper, this has affected PKS recruitment and caderization, as students, state university professors, and civil servants can no longer be officially members of PKS. In practice, however, members have suggested to me that they remain devoted cadres who are involved in all the activities of the movement, but they are no longer PKS card-carrying members, and they keep their political affiliation a secret.[20]

Now the party differentiates between the social and political cadres, and between "tarbiyah for the political sector, and tarbiyah for the social-sector."[21] Social activities continue to be centered around religious education. The political education, which involves PKS functionaries and

19. Interview with Wahyu Bhekti Prasojo, district level coordinator of PKS scout group, June 22, 2013, Depok, Indonesia.
20. Interview with PKS cadre, June 11, 2018, Depok, Indonesia.
21. Interview with PKS cadre, June 21, 2018, Depok, Indonesia.

government officials, includes classes, seminars on workshops on professional development on topics such as how to become a political figure, how to influence public policy, or how to communicate with other parties. For example, PKS has been organizing a "school for political leadership" at both the regional and the national level, which in 2017 and 2018 explicitly focused on anti-corruption training with officials from the Corruption Eradication Commission. In terms of their contributions, whereas the party has been historically funded in large part by membership fees, now cadres differentiate between their religious alms, which they give to registered religious organizations, and political donations, which they can make individually to the party.[22]

PKS members and experts on the party either perceive the movement and the party to be one and the same, or they suggest that they are separate entities, but work towards the same shared Islamic values. Because of recent legislation that prevents social organizations from mixing religion and politics, PKS is taking measures to separate the movement and the party. However, the division is mostly on paper. As a member pointed out, many PKS cadres work in education, health care, and religion, so they can no longer officially belong to the party. However, "they are still considered cadres, because they still do tarbiyah."[23] In recent years, however, PKS is more careful to differentiate between "tarbiyah for the political sector" and "tarbiyah for the social sector."[24] In the political realm, what the party defines to be tarbiyah, and therefore part of its religious mission, is in effect professional development – holding workshops on becoming a political figure, influencing public policy, communicating with the masses, etc. From this perspective, whereas some consider that the movement and the party are parallel structures that work towards the same religious values and long-term goal, others think that PKS is "a movement embodied with a political party, but the spirit is still bigger and longer than political interest."[25]

22. In addition to membership fees and contributions from the cadres, Muhtadi suggests that the party has been pursuing a threefold strategy for funding: It has instructed its MPs to donate part of their salaries to PKS, it has encouraged the spirit of entrepreneurship in the hope of attracting generous contributions from its wealthy cadres, and it has accepted contributions from companies and individuals who share their religious and political ideals. See Muhtadi 2008, 132-133.
23. Interview with PKS cadre, June 11, 2018, Depok, Indonesia.
24. Ibid.
25. Ibid.

This comment reflects how difficult it is to untangle party institutionalization from religious values and ideational factors when thinking about the resilience of PKS. When it comes to PKS ideology, most scholars recognize that the party was inspired by the Egyptian Muslim Brotherhood. What is missing from these discussions, however, is a closer attention to the organizational culture imported from the Muslim Brotherhood, which posits loyalty to the group as a key part of the ideology.

Ideology, Loyalty and the Legacy of the Muslim Brotherhood

Baswedan (2004) identifies six Islam-friendly parties, among which he differentiates between Islamist parties (PPP, PBB and PKS), Islam-inclusive parties (PAN, PKB), and Golkar as a secular-inclusive party. Out of the three Islamist parties, PKS is the only one that does not press for an Islamic state or the formal adoption of shari'a. Instead, PKS views shari'a as a long-term goal, and the party focuses on educating the masses on shari'a instead (689). Dropping the call for shari'a did not alienate the religious constituents of PKS because the party was able to re-frame its position within a coherent ideological framework. This framework was mainstream enough to attract additional supporters, but it also remained religious enough not to alienate its pious constituents. PKS's ideological framework can be described as gradualist pious pragmatism.

In terms of pious pragmatism, the cadres remain committed to the idea of an Islamic state, but they recognize that politically the party needs to accept Pancasila and focus on Islamic values and substantive manifestations of shari'a. PKS no longer brands itself as an Islamist party, but rather as a party that embodies Islamic principles while accepting Pancasila. Instead of pushing for the implementation of the Jakarta Charter, PKS speaks instead of the Medinah charter, which is generally considered a more pluralist and inclusive model, and as Hidayat Nurwahid argued, the basis for a civil society order and for the modern nation-state (Hilmy 2010, 199). Instead of focusing on how to institutionalize Islam as a state system, the party is more focused on how basic Islamic values are "embedded in the political practices of the state and in the management of societal affairs" (Hasan 2009, 7). As a political leader of PKS explained, "there are many aspects of Islamic laws that are implemented in daily life, and we don't have to restrict it to Islamic legislation; so it is Islamic to think about justice and welfare."[26] In 2009, the party campaigned under the slogan of "a party for all of us," and it affirmed its theological affiliation with mainstream Indonesian Islam (Hasan 2009, 20).

A member explained that "PKS accepts Pancasila as the rule of the game but not as the party ideology; Pancasila is how the people of Indonesia communicate with each other [...] but Islam is the ideology of the party."[27] Indeed, as Chernov Hwang notes, an internal poll found that the majority of voters chose the PKS because it was Islamic (Chernov Hwang 2014, 81). From the perspective of the political leaders, "Islamic values are not focused on artificial Islamic symbols but on the core values of Islam—fairness, justice, fight against corruption, democratic system based on values."[28] At the national level, the party also often chooses to focus on uncontroversial issues like Islamic banking and finance, or frames other concerns in non-religious terms.[29] At the local level, however, there has been a growing trend across Indonesia to pass shari'a bylaws (Sunny Tanuwidjaja 2010).

This ability to adopt a flexible approach to the religious mission is in line with the gradualist approach of the Muslim Brotherhood, which has a powerful influence on PKS. Al-Banna subscribed to the notion of 'comprehensive Islam' as a "perfect system of social organization which encompasses all aspects of life" (al-Banna 1978, 30) in which it is impossible to differentiate between religion and politics (al-Banna 1978, 36). For him, the revival of the Muslim community depended on gradual reform that proceeds from the individual to the family and then society, and eventually would lead to the reestablishment of the *umma* and the revival of the caliphate (al-Banna 2002, 46). Al-Anani argues that three key pillars of this Islamic identity were inclusiveness and comprehensiveness, elasticity and adaptability, and practicability and applicability (Al-Anani 2016, 56–58). Inspired by the Muslim Brotherhood, PKS cadres consider

26. Anonymous interview, June 10, 2013, Jakarta, Indonesia.
27. Interview with Wahyu Bhekti Prasojo, district level coordinator of PKS scout group, June 22, 2013, Depok, Indonesia.
28. Anonymous interview with PKS leader, June 18, 2013, Jakarta, Indonesia.
29. A PKS affiliate mentioned that, for instance on the issue of alcohol, PKS doesn't have to oppose it on the grounds of being haram, but it can instead emphasize health risks and use common reason. Thus, the party seeks to promote its Islamic mission by finding common values with others. Anonymous interview, June 18, 2013, Jakarta, Indonesia.

pragmatism and adaptability to be part and parcel of the religious identity. This helps explain why the party was able to reframe its political platform without alienating its religious constituents.

The Muslim Brotherhood ideology also influenced PKS organizational culture. Al-Anani argues that the Brotherhood has a unique organizational identity "that is largely characterized by obedience and submissiveness" (Al-Anani 2016, 119). From the beginning, al-Banna developed a socialization process centered around five norms: *bay'a* (allegiance), *ta'ah* (obedience), *thiqa* (trust), *iltizam* (commitment), and *intima* (loyalty) (Al-Anani 2016, 120). After the death of Hassan al-Banna, in response to the harsh crackdown on the Brotherhood, Sayid Qutb developed the idea of the Islamist vanguard, placing great importance on the need of a strong organization.[30] From Qutb's perspective, because the organization was the embodiment of the Islamist mission, the strength of the organization became essential and synonymous with the Islamic revival movement. This aspect of Qutb's thought had a powerful impact on the Muslim Brotherhood in Egypt, even if leaders did not adopt the violent aspects of the Qutbist thought. In response to external pressures, the response was not violent revolution but rather emphasizing the unity and cohesion of the organization. This meant obedience to the leader and strong party discipline were all in the name of promoting the Islamic mission.

In the case of the Brotherhood, the emphasis on loyalty, obedience, and conformity has devolved into organizational rigidity, and it has hindered in many ways internal ideological debates. This has alienated some of the most prominent reformers (who were often sidelined or silenced), as well as many of its youth members. One can recognize within the ranks of the PKS a similarly ideologically driven emphasis on group loyalty, but unlike the Brotherhood, the PKS prides itself both in a strong system of meritocracy, and in being a strong proponent of youth voices within the movement.

PKS values commitment and qualifications over nepotistic ties, it runs seminars on youth leadership, and it has run young candidates for parliament and governors (Chernov Hwang 2014, 69). In contrast, many young Brotherhood members today have either frozen their

30. Anonymous interview, June 7, 2012, Cairo, Egypt.

membership or left the organization, because they feel that the old leadership is unwilling to listen to the youth, or include young people and women in the decision-making structures. Since the 2013 military coup in Egypt and the ousting of the Brotherhood from power, the old leaders of the organization have once again emphasized saving the organization as the main response to the crisis. Rather than offering a new vision for how to adapt to the
new political situation, leaders have focused on reinforcing organizational loyalty, and saving the existing organizational structures.

PKS is able to maintain its strong party discipline at least in part because at the grassroots level activists understand the need for a strong party from the perspective of the Muslim Brotherhood's experience and ideological developments. Having a strong organization, with individual members embodying Islamic values and fully committed to the religious mission, is considered the foundation of transforming and reforming society. In the face of external challenges and pressures, loyalty and discipline become ever more important. This nuance, inspired by the history and experience of the Muslim Brotherhood, can explain why pious PKS activists might not defect in response to scandals involving the party leaders.

Beyond the pious cadres, however, PKS also received significant electoral support from swing voters. Some of the educated urban middle class voters that saw PKS as appealing in 2009 became disillusioned with the party after the corruption scandals. In the next section, I explore how the party adapted to this changing political landscape.

Strategic Adaptation

PKS has adapted to the shifting political landscape and to the potential damage caused by the scandals by adjusting its campaign strategies. In particular, the party has attempted to make inroads into rural areas, and it has capitalized on the growing conservative movement known as the 212 movement, as well as on the increasing disillusionment with President Jokowi. This strategic adaptation can help explain the electoral success of PKS in the 2019 elections.

When PKS first gained national prominence, the party was especially successful with urban educated religious constituencies. Since the corruption scandals broke out, however, PKS has actively sought to expand its appeal to rural areas. In the 2014 elections, the greatest losses for PKS came in some of its urban strongholds—Jakarta, Bandung, and Depok. In

West and North Jakarta, for instance, PKS saw a decrease of 9.3%, and in East Jakarta a decrease of 8.5%.[31] At the same time, however, the party made inroads in parts of Maluku, Papua, South Sulawesi, and East Java.

By the 2019 elections, PKS regained significant support in its traditional urban stronghold in Jakarta (8.33% increase) and West Java (4.47% increase), and made additional inroads in parts of Maluku, Sumatra, and Kalimantan.[32] Figure 1 shows the change in the percent of PKS vote between the 2014 and 2019 legislative elections, against the population of the different provinces.

Figure 1. *Change in PKS vote from the 2014 to the 2019 legislative elections*

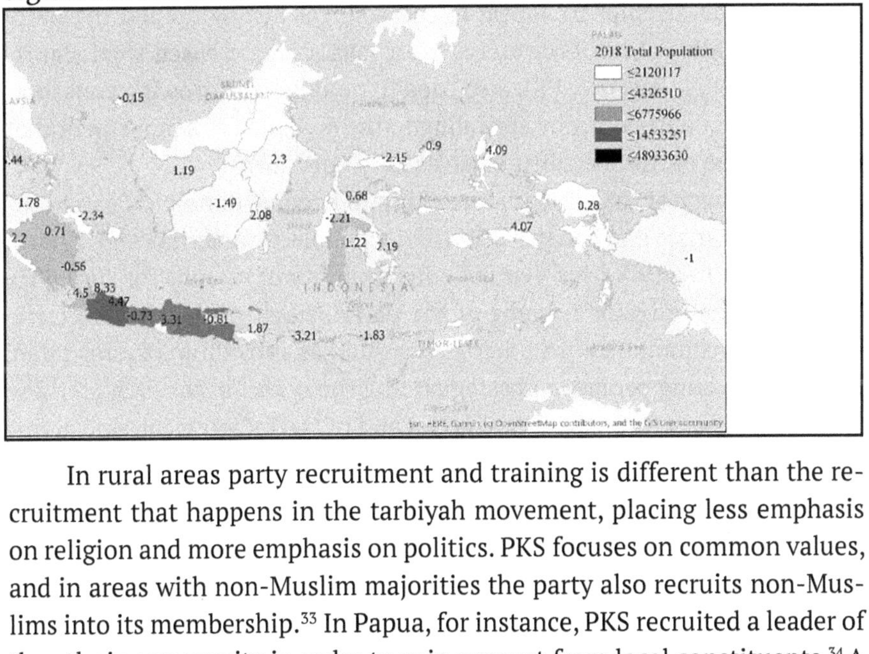

In rural areas party recruitment and training is different than the recruitment that happens in the tarbiyah movement, placing less emphasis on religion and more emphasis on politics. PKS focuses on common values, and in areas with non-Muslim majorities the party also recruits non-Muslims into its membership.[33] In Papua, for instance, PKS recruited a leader of the ethnic community in order to gain support from local constituents.[34] A frequent strategy in rural areas is also to attract respectable local figures, and focus less on PKS as the party.[35]

31. Data obtained from Adam Carr's Election Archive, http://psephos.adam-carr.net/countries/i/indonesia/.
32. Data obtained from Indonesian Election Commission, https://infopemilu.kpu.go.id/.
33. Interview with Hermawan Eriadi, November 8, 2012, Jakarta, Indonesia.
34. Interview with PKS member, June 11, 2018, Depok, Indonesia.
35. Interview with expert on PKS, June 8, 2018, Depok, Indonesia.

PKS's electoral strategy, however, did not rely exclusively on trying to appeal to rural voters. In Jakarta and West Java in particular, the party also tried to capitalize on the growing conservative movement and increasin disenchantment with Jokowi among the urban Muslim middle-class. Even though in regional elections PKS formed an alliance with President Jokowi's party in some areas, at the national level PKS became increasingly critical of President Jokowi, actively campaigning for Prabowo (Priamarizki and Dinarto 2019). The party's secretary-general Mardani Ali Sera popularized the hashtag #2019GantiPresiden (#2019ChangethePresident) on Twitter, and embarked on a social media campaign that targeted in particular the youth, and aimed to link opposition to President Jokowi with support for PKS. In an attempt to appeal to the younger demographics, the party organized flashmobs in Jakarta and West Java, and increased significantly its social media presence. PKS also tried to mobilize the growing conservative religious sentiments, by appealing to the so-called 212 movement that organized the protests against Jakarta Governor Ahok.

Some suggest that PKS is attempting to become more of a "catch-all" party (Priamarizki and Dinarto 2019). For example, Priamarizki and Dinarto (2019) point to a PKS flyer that included a variety of reasons for voting for PKS, from the religious framing of the party as being "close to the cleric and Islamic community" to other issues such as providing disaster relief, supporting young people, and safeguarding the poor. Yet for PKS, all these services can be seen as aspects of da'wa and of the religious mission. Some aspects might appeal more to swing voters, but for the religious cadres, the multifaceted activities of the party strengthen rather than compromise the religious mission of the party.

Conclusion

In this chapter, I have argued that PKS has been able to maintain a relatively stable base of electoral support in spite of scandals and leadership divisions thanks to its caderization and party institutionalization, its ideology, and its strategic adaptation to the shifting social and political landscape in Indonesia. Understood from this perspective, PKS is both a principled and a pragmatic actor. The party is the only da'wa party in Indonesia, and its core members are committed to a religious vision inspired by the Egyptian Muslim Brotherhood, which seeks to purify and transform society through gradual changes and reforms. Pious cadres are not affected by scandals because they understand that individual leaders are only human and may be flawed, but they trust the party's internal adjudication mechanisms, and they consider loyalty to the party as an important aspect of their da'wa. Perceiving the party as working towards their religious values, pious cadres also recognize that the party has to be strategic and flexible in the political realm. As a party, PKS has astutely adapted to its environment, shifting which outside constituencies to appeal to, depending on the political context.

PKS's evolution over the past two decades suggests that dropping the call for shari'a from a party platform does not have to mean either a drastic shift and fundamental ideological moderation, or the adoption of duplicitous rhetoric. The ideological underpinnings of gradualism inherited from the Muslim Brotherhood allow for pious pragmatism and for strategic adaptation to the political environment. The success of PKS also underlines that a focus on caderization that can combine an ideological emphasis on the religious need for a strong party with an emphasis on professionalism and personal development can be particularly effective.

The ability of PKS to maintain a relatively stable base of support in spite of growing pragmatism and political scandals also indicates that the "moderation" of religious parties in the face of political realities does not always alienate all the devout constituents. If ideological changes are framed in a way that is consistent with the original religious mission, the religious base will support a policy of pious pragmatism. While religious parties might seem particularly vulnerable to challenges of their members' integrity and character, this analysis has shown that there are instances where certain ideological tenets can shield the party from internal decay and defections, and make it less vulnerable to such external challenges than other parties.

The continued loyalty of PKS cadres to their party does not fit well within the existing debates on Islamist parties in Indonesia, or religion and politics more broadly. Rather than considering resource mobilization, group characteristics and religious appeals to be competing explanations, this chapter has argued that religious values and ideological tenets can inform and influence organizational structures, levels of institutionalization, and trust in party structures. This perspective on PKS suggests that the party may be distinctive from other parties in

Indonesia — the party is fairly highly institutionalized, it is not personality driven or clientelistic, and it is not really a "catch-all" party, even though it may try to appeal to a broad base of swing voters.

In order to understand why religion continues to be relevant in politics, we need to look not only at elites or at the masses, but rather at the ways in which top-down and bottom-up processes interact and reinforce each other. The political elites of PKS are strategic and politically astute actors who seek political power and who strive to maximize their votes. As a rule, they are also the most senior and devoted cadres of the party, who have risen up through the ranks of the movement, showing their religious commitments and values along the way. In this way, political elites shape the strategic calculations of the party, but the devout masses continue to infuse the party with a sense of identity and sacred mission.

If we accept that religious values are a key feature of the PKS cadres, and a key motivation for their support of the party, then we can expect that religious frames will continue to be relevant in Indonesian politics for the near future. The fact that PKS cadres have a powerful mobilization capacity during elections also means that they can represent an important ally for populist leaders, making it more likely that they would invoke religious frames in national politics.

Acknowledgements

The author is grateful for valuable feedback on earlier drafts received from Alex Arifianto, Julie Chernov Hwang, Amy Freedman and the participants in the workshop on the Religious and Cultural Drivers and Responses to Political Dynamics in Southeast Asia. This chapter is in part based upon work supported by the National Science Foundation under Grant No. SES-1160391. Any opinions, findings, and conclusions or recommendations expressed in this material are those of the author and do not necessarily reflect the views of the National Science Foundation.

Bibliography

Al-Anani, Khalil. 2016. *Inside the Muslim Brotherhood: Religion, Identity, and Politics*. New York: Oxford University Press.

Amnesty International. 2017. "Indonesia: Amendment of the Mass Organizations Law Expands Threats to the Freedom of Association." *Amnesty International*. https://www.amnesty.org/download/Documents/ASA2167222017ENGLISH.pdf.

Arifianto, Alexander R. 2014. "Unpacking the Results of the 2014 Indonesian Legislative Elections." Singapore: Institute of Southeast Asian Studies.

Banna, Hasan al-. 1978. *Five Tracts of Hasan Al-Banna' : (1906-1949) ; a Selection from the Majmu`at Rasa'il al-Imam al-Shahid Hasan al-Banna'*. Translated by Charles Wendell. Berkeley [u.a.]: University of California Press.

Banna, S.M. Hasan al-. 2002. *Imam Shahid Hasan Al-Banna: From Birth to Martyrdom*. Awakening Publications, Milpitas, CA.

Baswedan, Anies Rasyid. 2004. "Political Islam in Indonesia: Present and Future Trajectory." *Asian Survey* 44(5): 669–90.

Cammett, Melani and Pauline Jones Luong. 2014. "Is There an Islamist Political Advantage?" *Annual Review of Political Science 17*: 187-206.

Clark, Michael. 2009. "Valence and electoral outcomes in Western Europe, 1976–1998." *Electoral Studies 28*(1): 111-122.

———. 2014. "Does Public Opinion Respond to Shifts in Party Valence? A Cross-National Analysis of Western Europe, 1976–2002." *West European Politics 37*(1): 91-112.

Chernov Hwang, Julie. 2014. "Patterns of Normalization: Islamist Parties in Indonesia." *In Islamist Parties and Political Normalization in the Muslim World, eds*. Quinn Mecham and Julie Chernov Hwang. Philadelphia: University of Pennsylvania Press.

Collins, Elizabeth. 2003. "Islam Is the Solution: Dakwah and Democracy in Indonesi." *Kultur* 3.

Dhume, Sadanand. 2005. "Radicals March on Indonesia's Future." *Far Eastern Economic Review*, May.

Hadiz, Vedi R. 2004. "Indonesian Local Party Politics: A Site of Resistance to Neoliberal Reform." *Critical Asian Studies* 36(4): 615–36.

Hakim, Luqman-nul. 2016. "PKS Splits with Fahri Hamzah, Will the Red and White Coalition Be Next?" *Indonesia at Melbourne*, April 19. https://indonesiaatmelbourne.unimelb.edu.au/pks-splits-with-fahri-hamzah-red-and-white-coalition-next/.

Hamayotsu, Kikue. 2011a. "The End of Political Islam? A Comparative Analysis of Religious Parties in the Muslim Democracy of Indonesia." *Journal of Current Southeast Asian Affairs* 30(3): 133–59.

———. 2011b. "The Political Rise of the Prosperous Justice Party in Post-Authoritarian Indonesia." *Asian Survey* 51(5): 971–92.

Hariyadi, Mathias. 2017. "Jakarta Approves Law against Islamist Organizations." *Asianews.It*, January 28. http://www.asianews.it/news-en/Jakarta-approves-law-against-Islamist-organizations-42176.html.

Hasan, Noorhaidi. 2009. "Islamist Party, Electoral Politics and Da'wa Mobilization among Youth: The Prosperous Justice Party (PKS) in Indonesia." S. Rajaratnam School of International Studies. http://www.rsis.edu.sg/indonesia_prog/resources/working%20paper/WP184.pdf.

Hasyim, Syafiq. 2005. "Blending Dakwa and Politics: The Case of PKS (Justice-Prosperous Party)." In *The Rise of Religion-Based Political Movements*, ed. Darwis Khudori. Selangor, Malaysia: Strategic Information and Research Development Centre.

Hilmy, Masdar. 2010. *Islamism and Democracy in Indonesia: Piety and Pragmatism*. Singapore: Institute of Southeast Asian Studies.

Huntington, Samuel P. 2006. *Political Order in Changing Societies*. New Haven, CT: Yale University Press.

Jakarta Post. 2011. "IM Movement Inspires PKS Founding Fathers," March 28, sec. Expose.

———. 2013. "Luthfi Sentenced to 16 Years in PKS Beef Import Graft Scandal." December 9. http://www.thejakartaglobe.com/news/16-years-luthfi-jailed-until-the-cows-come-home/.

Jung, Eunsook. 2009. "Taking Care of the Faithful : Islamic Organizations and Partisan Engagement in Indonesia." Madison: University of Wisconsin.

Machmudi, Yon. 2008. *Islamising Indonesia: The Rise of Jemaah Tarbiyah and the Prosperous Justice Party (PKS)*. ANU E Press.

McCoy, Mary E. 2019. *Scandal and Democracy: Media Politics in Indonesia*. Ithaca, N.Y: Cornell University Press.

Muhtadi, Burhanuddin. 2008. "Thinking Globally, Acting Locally: A Social Movement Theory Approach of The Prosperous Justice Party (PKS) and Its Islamist Transnational Framing." Canberra: Australian National University.

Munhanif, Ali. 2010. "Different Routes to Islamism: History, Institutions, and the Politics of Islamic State in Egypt and Indonesia." Montreal: McGill University.

Priamarizki, Adhi, and Dedi Dinarto. 2019. "Capturing Anti-Jokowi Sentiment and Islamic Conservative Masses: PKS 2019 Strategy." 324. Singapore: RSIS.

Tanuwidjaja, Sunny. 2010. "Political Islam and Islamic Parties in Indonesia: Critically Assessing the Evidence of Islam's Political Decline." *Contemporary Southeast Asia: A Journal of International and Strategic Affairs* 32(1): 29–49.

Wiktorowicz, Quintan. 2004. Islamic Activism: A Social Movement Theory Approach. Bloomington: Indiana University Press.

Woodward, Mark, Ali Amin, Inayah Rohmaniyah, and Chris Lundry. 2012. "Getting Culture: A New Path for Indonesia's Islamist Justice and Prosperity Party?" *Contemporary Islam* 7(2).

Chapter 6

Indonesia's 2019 Elections: The Driving Factors Behind Political Movement of Conservative Female Muslim Groups

Susy Tekunan

Background

The Indonesian national election on April 17, 2019, was another democratic exercise in the fourth largest country in the world, proud to be the largest Muslim populated country in the world. There were notable problems with the elections: including high number of deaths among poll workers (Soeriaatmadja 2019), rampant money politics (Aspinall and Berenschot 2019), and riots rejecting election results (Lamb 2019); yet, by most accounts the elections were competitive and the problems didn't subvert the legitimacy of the exercise. One positive development in the 2019 election was the rise of female participation in the legislative election as representatives in the legislative body. Out of 245,106 total legislative candidates, 94,975 or 38.75% were female and 20.5% of the candidates elected were female. This is the highest percentage since 2004 election (KPU 2018). Aside from the elite political representation, simultaneously, there was a fascinating mobilization of women on the grassroots level, mostly among conservative female Muslims groups. This phenomenon is the focus of this research as an effort to identify the driving factors behind the movement. Understanding these dynamics may contribute to our ability to formulate efforts to prevent further conservatism and thus help us prevent radical ideas from spreading in Indonesia, especially among women, who play an undeniably crucial role in shaping the next generation.

The grassroots level political movement of conservative female Muslims groups supported the Prabowo-Sandi presidential ticket. This qualitative research observes one particular group with a large social media following and a network called PEPES (an acronym for *Perempuan Pendukung Prabowo Sandi* or Prabowo-Sandi female supporters). Due to the sensitivity of the issue, we did not gain interview access to the leaders or members of the group but conducted online and literature research on them. In addition to PEPES, we administered survey interviews to 82 members of Muslims study groups commonly known in Indonesia as *Majlis Taklim*. And, using a snowball approach, we conducted in-depth interviews with five legislative candidates from three different parties to collect data regarding the elite perspective on the movement and the politicizing of religious identity during the campaign.

The organization of this paper is as follows: the next section provides a brief introduction to the contestation of the presidential campaign in 2019 and the conservative Muslims supporters. It is followed by looking at the rise of conservative and radical ideologies in Indonesia as part of global rise in radicalism. Despite Indonesia's reputation as a moderate Muslim society, growing conservatism maybe changing the face of Islam in the country. We then discuss the role of social media as an important platform to spread radicalism and strengthen the sense of identity among conservative female Muslims. Data from interviews, field observations, and social media studies are presented, sorted, and analyzed in the next section. This part is organized into separate sub-sections based on the category of data. Lastly, we offer analysis and some preliminary conclusions on women's role in radical politics during the Indonesian 2019 campaign and election.

Competing Candidates and Conservative Muslims Supporters

The two presidential candidates for the 2019 election were Prabowo Subianto and Sandiaga Uno against the incumbent Joko Widodo (Jokowi) and Ma'ruf Amin. Divisions are Indonesian society is deepening the fissure that contrasts the differences between the tickets. Jokowi won the 2014 election with 53.15% of the votes against Prabowo with 46.85% of the votes. In 2019 Jokowi - Ma'ruf Amin won slightly higher percentage of votes compared to the opponent. In both elections, the percentage differences are relatively thin.

Religious issues were one of the most significant divides in the presidential election. Even though Jokowi is a Muslim, he is considered not religious enough in his support for key Islamic policies. The first example of this related to the 2016 blasphemy case of Ahok (Basuki Tjahaya Purnama), Jokowi's former partner in Jakarta's governorship. Jokowi did not explicitly help Ahok after he was accused of committing blasphemy (for

Table 1: *Election result of the last two Indonesian presidential elections*

Presidential Candidate/ Year – Vice President Candidate	2014 –Jusuf Kalla/ Hatta Rajasa (%)	2019 – Ma'ruf Amin/ Sandiaga Uno (%)
Joko Widodo	53.15	55.32
Prabowo Subianto	46.85	44.68

Source: https://kpu.go.id

encouraging Muslim voters to vote for him even though in the Qu'ran Muslims are encouraged to choose leaders who are Muslim). A Christian, Ahok was supported by Muslims and non-Muslims alike due to his proven effectiveness in making Jakarta better. The blasphemy case incited large demonstration and riots and Jokowi's position to punish those rioting was interpreted as a lack of support for the Muslim cause (*BBC* 2016).

The second case was Jokowi's decision to allow the police to pursue criminal penalties for Muhammad Habib Riziek for allegedly exchanging pornographic text messages with a Muslim woman. Riziek is a revered founder and leader of the Islamic Defenders Front also known as Front Pembela Islam/FPI (CNN 2019). The Front has aggressively promoted more conservative Islamic values and they are vocal in fighting against non-Islamic lifestyles including policing restaurants that do not observe the fast during Ramadhan or halal practices. Riziek was also influential in encouraging the masses to demonstrate against Ahok in the blasphemy case. Conservative Muslims consider Jokowi their enemy for his lack of support in protecting their group's interests. While Prabowo was not known for his religiosity, he established political networks with more conservative Muslim organizations and political parties such as two Islam-based political parties to form his five-party coalition: National Mandate Party (PAN) and Prosperous Justice Party (PKS). PKS is a hard line Islamic party calling for the inclusion of Islamic law as the broad stroke in the overall Indonesian law (PKS 2015) and it is the main party supported by conservative Muslims. He and his supporters were not afraid to use religious conservatism as a tool against rivals. Based on the perceived religiosity of each presidential ticket, conservative female Muslim groups along with other conservative Muslims, supported Prabowo-Sandi's candidacy during the campaign partly by organizing volunteers to canvass in the communities.

The Rise of Conservatism and Radical Ideologies in Indonesia

Political radicalism, according to Schmid (2013), is a process involving individual or collectives in political polarization between groups of diverging interests that may lead to conflict and confrontation. Schmid suggests that the radicalism includes non-violent coercion, forms of political violence or acts of terrorism. Radicalization is also a form of ideological socialization that departs from the mainstream (Schmid 2011). In this case, radicalism does not always have to lead to an act of terror but includes ideological influence and persuasive coercion to lead others into certain radical ideas and movements.

Radicalism is closely linked to terrorism and it became a more significant threat after the terror attack on the U.S. mainland in 2001. American legislators include the war on terror as part of their political agenda to provide security for the American citizens (*Rise of Radicalism* 2015). Several interest groups see the war as an opportunity to create a divide and promote Muslims solidarity to garner support against the war on terror. Many Muslims condemn terrorism but see the continuous attack on Muslim countries as a reason to see the West as an imperialistic power to suppress the Muslims. The rise of ISIS creates further division within Islamic communities, because some see ISIS as an ideal materialization of living out the faith while others disagree. Supporters of ISIS spread the ideology to convince many Muslims to join and support the caliphate. While were convinced to go to Syria, many others stayed home but were sympathetic to the movement and to more radical forms of religious practice. This radicalization spread to many countries with large Muslim communities. Indonesia, while known for being the largest Muslim population in the world, is also known for its moderate and diverse Islamic communities. This seems to be changing with the weakening of Nadhatul Ulama (NU), the largest moderate Muslim organization, due to internal problems and the radicalization movement on the grass roots level in rural areas (Syechbubakr 2018). The number of people supporting FPI (Front Pembela Islam), the embodiment of radical Islam organizations, is increasing as they become more mainstream and focus on domestic issues like pushing for more conservative legislation in society (Nurita 2019). The trial and conviction of Ahok for blasphemy marked a new era of conservative religiosity and growing intolerance. His case gave birth to the large radical movement of 212 (a huge rally on December 2nd) in Jakarta showcasing the huge number of radical Muslims mobilized by a number of top Muslim leaders. The case also negatively affected Jokowi, as he and Ahok had been close associates serving together in Jakarta governorship.

The Role of Social Media in the Social Construction of Conservative Identity

Radicalization can be analyzed through constructivist theory under social or international relations theory. Constructivism builds ideas around identity, culture, and understanding of the surrounding from perceptions toward the environment including who are friends and foes. Within the framework of constructivism, there is a changing perception that forms certain values that may shape a person or group's idea of self and others and provide the motivation to follow the ideology. This newly formed value or belief has the strong capacity to alter behavior especially when it is cultivated and reinforced by a supportive community. Identity as a member of a group has a strong impact for individuals, especially in a communal society such Indonesia, and can produce radical behavior reinforced through the group empowerment and a sense of belonging as part of the need narrative suggested by Kruglanski et al. (Kruglanski, Bélanger, and Gunaratna 2019). Furthermore, the sense of threat to the group values and existence helped form a common purpose against the source of threat. Groups with Muslim female members perceived a threat to their Islamic rights protesting against what they consider the government's lack of support for their religious-related concerns. As the majority, they prefer a government that can guarantee their preferences, including those whom they believe to be charismatic leaders of Islam.[1] The religiosity of the candidate matters much less than campaign promises to protect their rights as Muslims. This sense of identity through radical ideas has also been reinforced by cheap access to social media and thus the widespread use of it. Research on social media suggests that reinforcement in the form of "like" and positive comments have the driving impact as psychological elixir to repeat and intensify behaviors (Lin 2016).

Indonesia ranks sixth in the world with the largest number of cellphone users, 236.8 million (Wee 2016), and has the third largest number of

---

1. This argument is based on the interview responses at the *Majlis Taklim* in West Java.

Facebook users and ranks fourth for Instagram (*Statista* 2019). Aside from these two public social media platforms, Whats App is a very convenient form of group communication that allows different groups to chat simultaneously. Whats App is so ubiquitous that most Indonesians belong to at least three Whats App groups. Its popularity stems from a low entry barrier and the convenience of forming private chat groups. The convenience of this available technology serves as one of the driving force for ideas to circulate and to be germinated anywhere at a very low cost. Community leaders can instill their ideas and work within their network to influence a large number of people and gather supporters through these online platforms. The online chat rooms are particularly effective for female political activism. Women tend to be more active in communicating with others either in person or through other means. Several researches have found that women use social media more than men (Pew Research Center 2015). They tend to share information more and have stronger needs for community since many stay at home while their partners are working outside the house. The social media boom fits female characteristics and their tendency to engage with different communities while their partners deal with more public matters. Women who deal mostly with personal household affairs may experience the sense of contributing to public purpose by engaging in political activism. Savvy political candidates triggered the sense of female empowerment by acknowledging their power and encouraging them to participate in political campaigns.

Interviews and Observations

Legislative Candidates Interviews

In-depth interviews were conducted with five political party officials and legislative candidates. This interview used a snowballing approach to reach female representatives from different parties. One interview was done through a video call since the legislative candidate is located in Menado, North Sulawesi. The rest were face to face interviews in the Jakarta area. There were four female candidates and one senior male candidate. Interview questions aimed to determine campaign style and ideological content. We also tried to find their perspectives regarding radical campaign messages and their consideration of them as a political cost. This included whether the role of female political candidates/politicians in 2019 energized their bases with divisive messages to win votes/for their presidential candidates and if this may have been justified. The list of complete questions is included in the appendix and transcripts are recorded and archived.

The result of the in-depth interviews reveals that political candidates from PDI-P, Golkar, and PSI are all against radicalism and campaigned for unity of the country based on Pancasila as the nation's foundation. All political candidates shared their campaign experience including how they attract constituents to secure votes. Out of five candidates, three got elected and two did not.

Table 2: *List of legislative candidates being interviewed*

Name/Age	Political Party Afflication/ Region	Position at Interview
Jerry Sambuaga (34)	Golkar/ North Sulawesi	Senate Incumbent*
Puteri Lomarudin (26)	Golkar/ West Java	Won - Member of House
Regina Vianney Ayudya (N/A)	PDIP South Jakarta	Lost - Member of House
Sandra Rondonuwu (45)	PDIP/ North Sulawesi	Won - House Local District
Dara Nasution (24)	PSI/ North Sumatra	Lost - Member of House

Note. Since 2019, Jerry Sambuaga has served as the vice minister of trade under Jokowi's new cabinet.

The interviews suggest that candidates understand the important role of female voters in politics and their ability to influence others in their community to vote according to their preferences. The candidates are in agreement that pluralism is crucial in Indonesia and do not condone using religious issues for their political advancement. Out of the five interviewees, Putri and Dara are Muslims while the rest are Christians. Jerry and Sandra represent regions in North Sulawesi where the majority of the voters are Christian. Despite their religious differences, all candidates agreed that religion is a private matter and disapprove of politicizing religion. The fact that these candidates are all from pluralist political parties may play an important role in their ideology; they must represent their party's ideology despite /of their personal belief. Thus, their religion does not affect their political positions. However, most candidates interviewed, such as Puteri and Dara, were attracted to the party they belong to due by the pluralist ideology of the parties. They also noticed the intensifying identity politics by certain political parties and their candidates. Even the Muslim candidates from pluralist parties such as Golkar and PDI-P (Jokowi's party coalition) faced difficulties in entering areas known to support the Prabowo team and sometimes chose to skip the areas altogether and focus on areas with potential undecided voters. Female candidates said that while they realize the importance of female support, it is not the make or break of the campaign. Thus, they reached out to voters based on issues on their agenda. Puteri Komaruddin, for instance, did not just focus on the female voters. Her primary agenda during the campaign was to fight predatory lending, a genderless issue. The interviews suggest that first, Prabowo Sandiaga's team has successfully gained relatively solid support from Muslim conservatives quite early in the campaign. We see evidence of this in the next section from the results of survey interviews of members of the female *Majlis Taklim*: where the large majority pledged their support for the team. Secondly, gaining women voters can be achieved by convincing opinion leaders, both male and female, who will spread influence throughout their communities.

Administered Survey Interviews

In order to gather data from the grass-roots level, we worked with a student who has an extensive network in *Majelis Taklim*. *Majelis Taklim* is a gender-based group for Muslims to gather regularly for religious study and prayer. The term is used only in Indonesia and started in 1981 (Sasongko 2018). Women's *Majelis Taklim* groups flourish more than men's because the community aspect of the group tends to be more attractive to women. The groups are important forums to create close-knit Muslim communities to spread influence and ideas. The number of *Majelis Taklim* increased steadily with the growing influence of Arab Islamism (Alawiyah 1997; Rachmahlia 2017) and it is important to know the view from within. The Indonesian ministry of religious affairs issued regulation number 29 in 2019 requiring *Majelis Taklim* to register with the government and provide a learning module (Raharjo 2019). The regulation drew controversy; questioning the motive behind the regulation was government suspicion of radicalism spread through the informal groups. Thus, for the purpose of this research, we decided to gather information from some female *Majelis Taklim*. The administered survey interview has its drawbacks, but it is the best way to gather a relatively large number of respondents answering sensitive questions on politics and religion. The student who administered the survey is a member of the group and she is trusted by the members of the *Majelis Taklim* and its network. The questions were designed to gather information about the members' political experience including their political awareness, level of involvement, and sources of influence. The survey gathered information from 82 respondents from different *Majelis Taklim* in West Java.

Graph 1: *Administered Survey Respondent Age Group – primary source*

Respondent Age Group

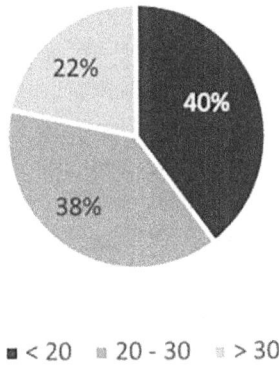

■ < 20   ▩ 20 - 30   ▨ > 30

Graph 2: *Administered Survey Answer for "Which Presidential Candidate can help you with issues that matter to you?" – primary source*

Which Presidential Candidate can help you with issues that matter to you?

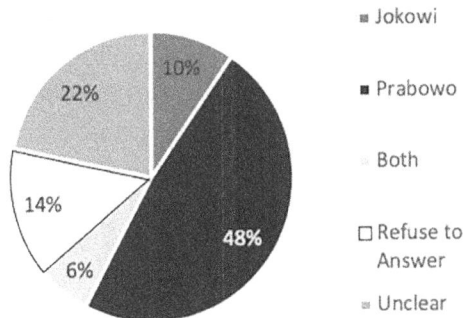

■ Jokowi

■ Prabowo

   Both

☐ Refuse to Answer

▩ Unclear

The age range of respondents is from 17–69 years old, with the majority under 30 years old: 39.75% are under 20 years old and 38.5% are between 20–30 years old. Due to the limitation of this survey, the result does not represent overall Indonesian female movement. Furthermore, some areas in Indonesia are more conservative than others. Indonesia also has Christian pockets such as in many areas in the East of Indonesia including North Sulawesi and North Sumatra. However, it may serve as a simple overview of female Islamic groups in West Java.

From 82 respondents, 48 gave direct answers regarding their presidential preference; others either refused to answer or gave unrelated answers. Out of 48 respondents, 40 supported Prabowo with the main consideration that Prabowo will be more supportive toward Islamic causes; one specifically mentioned that Prabowo is surrounded by devout Muslims so that he can better represent Muslims' interests or can sympathize with the Muslims. Only 8 out of 48 answered Jokowi and one explained that Jokowi will push for economic equality. Sixty-four respondents out of 82 mentioned religion as an important if not the most important issue in the election. Twenty-two of them said religion was the only important issue for them. One respondent who supported Prabowo said that it was suggested by a Muslim leader, two said a relative suggested it, and one said that she chose not to vote since according to Islam, democracy is forbidden or *haram* in Arabic. Four respondents said that they idolized Neno Warisman and one Ratna Sarumpaet, both are the radical female activists who used hate speech and radical content to mobilize constituents. From this data we suggest that there is a tendency for female Muslims in Indonesia to vote for Prabowo Sandi for religious reasons. Due to the limited scope of the survey, we cannot suggest that this phenomenon is found throughout Indonesia. We can only suggest that due to a targeted campaign in several Muslim pockets in Indonesia such as West Java, large numbers of female Muslims there supported Prabowo Sandi. The respondents were asked if there was anyone who pushed them or made them vote in the election and 49% or 40 of the respondents answered no one. From 41 respondents who answered there was someone, most of them said that they were influenced by family, and three said by Islamic leaders or organizations. Fourteen of the respondents said they had been influenced to participate in the election but did not specify by whom/what.

Graph 3: *Administered Survey Answer for "Who, if anyone, pushed or made you vote in the election?" – primary source*

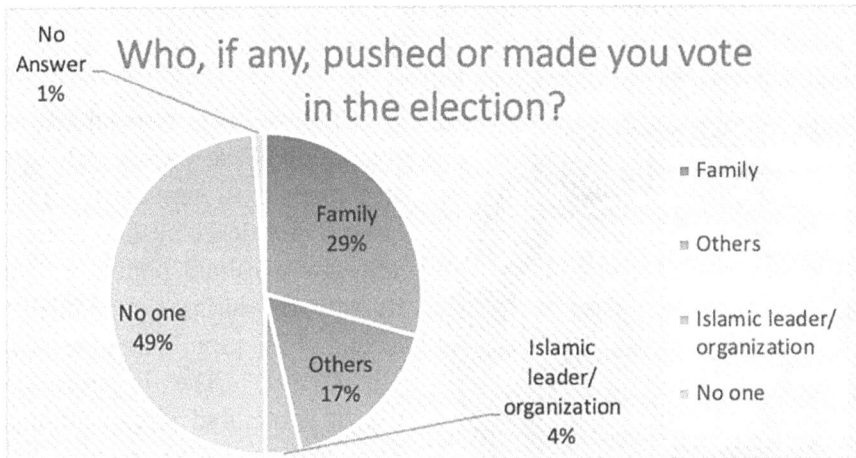

Social Media Study

We researched the social media postings of several women political candidates who were known to spread radical ideas related to the election. We found that some candidates, especially from PKS, are promoting religious radicalism through speeches and social media posts. Other candidates were active on closed group chats such as Facebook forums or Whats App, but did not publicly spread radical ideas. Certain individuals without real pictures or identity markers are more open about their support for radical Islamic causes. One example is @stevaniehuang, who uses cartoon pictures of a female with niqab and the tagline "#we are opposition" in Indonesian. Her account started in July 2018 and gained 39.9 thousand followers with over 9,500 tweets. Her tweets reflect her support for Prabowo Sandi, Islamic militancy, and the Islamic Defender Front (FPI), as well as humanitarian programs such as collecting donations for the smoke victims in Riau. While it is difficult to confirm, her account bears the signs of being a buzzer or a fake account administered to support certain political candidates. If the account is fake, the existence of accounts supposedly run by women and targeting women strengthens the suggestion that women have an important role in garnering political support during the campaign (*AsiaOne* 2019). And, it suggests that campaigns understand this dynamic.

PEPES (*Perempuan Pendukung Prabowo Sandi*) Prabowo-Sandi female supporters is one of the most organized female political groups that directly call themselves emak-emak (mothers). The acronym PEPES also means a popular Indonesian savory dish wrapped in banana leaves—pictured in the center of the logo below.

Picture 1: One of the logos of PEPES (Emak-emak party supporters of Prabowo-Sandi)

The group is also known as the emak-emak party with the sole mission to support the Prabowo Sandi ticket in the election. The group gained popularity for its activism during the campaign as one of the prominent groups of "emak-emak." The organization has a structured organizational form with a leader, membership procedure and card, and branches/activities in different regions. The group started on August 18, 2018 in Jakarta after being inspired by a statement made by Sandiaga Uno when he registered for the election. The group leader, Wulan, admitted to a reporter that the group saw the readiness of Sandiaga Uno to support the plight of "emak-emak" and formed the group to support the Prabowo-Sandi ticket (Bomantama 2018). The group has branches in many cities in Indonesia such as Aceh, Yogyakarta, Klaten, Padang, Lampung, Palembang, Jakarta, Bandung, Surabaya, Bali, Sidoarjo, Banyuwangi, Cilegon, and others. The organization sent volunteers to canvass voters with the aim of reaching women in their communities through a program called PEPES Kepung. PEPES Kepung is an acronym for "keliling kampung" which means going around villages; the acronym also means: aggressively surrounding a target (*SwaMedium* 2018; *Jerami* 2018). The women went to remote places introducing and encouraging people they met, mostly other women, to vote for the presidential candidate pair. In some areas they held programs such as health information workshops, giving out lunches for the poor, or administered free health checkups. During the campaign period, three PEPES volunteers were videotaped while spreading negative messages against Jokowi saying that if the president is re-elected then there will be no Muslim call for prayer and there will be many same sex marriages. In August 2019, the women were indicted and charged with violating the criminal law of 1946, article 14 (2), and were incarcerated for 6-months for spreading false information to induce hatred and divisions (Erdianto 2019). This is an example of the aggressive campaign efforts used by the members of this female organization to influence voters to give their vote to the Prabowo Sandi ticket. Aside from religious issues, the group was also using economic issues, particularly the price of goods, to suggest Jokowi's government was a failure (Ihsanuddin 2018). There was very little evidence that the Indonesian economic situation worsened during Jokowi's presidency and whether changing the government could improve the economy. In an interview with a woman who is a member of the movement, she admitted that a new government may not solve the economic issue yet they maintain the narration as the selling point.[2] Human rights proponents such as Munawir Sjadzali and Miriam Budiarjo suggest that economic disparity is at the root of religious conflicts in Indonesia (Bertrand 2003). Religious conflicts are the expression of dissatisfaction from the grass-roots level. It is thus very appropriate that presidential candidates use economic issues to encourage female activism in religious communities.

Religious identity is intensifying partly through the notion that there is a common threat attacking conservative Muslims in Indonesia. Members of the female political movement are mostly conservative Muslim women wearing headscarves and reaching out to other Muslims. The incident caught by video of three members of PEPES spreading black campaign information about Jokowi on religious issues suggests that the economy is only a part of the selling point to gather support for the Prabowo Sandi ticket. The formation and re-enforcement of a female identity construct started from Sandiaga Uno's recognition and encouragement of female power, *the power of emak-emak*, through his statement during the election registration. This statement celebrated Indonesian women, mostly Muslims, who started the movement, including the PEPES organization. Furthermore, members of the group re-enforced the Muslim conservative identity construct through social media and canvassing using conservative religious agendas and economic issues. Supporting Prabowo Sandi is viewed as a way to protect

---

2. The woman was part of a small protest group at a weekly car free day event in central Jakarta. Joana, was reluctant to speak but she eventually said that the economic issue is the main problem with the current president and was merely hoping for a change in governance.

way to protect Muslim identity and rights since Jokowi is considered 'not Muslim enough' and some argue he has not done enough to protect Muslim clerics. Jokowi's opponents point out the case of the prominent Indonesian Muslim leader Muhammad Rizieq Shihab, who was named as a suspect in a pornography case by Indonesian police and was summoned to court in May 2017 (*Jakarta Post* 2017). Conservative Muslims in Indonesia, including female political activists, criticized the government for charging Rizieq since he is considered a religious leader.

After the pair lost in the election and Prabowo met Jokowi to show reconciliation, the group changed its name and re-focused its mission to conduct trainings for small businesses and for those seeking to expand economic opportunities. Their new focus led them to encourage and support their members to start small culinary businesses and participate in street bazaars with logo endorsement of PEPES.

Field Observations

The effort to find PEPES members during car-free day (CFD) on September 8, 2019, was not successful. We looked for the banner on Twitter and found no vendor with it; those who we approached to ask if they knew about it, had never heard of the group. Eventually we tried to contact the Twitter account asking if they could direct us to to any of their members on site at Jakarta CFD; there was no response. We found a group at the center of the CFD, where people were not selling merchandise but

LisaAmartatara
@LisaAmartatara3

@PEPESOfficial Reborn

Hr ini Kami akan Bubarkan PEPES ~~> Partai Emak2 Pendukung Prabowo Sandi yg Kalian pernah Kenal dan Akhirnya Kita saling Kenal

Kami hanyalah Emak2 nekat yg hny memikirkan nasib anak cucu bangsa dan Kami BANGGA PERNAH BERJUANG UNTUK INDONESIA RAYA

Translate Tweet

Picture 2: PEPES Twitter account after Prabowo Sandi lost the election and the group's re-invention of its purpose

ideas, holding placards opposing the government: stop cheating etc. There were about seven people, mostly middle age females with headscarves, and one male who seemed to be the organizer. We approached them and asked about their demands to the government. They seemed reluctant to speak,

especially the man, but the woman that I approached said that economy is the issue. Prices are high and they are feeling the brunt. As mothers, they are the ones who know how much prices have increased and affect their purchasing ability. A woman named Joana said that she voted for Jokowi in 2014, but she saw that the situation is not improving but deteriorating so she wanted to make a difference and provide ways to help those who are in the lowest economic level by teaching them how to improve skills and find new economic opportunities. I asked her about PEPES and she knows the group and said that they shared the same goal and criticism against the government and sometimes collaborated on programs. The woman was critical of government law enforcement for using racist comments against Papuan students in Surabaya. She said that it is sad how there is a division in the society now, she has very good Chinese friends but now it is not the same. She blamed the president for the racial divide in the society and said that they want a change in the government.

The second field observation was conducted at a rally on September 20, 2019, in front of the parliamentary building in Senayan, Jakarta, following a protest by hundreds of students on September 19, 2019, protesting the new regulation for the Indonesian Corruption Committee (KPK) at the same location. The protest was called by the previous secretary of national volunteers for Prabowo Sandi campaign, Jalih Pitoeng, through a video that spread on social media. In the video, he is talking in front of the house representative complex next to a woman completely covered with sunglasses and gloves holding a sign that said "rejecting legislative proposal on eliminating sexual violence." Pitoeng called for all people who care about Indonesia to come on the 20th to protest various pieces of legislation to show people's dissatisfaction. The announcement spread to different groups including the Muslim female supporters of Prabowo Sandi and those that call themselves militant mothers (*emak-emak*). The protest was supposed to start at 1 pm and there were only about six middle-age females with colorful Muslim outfits gathered under the shade of a gate. They were talking and taking pictures of themselves. I talked to them and they were careful but quite friendly. They said that they came out because they care about the future of their children. They want a change of government because the situation is worse now compared to the previous administration. They came from all over Indonesia, including Padang and Balikpapan. Most came from around the Jakarta area. More people arrived after 2 pm. There were about four different groups of 'mothers' who stayed in their own groups. Women were asked to wear identification to distinguish themselves from the other groups. When asked what organization they were with, many just said they were from many different parts or that they were not part of an organization and came with friends. Joana was not in sight, but she might have been there. The male who led her group was there orchestrating a photo op of women standing in line, wearing colorful head decorations on top of their headscarves, holding placards reading "Government is thief," "Indonesia is not for thieves," "Stop corruption," and so on. On the gate of the complex some posters were put up with words that supported Pancasila, and pictures of the leaders of the movement. Sri Bintang Pamungkas, a self-claimed reformist and a figure that openly tried to create a movement to block Jokowi's inauguration, was present and received a positive welcome from the crowd. He said to a reporter that he was demanding the government step down because of their incompetence. He provoked the crowd by mentioning that the government had allowed ten million Chinese workers into the country and this would lead to Indonesians becoming servants to these Chinese who own factories and are paid high salaries. The female groups also demanded the return of Habib Riziek without conditions. He left Indonesia and remains in Saudi Arabia to avoid trial for his 2017 crime of spreading pornographic content electronically (BBC 2018b).

The Tauhid rally on September 28, 2019, was scheduled to follow up the 212 movement. It called for all believers to participate in the peaceful rally. From the rally on September 20, 2019, to the Tauhid rally, students demonstrations occurred almost daily and were marked by violent protests and anarchic destruction of public property. There was a rumor that the student movement was infiltrated by irresponsible elites, including a senior professor at the Bogor Institute of Agriculture, who was suspected of making Molotov bombs to supply the demonstration (Triyadi Bempah 2019). The suspicion turned out to be false since the bombs found in his house belonged to his guests who were members of HTI, a hard line Islamic group banned by the government. There was no unified voice in the Tauhid rally and there was no clear demand or sense of whether they were demanding action from the executive or the legislative branch of government. Security forces at the rallies were substantial with a strong police presence and around ten visible military tanks and bullet-proofed police special force vehicles. Even though tensions ran high between some female rally participants and the police force, mostly regarding road blocks, there were no reported casualties at either rally.

Analysis and Conclusion

Based on the observations, this research finds three main driving factors behind the political movement of conservative female Muslims groups in Indonesia during the national election in 2019. The factors include the rise of global conservativism, contribution of social media in intensifying religious identity among Muslims women, and political candidates' strategic targeted soliciting. First, the rise of global conservatism and the spread of radical ideologies promoted by Islamic radical groups and individuals. As a country with moderate Muslims, Indonesia is not immune from radical influence as a form of religious transnational solidarity. Similarly, the sense of threat to the Islamic plight against secularism or pluralism further strengthens the community's sense of urgency to fight back. The blasphemy case of Ahok, who challenged the rights and privilege of the Muslim majority in Indonesia, served as a watershed for the conservative movement in the country. Secondly, social media accessibility allows for a sense of community and power in numbers. The construct of religious identity formed through the rise of radicalism has been conveniently reinforced through social media. These communication platforms allow opinion leaders to spread ideas and increase followers at a very low cost. Community confirmation also encourages conservative female Muslims to participate in meaningful activities as part of a need for self-actualization. This is particularly effective among female voters since women tend to engage closely with their community both online and off line. Lastly, the groups were encouraged by political candidates, who are aware of their potential role and strong loyalty, to support their campaigns. Politicians can recruit opinion leaders to convince female followers to support them or diplomatically empower the female directly, as Sandiaga Uno has demonstrated (BBC 2018a; CNN 2018). This form of cooptation by certain candidates and parties can strategically appeal to this demographic through issues such as the economy and religion. Economic issues were particularly relevant to this group since they are the managers of the house and most often are responsible for daily household spending. Political candidates are aware of the potentially significant role that females can play in influencing others by being opinion leaders.

From the field observations, it is apparent that the rally participants were comprised of various interest groups who are not necessarily connected; in fact, there was an apparent disunity among the groups despite their supposedly shared purpose. Many of the mothers participated because they were mobilized by opinion leaders who may or may not have been female themselves. Some groups were led or noticeably orchestrated by men. The demonstration was called by a man whose arrival and speech was central to the particular protest. From the groups, only a handful of females were seen to be leading the groups. One in particular showed aggressive and feisty behavior and identified mostly with alpha male characters. She talked loudly on the phone and to other females inciting excitement for the rally. She provoked the police and was definitely welcoming the attention. Other women seemed to just follow the directions that in some cases came from the men, such as the one from Joana's group. There was a sense that they were being co-opted with economic fears and without having correct references, they relied on the confidence of the number of people supporting the same issue who came from circles they were familiar with. The rise of nationalistic and isolationist feelings were fueled by certain political interests, pushing the voters toward radicalization and division. The intensifying of radical ideas spread among female Muslims. Another strong indication that the female movement is being driven by men, is the apparent campaign strategy by the Prabowo Sandi team to dispatch Sandiaga Uno to engage the mothers/*emak-emak* group as their supporters.

The interviews with Muslim prayer groups or *Majelis Taklim* members show that the large majority of the respondents supported Prabowo. They believed that Prabowo would support Islamic causes while Jokowi might not. The existence of this supporting community through the prayer groups also strengthened and confirmed each other's convictions. Jokowi is a pluralist and most Muslims think he will not represent Muslims despite having Ma'ruf Amin, known to be a prominent Muslim leader, as his running mate. This construct of Jokowi's 'secularism' was built up over time, including playing up his closeness with Ahok, the perception of his lack of sympathy for rioters pushing for Muslim rights, his policy of freeing visa requirements for Chinese tourists, and his firm position on fighting radicalism (Hermawan 2019); these were all used against him by Probowo and Islamist groups. The belief construct was also reinforced by groups of radical female activists, encouraged and coopted by Prabowo-Sandi, mostly through the strategic charm of Sandiaga Uno who called for the mothers or *emak-emak* to support his ticket. Uno maintains connections with the group that supported his team by speaking at their seminars and gatherings that mostly focus on economic programs.

The result of this research can provide an understanding of relations between women voters and activists, their political contributions, and religious polarization in Indonesia. And, it may contribute to the larger scholarship on gender and identity politics. The three main factors found in this analysis are not the only factors that encouraged the movement. There are other variables that may contribute to our understanding of radical movements, such as cultural and religious teachings. Factors not covered in this research are no less important but they are beyond our focus and scope of this paper.

Acknowledgements

I thank Universitas Pelita Harapan (UPH) for the support and funding. This chapter is a result of in-depth discussions and ideas exchanges with Siti Nurjanah with her valuable perspective as the director of the Women and Youth Development Institute of Indonesia. I also thank Kim Litelnoni, Indira Purnami and Fauziah Rizky Ayu for their data collection and research assistantship contribution.

Bibliography

Alawiyah, Tutty. 1997. *Strategi Dakwah Di Lingkungan Majelis Taklim.* Bandung, Indonesia: Mizan.

AsiaOne. 2019. "Social Media Teams Paid to Drive up Buzz on Indonesian Presidential Rivals." March 13. https://www.asiaone.com/asia/social-media-teams-paid-drive-buzz-indonesian-presidential-rivals.

Aspinall, Edward, and Ward Berenschot. 2019. *Democracy for Sale: Elections, Clientelism, and the State in Indonesia.* Ithaca, NY: Cornell University Press.

BBC. 2016. "Ketua HMI: Presiden Jokowi Memecah Belah Umat Islam." *BBC News Indonesia*, November 9. https://www.bbc.com/indonesia/indonesia-37910983.

———. 2018. "Istilah 'emak-Emak' Dan 'Ibu Bangsa': Cara Jokowi Dan Prabowo Memikat Pemilih Perempuan." *BBC News Indonesia.* https://www.bbc.com/indonesia/trensosial-45563444.

———. 2018. "Rizieq Shihab Dibawa Ke Kantor Polisi Arab Saudi Terkait 'kasus Bendera.'" *BBC News Indonesia.* https://www.bbc.com/indonesia/indonesia-46113565.

Bertrand, Jacques. 2003. *Nationalism and Ethnic Conflict in Indonesia.* https://doi.org/10.1017/CBO9780511559341.

Bomantama, Rizal. 2018. "Partai Emak-Emak Pendukung Prabowo-Sandi Dideklarasikan." *Tribunnews.* https://www.tribunnews.com/pilpres-2019/2018/08/23/partai-emak-emak-pendukung-prabowo-sandi-dideklarasikan.

CNN. 2018. "Kampanye Sandi, Upaya Menambal Elektabilitas Mentok Prabowo." *CNN Indonesia.* https://www.cnnindonesia.com/nasional/20181015193054-32-338681/kampanye-sandi-upaya-menambal-elektabilitas-mentok-prabowo.

———. 2019. "FPI: Insya Allah Rizieq Shihab Pulang 2020." *CNN Indonesia.* https://www.cnnindonesia.com/nasional/20191231144117-20-461335/fpi-insya-allah-rizieq-shihab-pulang-2020.

Erdianto, Kristian. 2019. "5 Fakta Vonis Emak-Emak Pepes, Dihukum Ringan Hingga Klaim Kerja Keras Gerindra Halaman All." *Kompas.* https://nasional.kompas.com/read/2019/08/01/11082051/5-fakta-vonis-emak-emak-pepes-dihukum-ringan-hingga-klaim-kerja-keras?page=all.

Hermawan, Ary. 2019. "Choose Freedom over Fear: Illiberal Pluralism Is Threatening Our Democracy." *The Jakarta Post.* https://www.thejakartapost.com/academia/2019/07/04/choose-freedom-over-fear-illiberal-pluralism-is-a-threat-to-our-democracy.html.

Ihsanuddin. 2018. "Jokowi Minta Emak-Emak Tak Termakan Hoaks Soal Harga Sembako." *Kompas* https://nasional.kompas.com/read/2018/10/30/11083731/jokowi-minta-emak-emak-tak-termakan-hoaks-soal-harga-sembako.

Jakarta Post. 2017. "Rizieq Shihab Named Suspect in Pornography Case While Abroad." May 29. https://www.thejakartapost.com/news/2017/05/29/rizieq-shihab-named-suspect-in-pornography-case-while-abroad.html.

Jerami. 2018. "PEPES KEPUNG, Malam-Malam Ini Yang Dilakukan Emak-Emak Pendukung Prabowo Sandi Di 3 Kabupaten." http://www.jerami.info/2018/11/16/pepes-kepung-malam-malam-ini-yang-dilakukan-emak-emak-pendukung-prabowo-sandi-di-3-kabupaten/.

Komisi Pemilihan Umum [General Elections Commission of Indonesia]. 2018. "KPU Portal Publikasi Pileg 2019." https://infopemilu.kpu.go.id/pileg2019/verpol/skparpol.

Kruglanski, Arie W., Jocelyn J. Bélanger, and Rohan Gunaratna. 2019. *The Three Pillars of Radicalization.* https://doi.org/10.1093/oso/9780190851125.001.0001.

Lamb, Kate. 2019. "Jakarta Riots: Indonesian President Says He Will Not Tolerate Threats to Unity." *The Guardian,* May 22. https://www.theguardian.com/world/2019/may/23/indonesia-pm-riot-deaths-jakarta-joko-widodo.

Lin, Jih Hsuan. 2016. "Need for Relatedness: A Self-Determination Approach to Examining Attachment Styles, Facebook Use, and Psychological Well-Being." *Asian Journal of Communication* 26(2): 153-73. https://doi.org/10.1080/01292986.2015.1126749.

Nurita, Dewi. 2019. "Mayoritas Partai Di DPR Setuju Pengesahan RKUHP Ditunda." *Tempo* [blog], September 22. https://nasional.tempo.co/read/1250835/mayoritas-partai-di-dpr-setuju-pengesahan-rkuhp-ditunda.

Partai Keadilan Sejahtera. 2015. "Hukum Islam Harus Mewarnai Hukum Nasional." http://pks.id/content/hukum-islam-harus-mewarnai-hukum-nasional.

Pew Research Center. 2015. "Men Catch up with Women on Overall Social Media Use." https://www.pewresearch.org/fact-tank/2015/08/28/men-catch-up-with-women-on-overall-social-media-use/.

Rachmahlia, Andini. 2017. "Perkembangan Majelis Ta'lim Dan Pengaruhnya Di Kelurahan Batu Ampar Condet Jakarta Timur Tahun 1965–2010." Universitas Negeri Islam Syarif Hidayatullah.

Raharjo, Budi. 2019. "Majelis Taklim Tak Perlu Ditakuti." *Republika Online.* https://republika.co.id/berita/q2dk76415/majelis-taklim-tak-perlu-di-takuti.

Rise of Radicalism: Growing Terrorist Sanctuaries and the Threat to the US Homeland: Joint Hearing Before the Committee on Homeland Security and the Committee on Foreign Affairs, House of Representatives, 114th Cong. (2015)

Sasongko, Agung. 2018. "Memahami Istilah Majelis Taklim." *Republika Online.* https://republika.co.id/berita/p4suiq313/memahami-istilah-majelis-taklim.

Schmid, Alex. 2011. *The Routledge Handbook of Terrorism Research.* London: Routledge. https://doi.org/10.4324/9780203828731.

Soeriaatmadja, Wahyudi. 2019. "318 Election Officials Die, More than 2,000 Ill after Indonesia's Mammoth Single-Day Poll." *The Straits Times,* April 30. https://www.straitstimes.com/asia/se-asia/318-election-officials-die-more-than-2000-ill-after-indonesias-mammoth-single-day-poll.

Statista. 2019. "Countries with Most Instagram Users 2020." https://www.statista.com/statistics/578364/countries-with-most-instagram-users/.

SwaMedium. 2018. "PEPES KEPUNG, Gerilya Ala Emak-Emak Pendukung Prabowo-Sandi." https://www.swamedium.com/2018/11/02/pepes-kepung-gerilya-ala-emak-emak-pendukung-prabowo-sandi/.

Syechbubakr, Ahmad Syarif. 2018. "Nahdlatul Ulama and Muhammadiyah Struggle with Internal Divisions in the Post-Soeharto Era." *Indonesia at Melbourne,* University of Melbourne. https://indonesiaatmelbourne.unimelb.edu.au/nahdlatul-ulama-and-muhammadiyah-struggle-with-internal-divisions-in-the-post-soeharto-era/.

Triyadi Bempah, Ramdhan. 2019. "Seorang Dosen IPB Diduga Gerak-kan Pembuatan Bom Molotov Untuk Aksi Mujahid 212." *Kompas*. https://megapolitan.kompas.com/read/2019/09/29/22264441/seo-rang-dosen-ipb-diduga-gerakkan-pembuatan-bom-molotov-un-tuk-aksi.

Wee, Rolando. 2016. "Which Country Has the Largest Number of Cell-phones?" *WorldAtlas*. https://www.worldatlas.com/articles/10-coun-tries-with-the-highest-rates-of-cell-phone-subscriptions.html.

Appendix

Questions for Female Legislative Candidates:

1. What is the mechanism of legislative candidate in your party?

2. Who determine type and which constituent you will reach in campaign? Which group/ type of constituents are most enthusiast in giving you support? Why?

3. Is there any of your constituent organize campaign for you or involve in other political actions, for example demonstration or attending campaigns?

4. Any of your constituent actively upload video or update status for you on social media? What type of material?

5. Have you ever given incentive to constituents in any form (money, rice, headscarves)?

6. Is there special training, program for you during campaign season relate to religion or political ideological material? Why is there or there isn't?

7. In your campaign do you have attitude, statement or thoughts along the line of: keeping the purity of religious teaching (Islam/ Christian), concerns over domination of other religion, conditional tolerance, anti Ahok, anti Jokowi etc.

8. What is the usual form of reaction/ action from your constituents? Campaigning, social media postings etc.

9. What is your thought regarding Neno Warisan action especially leading prayers as female in political campaign?

10. With the recent development of reconciliation between Prabowo and Jokowi, do you consider the necessity of campaign with hatred and division content (as political pursuit)?

11. Do you consider there is a strategic benefit derived from the identity politics campaign? Why?

12. Does anyone need to be radical in order to achieve political/ religious goal?

13. What defines radicalism and liberalism in your view?

14. Do you consider yourself to be more radical or liberal? What is the distinction?

Questions for the Female Constituents/ Voters :

1. Are you a first time voter?

2. Are you affiliated to a political party? Or which political party do you support?

3. What or who are the people that makes you vote in the election? Possible follow up questions:
   a. How these people influence your decision to vote in the election
   b. Why these people can make you vote in the election

4. What are the issues that you care about? (you may follow up with these options: economy, education, law, education, religion)

5. Which candidate you think can help you with that issue?

6. Why do you think the candidate can help you attain or pursue (can speak for you) the issues you care about?

7. How involved were you in the election?
   a. Vote only;
   b. Volunteer on the election day;
   c. Participated in campaign (how).

Chapter 7

A Righteous Intervention: Megachurch Christianity and Duterte's War on Drugs in the Philippines

Jayeel Cornelio and Ia Marañon

Duterte's administration claims that the war on drugs in the Philippines is successful. To the government, the figures are undeniable. As of late 2018, around 165,000 drug-related individuals have been arrested, almost 10,000 local villages declared drug-free, and USD 364 million worth of methamphetamine seized (Philippine Information Agency 2018). By invoking these figures, the administration refutes accusations that the war on drugs is only about killing drug addicts, which has been widely reported by journalists. At the same time, the government's official count also shows that the total number of drug-related deaths is around 5,000 to date, far below the estimates of human rights activists (Qintos 2018). Responding to the policy's critics, government officials have repeatedly asserted that the "majority of Filipinos actually feel much safer now" (Viray 2018).

A few religious entities could not turn a blind eye. Some influential members of the Catholic Bishops' Conference of the Philippines (CBCP) have spoken up. In a letter read in all the parishes of the Archdiocese of Manila, Cardinal Tagle admits that "the menace of illegal drugs is real and destructive." He also appeals to "the consciences of those who kill even the helpless, especially those who cover their faces with bonnets, to stop wasting human lives." Here he refers to killings involving unidentifiable vigilantes, who may or may not be connected to the anti-illegal drug campaign itself. By contrast, Archbishop Villegas of Lingayen-Dagupan has written a more forceful letter. In Filipino, Villegas offers his critical reflections: "They say that a nation that rejects drugs should give its consent to the murder of drug pushers. If you take a stand for the murdered victims, you would be for sure cursed and threatened...Is this the new normal?" (*Philippine Star* 2017). Adding to this voice is the Association of Major Religious Superiors in the Philippines. Its statement declares that "we cannot be party to a war that kills and kills. We cannot accept a war that targets the poor and the powerless" (*CBCP News* 2017). In their own ways, local Catholic parishes have done their part too. The National Shrine of Our Lady of Perpetual Help in Parañaque has put up an exhibit of photos of corpses and grieving families (Evangelista 2016).

The response is not limited to influential Catholic figures and groups. The Philippine Council of Evangelical Churches (PCEC) has lauded the "determination" of the administration to end the drug problem. But, it is concerned "with the daily bloodshed of those who are accused of being a pusher, addict, or involved in some way in prohibited drugs" (Esmaquel II 2017). PCEC is a nationwide network of various denominations and local churches that consider themselves evangelical (Lim 2009, 1989). Similarly, the National Council of Churches in the Philippines (NCCP) came up with a statement in the wake of the death of at least five teenagers. It asks why "young people and the poor have become vulnerable to impunity while suspected big-time drug syndicates have their day in court" (Esmaquel II 2017). NCCP is an ecumenical network of mainstream Protestant denominations and churches associated with progressive issues such as peace and justice. On their own, some other evangelical churches have also pitched in. When it celebrated its 39th anniversary in 2017, the founding pastor of Jesus is Lord Church, Brother Eddie Villanueva, took police offers to task: "The problem is killings left and right...As a Christian, I could not accept this...These could be abuses of the scalawag members of the police system who decided to impress their superiors" (*ABS-CBN New*, 2017). Brother Eddie is convinced of this allegation based on confessions of police officers who have come to him for help.

How influential are these statements? Inasmuch as they have been made by influential leaders of the Catholic Church and other blocs such as PCEC and NCCP, it is important to note that they are not necessarily echoed by their constituent congregations or local religious leaders. It is in this manner that one can complicate the religious context insofar as Duterte's war on drugs is concerned. Making distinctions between churches and denominations in terms of their official statements about the campaign is useful only to a certain extent. But to suggest that religious groups are unified against the war on drugs is a mistake.

Indeed the situation in communities is more complex. For example, these statements do not reflect public sentiments in contemporary Philippine society. The war on drugs is a welcome intervention on the part of the majority. A national survey reveals that 88% of Filipino adults support it.

This is even if 73% also believe that extrajudicial killings accompany the campaign (*Pulse Asia* 2017). Furthermore, other religious groups, especially in local communities, have been noticeably quiet about the issue. One major study in an urban poor community that has been tagged as a hotspot in the war on drugs reveals that only a handful of religious groups—Catholic and evangelical alike—confront the reality of killings in their neighborhood (Cornelio and Medina 2019). The majority of religious leaders in this community support the campaign, even invoking Scripture to make their case. They come from different Christian groups including Baptists, evangelicals, and even non-denominational churches. They even claim that the war on drugs has been a blessing in disguise for creating new opportunities for evangelism around the country (Christian Aid 2018). In other communities, some Catholic priests have been vocally supportive of the campaign (Bladwin and Serapio 2016), while others have spoken out against the campaign. In other words, depicting the religious response to the war on drugs along denominational lines or religious affiliations is inadequate.

Focusing on Megachurch Pastors

This situation serves as a backdrop to the main point of the article, which is to account for the seeming silence of other influential religious groups on the war on drugs. Our argument is that religious frames inform their political attitudes towards the campaign, chief of which is that it is a "righteous" intervention. In particular, we focus on the pastors of evangelical megachurches in Manila. By and large, megachurches have been apolitical towards the war on drugs. We investigate megachurch leaders not only because they lead influential congregations that are among the fastest-growing religious groups in the country, but also because they have not, for example, released any official statement in relation to the war on drugs. At the same time, they have chosen to focus on the rehabilitation of substance users and organize workshops for the moral renewal of police officers.

Several observations have compelled us to embark on this study. The response of megachurches, for one, stands in contrast to that of their evangelical and Catholic counterparts described above. Furthermore, the literature shows that historically, evangelical Christians were at the forefront of democratic participation in the country. During the People Power Revolution in 1986, PCEC declared that "where Caesar conflicts with Christ, we declare that Jesus is Lord. Divine law supersedes human law. Therefore, our obedience is not absolute. Whenever government rules contrary to the will of God, then civil disobedience becomes a Christian duty" (Lim 1989). Given this contrast, the current political silence of megachurches calls for a deeper probe into the theologies surrounding the war on drugs and the publics they choose to engage. It is in this manner that we align with studies that show that religious beliefs affect how people "understand drug use and abuse" and also "what they think should be done about it" (Courtwright 1997).

This article draws from interviews with megachurch pastors from two of the most prominent megachurches in Metro Manila. In the interest of confidentiality, we have chosen not to disclose their real identities or even the names of the churches to which they belong. Nevertheless, we can describe that the prominence of these megachurches in the country is unmistakable. Most megachurches will have their headquarters in Manila, with satellite branches in urban centers around the Philippines. Their headquarters alone are spectacular buildings in their own right, with members in the thousands. Their satellite churches, located in cities around the country, are often in the form of movie theatres that become worship halls on a given Sunday or rented office spaces converted for the purposes of fellowships and discipleship activities. In terms of our informants, we chose to interview a diverse range of leadership positions. Some occupy top leadership roles in the respective headquarters of their megachurches while the rest are assigned to local congregations in different parts of Manila. We also interviewed youth ministers among them. All of them are male, with the youngest in his 30s, indicative of the predominantly male leadership structure in these religious organizations. Some of them have also played important roles for the activities of their church to address substance abuse.

We understand that fine differences are discernible between the evangelical megachurches in our study, especially along theological lines and religious practices, but we also recognize that by and large, these megachurches attract a predictable demographic: the youth, middle class families, and highly educated young professionals (Teledo 2018). In this sense, these megachurches are religious spaces for aspirational Filipinos. So, even if they have special ministries catered for the urban poor, as we will mention later on, they generally compete for exactly the same segment of the population that benefits from the country's economic development. The proclivity for social stability is thus to be expected. We will revisit the importance of this point towards the end. For now, what is important to recognize is that their institutional dispositions are very different from that of independent evangelical churches and older denominations that have taken root as small congregations in suburbs or rural areas. They are also different from indigenized megachurches like Jesus is Lord whose religious nationalism is worth investigating in relation to the war on drugs (Cornelio 2018).

Religion and Drug Abuse

Psychologists have dominated the scholarship on religion and substance abuse. Their studies focus on how beliefs and practices affect individual dispositions toward abuse. In fact, many of them validate the religiosity hypothesis, which posits that being religious is a protective factor against substance abuse (Wallace 2003). Some studies show, too, that religious support is helpful in the recovery phase (Al-Omari, Hamed, and Tariah 2015). How is religion influential in framing people's attitudes towards policies concerning substance abuse? To us this is an inescapable question because of the wide support for the war on drugs in the Philippines. Given that the country is among the most religious societies in the world, the underlying premise of our study is that the support for the war on drugs has an inherent religious dimension (Smith 2012). There are three ways to unravel the religious dimension.

The first is by recognizing it as a moral crusade. The mere idea of drugs is already loaded with moral judgments. For Jacques Derrida, "the concept of drugs is not a scientific concept, but is rather instituted on the basis of moral or political evaluations" (Derrida 2003, 20). To him, before one even talks about addiction, the mere mention of drugs already carries a set of norms and prohibitions. The state plays a big role in defining not only what constitutes drugs but its public acceptability as well (Lopes and Costa 2018, 2). In this light, that illegal drugs are framed as a public enemy demands that a war be waged against it. In the US, the anti-drug campaign launched by President Nixon in the 1970s was punitive and oriented towards eradication and incarceration. It received much public support especially because it claimed "morality and protection of our children as its goals" (Boyd 2002, 845). For the general public then, sacrificing some liberties was justified because the nation and the future of children were sacred. Indeed, the US war on drugs had lasting negative consequences on freedom of religion, freedom of speech, and freedom from unreasonable searches and seizures. To sacralize the nation explains why the imagery of any war on drugs is militant. That it is a war means that certain sacrifices—or collateral damage—are to be expected.

The second approach interrogates religious support for specific policies concerning substance abuse. In the literature, these policies range from less restrictive models to more. Less restrictive models such as taxation and laissez-faire follow libertarian principles. More restrictive models, by contrast, impose criminal sanctions in terms of incapacitation and deterrence. In between is the medical approach that calls for therapy and rehabilitation as viable interventions. How then is the religious worldview influential here? Research shows that religious conservatives who generally frame drug abuse as an excessive behavior are likely to favor coercive tactics often associated with drug wars around the world. Progressive Christians, on the other hand, are more supportive of medical approaches. The theological underpinning is that treatment expresses compassion to victims of social circumstances. Individuals with no or nominal religious affiliations may be more libertarian (Courtwright 1997).

Third, beliefs inform how religious people respond to illegal drugs as a social problem. Some religious worldviews, on the one hand, are inclined to take drug abuse as an immediate concern, which the church could practically address. In Brazil, Protestant churches whose members are poor have provided support for the therapy and treatment of drug users. Other churches, however, treat it as a "spiritual illness." They have thus designed a 12-step program that "begins with surrendering to Jesus and ends with prayer, fasting, and actively saying 'no' to the temptations of the world" (Lopes and Costa 2018, 9). For these churches, substance abuse opens up opportunities for ministry and outreach. There are, on the other hand, churches that see the proliferation of illegal drugs as a social evil. Echoing recent findings about the use of illegal substance among the poor in the Philippines, these churches treat users as victims of social injustice (Lasco 2014, 784). Apart from the provision of welfare and support, they have also extended legal help.

Some scholars claim that religious people are "quietist by instinct and would prefer to avoid political engagement" (Griffith-Dickson 2018, 70), but the studies we have covered thus far demonstrate that political silence is not so much about the instinct as it is the religious lens through which they view issues. As we have pointed out above, social issues like

substance abuse are based on moral evaluations that have consequences on how churches respond especially at the level of communities in
which they are embedded. By interrogating these moral evaluations, our
study brings to the surface different visions of the Christian gospel "as
a blueprint for making the world a better place" or "as a mandate calling
on individuals to repent as humanity heads toward its imminent demise"
(Elisha 2011, 2). For scholars to be aware of these differences is crucial to
understanding churches' engagements with the public. At the same time,
we argue that the distinction cannot be painted in broad strokes. The
nature of the specific public concern, such as the war on drugs, matters
as well. We will revisit this idea in the succeeding sections.

Megachurches, which are among the fastest growing religious organizations in the Philippines, have been apolitical towards the war on
drugs. In contrast to the religious groups mentioned above, that they
have not released any official statement is glaring. At the same time,
megachurches have adopted interventions that aim at the rehabilitation
of drug-dependent individuals and the moral renewal of police officers.
What accounts for these actions? From the point of view of megachurch
pastors in the country, the war on drugs is a "righteous intervention" on
the part of a God-ordained administration, whose actions seek the safety
and welfare of the public. At the same time, addressing the proliferation
of illegal drugs and criminality is "humanly impossible." Responding to
substance abuse, in other words, can only be a spiritual matter. Thus the
task of the church is to treat substance abuse as a spiritual condition to
which the answer is conversion and moral recovery. Reinforcing this position are their convictions that Christians are to submit to authority and
that extrajudicial killings are a divisive political matter that cannot be
mentioned at the pulpit. We end this article with a critical reflection on
how these theological views ultimately reflect the interests of the class
these megachurches represent.

Megachurch Pastors and the War on Drugs

What do the pastors think about the war on drugs? In this section,
we spell out several ideas that articulate the theological position of megachurch pastors on the war on drugs. The first one frames the war on drugs
as a righteous intervention insofar as it addresses people's desire for swift
justice. The second frames it as an opportunity for evangelism. Both, in

effect, deflect moral and political responsibility. The deflection becomes much more acute in relation to their views on extrajudicial killings that have accompanied the war on drugs and their theological position concerning submission to authority.

Framing the War on Drugs

During the interviews, we repeatedly heard pastors describe substance abuse and the crimes associated with it as "humanly impossible to solve apart from a supernatural intervention." The idea that it is "humanly impossible" needs to be teased out as it serves as their moral justification for the war on drugs. For Pastor Boggart, 33 years old, the proliferation of illegal drugs is a reality encountered by Filipinos in their daily life. But to solve the problem, in his view, is "humanly impossible" because human beings, "are imperfect creatures incapable of doing completely godly or good things." Thus, he believes that the war on drugs is righteous insofar as it responds to a certain need, a "cry of the people" for safety and swift justice. In effect, the phrase is not just theological shorthand. It articulates deep anxieties locals feel about their safety in their respective communities, validating observations about the effectiveness of Duterte's presidential campaign to turn local anxieties into a national concern (Holmes 2016, 18). Pastor Boggart then makes the case that if the president wants to rid the Philippines of illegal drugs, then there will be trade-offs, referring to people dying in its wake. He admits that killings do happen—whether state-sanctioned or caused by vigilantes.

Indeed, killings have taken place even within the congregations some of our pastors lead. A member in Pastor John's congregation was found dead more than a year ago. This congregation, which has outreach ministries to the urban poor, is located in an area in Manila notorious for extrajudicial killings. Marlon, who drove a pedal-operated sidecar for a living, was converted in Pastor John's congregation where he had already been undergoing discipleship activities with other members. Marlon was even part of a small or "cell" group, in which the main work of discipleship is facilitated. These small groups often spend time outside of church hours and do Bible studies together. In the wake of his death, Pastor John, 34 years old, sought to protect this group from being associated with Marlon lest the other members be targeted next. Since Marlon did not have any next of kin, his group wanted to claim the body and give him a proper burial. Pastor John discouraged and warned the group not to do that because they might be mistaken for Marlon's drug network. The group took note of Pastor John's advice. Pastor John finds consolation in the fact that although Marlon was a drug user, what happened to him was that "past sins...merely haunted him." Pastor John is convinced that Marlon's death is "not in vain...as he is now with the Lord."

Megachurch pastors have also framed the war on drugs as an "opportunity," another word we repeatedly heard during the interviews. For our interlocutors, the war on drugs has empowered them to 'reach out' to those who are normally 'resistant' to evangelization. This has happened in a very concrete manner for some of our pastors. The government's Dangerous Drugs Board (DDB) sought the help of their megachurch to lead a drug rehabilitation effort. DDB was in particular interested in a faith-based intervention to address drug problems. Because there was already a pre-existing relationship between DDB and the megachurch's leadership, the initiative quickly took shape. The intervention, placed under a non-governmental organization connected to the megachurch, adopted a self-confessed Filipino response to addiction. The program involves admitting one's mistakes and re-centring one's life back to the family. The NGO employs a 12-step program that is hinged on moral recovery. It partners with local churches of different religious denominations to target drug-dependent individuals both apprehended by the police and those identified at the village level. Through the NGO, pastors have the opportunity to connect with these entities who otherwise would not be willing to go through the process.

The "righteousness" of the war on drugs and the evangelistic opportunities it has opened up for megachurch pastors ultimately rest on the worldview that drug addiction is a spiritual condition. This worldview arrests any proclivity to recognize the structural injustices that account for the proliferation of drug abuse and accompany the war on drugs as it has taken place in urban poor communities around the country. This to us is a very important finding. Other studies show that the death of a member in the war on drugs is pivotal to the political awakening of a congregation. This is the observation of Cornelio and Medina (2019) in another poor urban hotspot in Manila. Also, the megachurch pastors' worldview might be understandable if they had already been dealing with "compassion fatigue" as a result of unsuccessful faith-based activism (Elisha 2008, 155). Yet, this was not the case. As we have observed during the fieldwork, for these pastors, killings, while not necessarily acceptable, are in a sense to be expected because "past sins" are still to be answered for even after conversion. In effect, the renewal of Philippine society necessitates that certain sacrifices are to be made. At the same time, what this means is that pastors can only accept that people getting killed in this war on drugs is a "trade-off."

Extrajudicial Killings?

As a policy, the war on drugs involves different schemes addressing supply and demand for illegal substance. The government regularly releases its reports that include data on surrenders, rehabilitation, and investigations of the supposed killings that take place in both government and non-government operations (Philippine Information Agency 2018). But the campaign is mainly associated with extrajudicial killings, which take place in different forms. For example, dead bodies found with placards that read "I'm a pusher" are linked to vigilante killings. The Philippine National Police makes a distinction between these and deaths that take place during operations where drug suspects allegedly fought back. But accounts by journalists and human rights activists reveal that police officers themselves are "incentivized to murder drug users" (Gallagher, Raffle, and Maulana 2019, 8). As a result, some scholars argue that the state fails in its responsibility to protect those that are being systematically targeted in the war on drugs (Gallagher, Raffle, and Maulana 2019;).

So, how do church leaders deal with the moral gravity of the situation? Above we mentioned that deaths are seen as a "trade-off" even if pastors would not consider them "legitimate." We wish to deepen that discussion here. One aspect is that the pastors treat the killings as a concern secondary to the priorities of the church. In the words of some of our interlocutors, their priorities are "the concerns of the living," referring to conversion and discipleship. Others question the prevalence of the problem. Pastor Justin, who has been in the ministry for two decades, says that the term extrajudicial killings "is not an accurate way" of rendering the problem in the war on drugs. Although he admits that there is enough proof that extrajudicial killings do indeed occur, for him it is not fair to paint the entire war on drugs as such. Pastor George, 40 years old, shares in this discomfort, as there are too many "unconfirmed reports," casting doubts on claims that police officers are responsible for all the killings that have taken place. To him due process must take place to ascertain their guilt. At the same time, Pastor George and his peers are wary about news reports that they feel might be skewed. Pastor George thus explains that the church cannot proceed with any political action. It will be a "Pandora's box," causing division within the church. For the pastors we interviewed, this situation would not be acceptable.

There are, however, dissenting voices, even if they remain marginal. In confidence, Pastor Ben tells us that the killings and the war on drugs are one and the same. Thus, it is "not in any sense godly." During the interview, he repeatedly points to disparities between high-profile drug lords being afforded due process and poor drug-dependent individuals murdered in the streets. His position stands in contrast to that of his peers who believe that substance abuse happens because people do not have a "Biblical standard" by which they lead their lives. The fixation on spiritual explanations characterizes much of contemporary conservative evangelicalism (Elisha 2011, 4). One possible explanation for his dissenting opinion is that Pastor Ben is the head of a congregation in a university area where students have been involved in protesting the war on drugs.

Submission to Authority

During the interviews we asked pastors to explain the Biblical or theological bases of their perspectives about the war on drugs. Repeatedly we heard them quote Romans 13 to insist that the Bible mandates Christians to submit to authority. The passage asserts that God has appointed government authorities as "agents of wrath to bring punishment on the wrongdoer" (Rom. 13:4). Based on the literature, there are two competing interpretations of this text. Adopting a literalist approach, the first highlights submission to the governing authority as a matter of duty (Cranfield 1959). At the very core of civil government is a good worth honoring. Rebelling against the government is thus in effect rebelling against God (Stein 1989, 325). By contrast, the postcolonial reading of Romans 13 paints Paul as a subversive voice within the Roman Empire. This reading recognizes the precarious situation of Christians who were under persecution at that time. To settle the debate is not the point of this paper, but it is telling that most of our interlocutors adhere to the literalist view of Romans 13. Pastor Justin, for example, emphasizes the civil government's "God-ordained function," which, he explains, is to "promote righteousness and punish evil." Echoing his initial statements above, this is why the war on drugs, "as a matter of principle," is "righteous." Convinced that the war on drugs is "righteous," Pastor Justin believes the church as an institution must support the government. This includes members who are also critical of the campaign.

Other pastors would agree with this position, but not without caveats. Pastor Ben, whose dissenting voice we mentioned above, asserts that there are limits to submitting to authority. For him it lies in legality, appealing to the principles of the Philippine Constitution. He believes that every Christian must critically assess whether what Christians submit to is in fact constitutional. Outside of that is space for outright dissent. Dissent is what he brings up in talking about the war on drugs. For him, it is "disappointing" that Christians are silent on this matter. He questions why evangelicals have been immensely more vocal about Lourdes Sereno than they are about extrajudicial killings. Sereno is the former Chief Justice of the Supreme Court, an avowed evangelical whose leadership was opposed by President Duterte himself. Other pastors, however, are not as forthright. For them one's submission is a delicate balance between duty and dissent. This means that the church must be able to "prick the conscience" of the larger society, while at the same time "honoring and praying" for public officials. To them it is not yet clear whether the time has come for them to "call for public accountability" on the part of the government. These two caveats reveal that the nature of issues matters in determining a church's "moral ambition" in civil society—whether a church participates, how it does so, and what values it embraces (Elisha 2011, 1). Whereas Sereno's ousting has compelled evangelicals and the leaders of these megachurches to come out to the streets in a show of force, the war on drugs has not. It is because the latter is a "righteous" intervention.

The Apolitical Pulpit

For the pastors we interviewed, the pulpit must be apolitical. Megachurch pastors are cautious for various reasons. First, they are convinced that using the pulpit to discuss political matters will only lead to divisions within the megachurch. Second, they have repeatedly pointed out that they have little credibility in speaking about political matters. For them their role as religious leaders must concern the spiritual. This is why, they believe, that they are "pastors in the first place." Third, they also assume that politics is alienating, especially to newcomers. For Pastor Justin, this will defeat the main purpose of the megachurch, which is to "reach out" to those who need to hear the good news. Clearly to convert is their vision of the Christian gospel (Elisha 2011).

The last point is crucial. The leaders in this study understand the importance of speaking out, but choose to focus on the potential implications of any political statement. For them, the call for Christians is to lead and practice a Christian life, which is about involving themselves in ministry and evangelism. To them the megachurch has to be an "open space" in which everyone is welcome—pro-Duterte or otherwise. In our interview with him, Pastor George stresses the importance of honoring the separation clause, by characterizing it as "reducing the friction between church and state." We need to reiterate, however, that this position is not necessarily consistent for these megachurches. As we have recounted above, their leaders and members have organized themselves to pray and even stage vigils at the Supreme Court when their fellow evangelical Chief Justice Sereno was under attack.

In this light, their hesitancy to treat the war on drugs as a political matter is very telling. This is not just about the inability to dissent because it does not honor the civil government. Instead, the war on drugs is to them a "righteous intervention" that becomes even more welcome because it has expanded their opportunities to evangelize through their programs with drug offenders and police officers. In effect, these megachurches have taken on the role of assisting, in the spirit of Romans 13, "God-ordained institutions." What accounts for this position?

The first is institutional. Although Pastor Ben tackles the war on drugs in his own circles, he could not bring this up in the megachurch at large because he is aware that his views are unpopular. John, another pastor, struggles with the same dilemma but on a different level. For him, there is a split when he talks about social issues—that his convictions as a citizen are very different from those as a church leader. He says that what keeps him from "filling his home with guns" is the fact that he has to live a life of "righteousness." To him, his identity as a churchman supersedes his identity as a citizen with democratic rights and obligations. Being a religious leader in an institution that renders the pulpit apolitical means that he has to disentangle these two identities.

The second is structural. These megachurches have a strong aspirational middle class disposition. They are located in urban centers and attract young and educated members. Some of their congregations may not necessarily be affluent, but these megachurches imbibe the middle class disposition. From the English songs they sing to the high-energy sermons that focus on individual purpose, happiness, and peace, these megachurches imbibe the aspirations of an upwardly mobile segment of the Philippine population. In many ways, this replicates the social location of megachurches described by researchers elsewhere, such as in Singapore. In Singapore, not all their members are established middle class, especially because many of them are still in university. But being in university is indicative of their aspiration for economic stability in an otherwise competitive society (Chong 2015, 215). The resonance with the megachurches we have included in this research is unmistakable, especially when they are approached from the vantage point of a competitive religious economy where numbers, finances, buildings, and programs are indicators of success and blessing (Cornelio 2020; 2017). Part of the process of wanting a "better life" is securing a space in which the megachurch does not invite conflict upon itself, and by extension, its members. Furthermore, the leaders often invoke a functionalist take on what it means to be a Christian church: that they have a part to play, much like the government and the police have their own. In this sense, the structural location of these megachurches in Philippine society makes them very selective when it comes to public issues they are to engage. That they are willing to invoke Scriptures and the separation clause to justify their selectiveness sets them apart from Catholic, evangelical, and other religious groups that historically have a very strong orientation towards politics and social justice (Lim 2009; Cornelio 2018).

Conclusion

In the literature, the war on drugs has been largely assessed from the point of view of policy and human rights (Gallegher, Raffle and Maulana 2019, 1). Our contribution in this article has been to understand the religious underpinnings of a church's institutional action towards the campaign. Doing this is a necessary intervention in several respects. For one, the war on drugs is not just any other policy. It strikes at the core of the message of the Christian gospel, which calls for renewal and hope. How Christians, especially those who come from affluent and influential churches, position themselves in relation to the killings interrogates how much their moral worldview affects their social action. Second, megachurches are among the fastest growing religious groups in the Philippines today. Mirroring the work of other influential religious groups in the history of the country, they have the social capital that can influence politics (Cornelio 2018, 137). Whether they use it or not and on what issues they do are key questions for observers of religious change in the Philippines. At the onset we pointed out how Catholic groups and some of their Protestant counterparts have historically been involved in progressive politics. Third, the war on drugs is not an isolated issue. It is part of the wider political environment that embraces anti-crime rhetoric and action, even at the expense of the rights to speech, life, and due process. This new environment includes calls for the reinstatement of the death penalty and the lowering of the age of criminal liability.

The religious frames have been very instructive in making sense of what megachurch pastors have done in relation to the war on drugs. For them, the campaign is in itself a righteous intervention insofar as it seeks the safety and welfare of the public. In addition, it has created opportunities for evangelistic expansion in the form of partnerships with government agencies that aim to bring religion into the operation. Megachurches have thus taken advantage of the opening by running programs for rehabilitation and moral renewal. Reinforcing this position are their views that treat extrajudicial killings as a "trade-off" and submission to authority as a divine mandate. Whether this is a form of religious co-optation by the government to sacralize its otherwise controversial public action is open to debate. Instead we have been more interested in offering critical assessments of the megachurches' middle class position that seeks stability to uphold the aspirations of their adherents.

The implication is clear. That megachurch pastors have spiritualized the war on drugs, as it were, fails to recognize the structural causes and consequences of substance abuse in the country (Lasco 2014, 783). While we have argued that this perspective is ultimately derived from their class location, it is the consequences on their political engagements that we wish to highlight in this conclusion. The first has to do with the morality of the war on drugs itself. The implications of an apolitical megachurch at a time when thousands have been killed raise questions on how these churches adapt to the needs of their congregation, and what these megachurch leaders ultimately enable by their continued silence. This selective silence on the war on drugs reaffirms certain biases that may at some point appear contradictory: Is the war on drugs not worth mobilizing for, even if thousands of people have lost their lives? Can the theology that implicitly dismisses killings as a "trade-off" still be contested? The second consequence concerns their place in relation to democracy. Given the rise of right-wing populism and illiberal reforms around the world, can churches reimagine their contributions especially in societies such as the Philippines where they have played prominent roles as civil society actors? What visions of the Christian gospel are appropriate in such political environments? These questions, while important for observers, are ultimately more so for megachurch leaders themselves who need to ask what it means to be Christian when core values of life and human dignity are under attack.

Bibliography

ABS-CBN News. 2017. "JIL Leader Villanueva Hits Unsolved Drug Killings, Blames 'Scalawags'" http://news.abs-cbn.com/news/10/28/17/jil-leader-villanueva-hits-unsolved-drug-killings-blames-scalawags.

Al-Omari, H., R. Hamed, and H. Abu Tariah. 2015. "The Role of Religion in the Recovery from Alcohol and Substance Abuse among Jordanian Adults." *Journal of Religion and Health* 54(4): 1268-77.

Baldwin, C. and M. Serapio. 2016. "Once-Powerful Philippines Church Divided, Subdued over Drug Killings." https://www.reuters.com/article/us-philippines-duterte-church-insight/once-powerful-philippines-church-divided-subdued-over-drug-killings-idUSKCN12A07Y.

Boyd, G. 2001. "Collateral Damange in the War on Drugs." *Villanova Law Review* 47(4): 839-50.

CBCP News. 2017. "Religious Superiors Call for an End to 'War on Drugs.'" http://cbcpnews.net/cbcpnews/religious-superiors-call-for-end-to-war-on-drugs/.

Christian Aid. 2018. "Trouble, Strife – and Unexpected Opportunity." https://www.christianaid.org/missions-insider/2018-trouble-strife-and-unexpected-opportunity/.

Cornelio, J. 2017. "Religious Worlding: Christianity and the New Production of Space in the Philippines." In *New Religiosities, Modern Capitalism and Moral Complexities in Southeast Asia,* eds. Juliette Koning and Gwenaël Njoto-Feillard, 169-97. New York: Palgrave Macmillan.

———. 2018. "Jesus Is Lord: The Indigenization of Megachurch Christianity in the Philippines." In *Pentecostal Megachurches in Southeast Asia: Negotiating Class, Consumption and the Nation*, ed. T. Chong, 127-55. Singapore: ISEAS.

———. 2020. "The Philippines." In *Edinburgh Companions to Global Christianity: Christianity in East and South-East Asia*, eds. K. Ross, T. Johnson, and F. Alvarez, 242-253. Edinburgh: Edinburgh University Press.

Cornelio, J. and E. Medina. 2019. "Christianity and Duterte's War on Drugs in the Philippines.'" *Politics, Religion & Ideology* 20(2): 151-69.

Courtwright, D. 1997. "Morality, Religion, and Drug Use." In *Morality and Health*, eds. A. Brandt and P. Rozin, 231-50. New York and London: Routledge.

Cranfield, C.E.B. 1959. "Some Observations on Romans XIII: 1-7" *New Testament Studies*, 6: 245.

Derrida, J. 2003. "The Rhetoric of Drugs." In *High Culture: Reflections on Addiction and Modernity*, eds. A. Alexander and M. Roberts, 19-44. Albany: SUNY Press.

Elisha, O. 2008. "Moral Ambitions of Grace: The Paradox of Compassion and Accountability in Evangelical Faith-Based Activism." *Cultural Anthropology* 23(1): 154-89.

———. 2011. *Moral Ambition: Mobilization and Social Outreach in Evangelical Megachurches*. Berkeley: University of California Press.

Esmaquel II, P. 2017. "Christian Churches on Drug War: 'Stop the Slaughter!'" *Rappler*. https://www.rappler.com/nation/182059-christian-churches-nccp-drug-war-killings-stop-slaughter.

———. 2017. "Christians Hit 'Daily Bloodshed' in War on Drugs." *Rappler*. https://www.rappler.com/nation/143207-evangelical-christian-churches-killings-war-drugs.

Gallagher, A., E. Raffle, and Z. Maulana. 2020. "Failing to Fulfill the Responsibility to Protect: The War on Drugs as Crimes against Humanity in the Philippines." *The Pacific Review* 33(2): 247-77.

Griffith-Dickson, G. 2018. "Religion, Security, Strategy: An Unholy Trinity?" In *Religion and the Public Sphere: New Conversations*, eds. J. Walters and E. Kersley, 62-71. London and New York: Routledge.

Holmes, R. 2016. "The Dark Side of Electoralism: Opinion Polls and Voting in the 2016 Philippine Presidential Election." *Journal of Current Southeast Asian Affairs* 35(3): 15-38.

Lasco, G. 2014. "Pampagilas: Methamphetamine in the Everyday Economic Lives of Underclass Male Youths in a Philippine Port." *International Journal of Drug Policy* 25(4): 783-88.

Lim, D. 1989. "Church and State in the Philippines, 1900–1988." *Transformation* 6(3): 27-32.

———. 2009. "Consolidating Democracy: Filipino Evangelicals between People Power Events, 1986-2001." In *Evangelical Christianity and Democracy in Asia*, ed. D. Lumsdaine, 235-84. Oxford and New York: Oxford University Press.

Lopes, O. and J. Costa. 2018. "Drugs and Religion: Contributions to the Debate on the Science–Religion Interface." *Religions* 9(4): 1-13.

Philippine Information Agency. 2018. "#Realnumbersph." http://pdea.gov.ph/pdea-map/2-uncategorised/279-realnumbersph.

Philippine Star. 2017. "Full Texts: CBCP Officials' Statements on Drug-Related Killings." https://www.philstar.com/headlines/2017/08/20/1730992/full-texts-cbcp-officials-statements-drug-related-killings.

Pulse Asia. 2017. "September 2017 Nationwide Survey on the Campaign against Illegal Drugs." http://www.pulseasia.ph/september-2017-nationwide-survey-on-the-campaign-against-illegal-drugs.

Quintos, P. 2018. "Are #Realnumbers Real? Rights Defenders Question State Data on Drug War." *ABS-CBN News.* http://news.abs-cbn.com/focus/04/06/18/are-realnumbers-real-rights-defenders-question-state-data-on-drug-war.

Smith, T. 2013. "Beliefs About God across Time and Space." http://www.norc.org/PDFs/Beliefs_about_God_Report.pdf.

Stein, R. 1989. "The Argument of Romans 13:1-7." *Novum Testamentum* 31(4): 325-43.

Tejedo, J. 2018. "Pentecostal-Charismatic Megachurches in the Philippines." In *Pentecostal Megachurches in Southeast Asia: Negotiating Class, Consumption and the Nation*, ed. T. Chong, 156-78. Singapore: ISEAS.

Viray, P. 2018. "Cayetano Slams HRW Anew: You Owe Us an Apology." *Phil-ippine Star.* https://www.philstar.com/headlines/2018/01/26/1781590/cayetano-slams-hrw-anew-you-owe-us-apology.

Wallace, J., T.N. Brown, J.G. Bachman, and T.A. LaVeist. 2003. "The Influence of Race and Religion on Abstinence from Alcohol, Cigarettes and Marijuana among Adolescents." *Journal of Studies on Alcohol* 64(6): 843-48.

Conclusion

Amy Freedman

Chapters in this volume have looked at Indonesia, Thailand, Cambodia, and the Philippines. What have we learned from them about the relationship between religion and politics? Can we offer any assessments or answers about the sources of greater entwining of religion and politics? Is it elite-driven, or coming from increased religiosity in society? And, what can we draw out and understand about the implications for future political dynamics?

There are a few sweeping points we can make: different countries demonstrate different dynamics in how we think about religion and politics, but there are some similarities. Anti-democratic leaders are finding common cause with conservative religious forces. From Indonesia, to the Philippines, Thailand, and Cambodia (one could also include Burma as well, although this volume does not address the situation there), increased appeals to piety and conservative religious practice are operating in tandem with political processes that weaken civil rights protections. Second, while we cannot say definitively that this process is only being driven by elites, elites are a key part of what is going on as they are using religious politics to their advantage. Third, this dynamic is taking places across different types of political systems: from partly-free countries like Indonesia, the Philippines, and Malaysia, to military-dominated Thailand, and one-party state Cambodia. The variation in regime type forces us to look at more complex factors at the political level. As Ionana Emy Matesan writes in her chapter on PKS in Indonesia, the link between religion and politics is both a bottom-up and top-down process.

In countries where electoral politics matters, and where politicians need to campaign to win seats in office, parties must compete with each other for voter support. This support will translate into holding positions in government and the ability to make policies and assert political influence. One of the strategies the parties and individual office seekers have used is religious politics. This is manifest in two ways: one in identity politics, where candidates for election trumpet their identity and piety: this can include things like photo ops with religious leaders, or attending religious services, or getting the endorsement of religious leaders. We see this in Malaysia and Indonesia, and with Dueterte's support from mega-churches in the Philippines. Second, candidates can openly assert particular positions on religious and moral policies. For example, in Malaysia and Indonesia candidates can and do express their support for anti-blasphemy measures, and anti-pornography laws, or crack downs on clubs serving alcohol, or on the adoption of explicit elements of shari'a law. An interesting element of this is that we see candidates supporting these kinds of measures from both religious parties and secular parties. (Tanuwidjaja 2010; Buehler 2016) Because these kinds of issues attract a growing segment of voter support, such policies have been promoted or supported by both religious and non-religious parties. The reality of political competition where electoral candidates use religious issues to help win office is a problem for religious minorities; often the resulting religious legislation harms their interests, and it also demonstrates their weak political position (Sumaktoyo 2020).

In 2008, the journal *Asian Security* published a special issue on "Faith and Security: the Effects of Democracy on Religious Political Parties." The four articles in the journal looked at Indonesia, India, Israel, and Italy and the broad thesis of the comparison was

> that religious political parties in democracies can be "tamed" with access to patronage, power, and policy. While democracy tends to have a moderating influence, we identify the conditions and circumstances under which extremism may not be quelled merely by the party's participation in the government. (Elman and Warner 2008)

The need to win votes in elections, and then to have an effect on policy-making in multi-party parliamentary systems (at the time), led religious parties to moderate the most conservative religious elements in their platforms, Elman and Warner's volume found. For Israel, Indonesia, and India these findings no longer hold up. Instead, religious parties have become more powerful and more religiously conservative in how they both appeal to voters and how they govern. Thus, they may no longer need to moderate their positions to get access to power, patronage, and policy-making.

Why might elites use religious politics as an electoral strategy? The answer to this may be similar to answers about populist appeals more generally. In political systems where political parties are non-ideological (like

Indonesia, Thailand, and the Philippines, and to a lesser extent, Malaysia), parties and politicians tend to run for election using strategies based on charismatic identities of those at the top of the ticket, or based on appeals to self-interest. Literature on populist mobilization sees populism as a flexible way of animating popular support (Jansen 2011). We used to believe that populist mobilization was most salient during economic downturns; that is no longer the case (Mols and Jetten 2015). Populism, at its core, uses anti-elite rhetoric, and appeals can be based on nationalism, or other forms of identity politics, which can be based on race, ethnicity, or religion. The appeal is to citizens' feelings of relative deprivation; that one's position and well-being is at risk due to threats from some other group or force in society (Mols and Jetten 2016; Crosby 2018). In Indonesia, religious populism provides an easy-to-understand appeal to people's religious identities and values. By denigrating "liberal" or multi-religious or pluralist values, candidates and their proxies in the Jakarta governor's race and the 2019 Presidential race conservative candidates tried to stake out a zero-sum competition between properly Islamic candidates and those who would not uphold Islamic values. The strategy worked in the Jakarta election, but not in the Presidential one. It is possible that populist mobilization is especially tempting when other possible electoral strategies are difficult. In an ideal world, candidates would appeal to voters with different policy ideas on how to address significant societal problems such the need for infrastructure improvements, the need for better social safety net provisions, and public goods like education and healthcare, and the over-all need to create economic growth and jobs, and the need to tackle endemic corruption. However, populist candidates often only make the most basic passing references as to how they will address these needs. Seemingly, it is much easier to appeal to voters based on visceral identity politics and demonization of the "Other" than to provide clear, workable policy ideas on solving big needs.

There is an economic argument in this volume as well. As Cornelio and Marañon find in the case of Evangelical churches in the Philippines, pastors don't want to dwell on the war on drugs with their upwardly mobile congregants. The implication of this is that members don't want to be reminded of the problems of poverty in neighborhoods and communities that they are removed from. Likewise, as Christopher Ankersen frames for us in his chapter on Thailand, ideological frameworks (including the use of religion and identity) are a convenient way to legitimize the "inequality regime" and it allows for a glossing over of low levels of social mobility and efforts to maintain systems of privilege by those at the top of the socioeconomic ladder. Societies in Southeast Asia have grotesque levels of inequality. Focusing on religious identity and issues of morality allows elites to deflect attention away from this glaring problem, and protects the system of privilege for those at the top.

Increased use of religious appeals and religious legislation also prompts us to ask questions about the role of the judiciary in protecting minority rights in Southeast Asia, and the role of checks and balances more generally. We have seen courts in Indonesia and the Philippines go along with policies harmful to minorities. The blasphemy laws in Indonesia have been turned into a political tool (in the Jakarta governor's race), and used against Muslim and non-Muslims alike. The courts in the Philippines have also been compliant with polices which violate civil rights of activists pushing back against Dueterte's war on drugs (Suryana 2018). Likewise, the courts in Thailand have served as a tool for the military; in February 2020, the Thai courts disbanded the new popular opposition party, the Future Forward Party. The Constitutional Court found that the party had violated election law by accepting a loan from its leader. The Party argued that campaign financing laws are ambiguous and that other political parties have taken out loans without any legal repercussions (Beech 2020). One of the cornerstones of democracy is the idea and practice of checks and balances. If there are few institutional checks on executive or legislative power, then we are likely to see a concentration of power. If courts simply go along with curtailing political or civil rights and liberties, it is a clear sign of the weakening of democracy and bad news for minority and other opposition groups. Levitsky and Ziblatt's (2018) work, *How Democracies Die*, demonstrates how democratic countries slide into authoritarianism when citizens are polarized and elites in power support the weakening and undermining of checks and balances like an independent judiciary and a free press. Often, the first set of rights to be undercut or pushed aside are political and civil rights for minority groups. If the slide continues and there are few or weak attempts to reassert checks on the concentration of power, the political system ends up looking more like authoritarianism than democracy (Levitsky and Ziblatt 2018).

In Thailand, it is clear that changes are coming from the top down. The king and the military are each (separately) acting from positions of weakness. Their legitimacy has eroded over time, and thus they need to create new ideas, beliefs, and norms to maintain their positions of economic and political power. They are reaching for all the tools at their disposal: fear, the judiciary, rigging elections, and yes, trying to assert religious control. Religious control will aid in the reassertion of ideological and normative legitimacy, which the king and military elites both crave. Ankersen's chapter helps us understand the importance of this normative power as it provides additional justification for the continued hold on power by the military and the monarchy at the expensive of any semblance of democracy.

Noseworthy's chapter on Cambodia adds to this line of thinking. Hun Sen has eroded almost all democratic elements in Cambodia. None-the-less, he, like other authoritarian leaders, needs to maintain popular support and a veneer of legitimacy. To this end, he has actively sought out the Muslim community's approval. Some Muslim clerics have decided that ties to Hun Sen may afford the community a measure of acceptance and protection. As a minority community with a history of being persecuted, this strategy makes sense. It is worth noting, however, that photo opportunities, and rhetorical respect, do not always translate into economic or political privileges, despite Muslim clerics' support of Hun Sen, it is unclear that Cham Muslim communities more generally have reaped much benefit from these patronage ties.

In Indonesia, Islam and politics have a long and complicated history. Islamic parties have vied for political power and have competed in elections going back to the struggle for independence. Not all Islamic parties or groups are antithetical to democracy, nor do all Muslims respond to religious appeals and the demonization of others. What the chapters in this volume show is that the link between religion and politics will continue to be a powerful factor in electoral and non-electoral politics going forward, and have differring impacts for elites and the masses.

Danielle Lussier, M. Naji Azca, Hakimul Ikhwan, Wahyu Kustiningsih's chapter on religious practice and political participation in Yogyakarta demonstrates that religious engagement has differing impacts on Muslims and Christians. Both groups are engaged with their religious communities at similar levels and both groups vote at similar rates in elections. For Christians, there is little statistical correlation between the frequency of religious engagement and/or leadership activities and non-voting forms of political activity (attending political meetings or rallies, or petitioning the government in some way). For Muslims, there is a correlation. Those who are engaged in their mosques are more likely to engage in non-voting political behavior, and the relationship is even stronger for those who serve in leadership positions. There is also variation based on where one worships. Mosques and their communities are not all the same. Thus, mosques are not automatically political mobilizers. Future research will help illuminate which ones are and why.

There is enormous durability of Islamic parties like PKS. Matesan's chapter demonstrates that PKS has been able to overcome scandals and challenges and has maintained and even increased their popular support. They are able to do so by building up the party's social networks and have been able to capitalize on the overlap between religious, social, and party networks. The well-institutionalized nature of the party has helped it move beyond earning support based on a candidate's personality, name recognition or charisma. Matesan's chapter shows how support for the party from the population continues both through changes in the party platform, and despite scandals, and party leaders have been savvy in adapting the party to continue and expand their base of support, thus we can think of this as an example of top-down and bottom-up processes.

Susy Tekunan's chapter on women's role in radical movements finds that Indonesia, like other Muslim countries, is seeing an increase in religious conservatism and this has increased in tandem with the increased perception of threats to Islam from secularism and pluralism. Social media fosters both a sense of community and reinforces in-group identity, and it helps stoke a sense of outrage against those who seem to pose a threat to this cohesion and insular worldview. Social media also helps create a sense of efficacy among like-minded groups of individuals, particularly with women. Tekunan's research finds that men are often the leaders of networks and mobilization efforts. One prominent example of this was in the presidential election of 2019. Vice Presidential candidate, Sandiaga Uno played a role leading the women's emak-emak group. Tekunan's work finds that religiously based groups have been politicized around perceived threats to their beliefs and values, and that women are a key part of this phenomena, but that the mobilization is often driven by men at the top.

Finally, Jayeel Cornelio and Ia Marañon's chapter on the Philippines demonstrates the diversity in links between religion and politics. Megachurches in the Philippines view themselves as staying away from politics (so as not to turn off or alienate congregants). Pastors in these congregations see the church as separate from politics and that the church should be a spiritual space open to all; they fear that weighing in on Duetere's policies and particularly the anti-drug campaign would polarize churchgoers. Leaders of the megachurches see their members as upwardly mobile, middle-class strivers and for many, the anti-drug policies (and the extrajudicial killings that go with these policies) are a part of creating a more stable and ordered society and thus this is a higher good then advocating for the rights and protection for those targeted by the campaign. The anti-drug program is thus a "righteous intervention" meant to aid middle class, law-abiding members of society. Megachurches furthermore have participated in government programs for rehabilitation and moral renewal, and so are further invested in Duterte's efforts. While pastors may believe that staying silent on the civil rights violations constitutes being neutral, in actuality, the megachurches are, in fact, taking sides. By not standing up against the human rights atrocities, and by taking part in rehabilitation activities (and taking government money), the churches are assisting Duterte's campaign. Thus, in the Philippines, we see religious actors siding with the government and thus helping provide legitimacy and moral weight to the President's policies.

Each of these chapters provides us with a piece of a puzzle, but we have yet to assemble the whole scene. Further research is needed to understand more of the dynamics driving the relationship between religion and politics. The scholars writing in this volume, who presented at the conference in November 2019, are continuing to help us understand these links by helping to uncover who stands to benefit and who loses out when religion and politics collide.

Bibliography

Beech, Hannah. 2020. "Thailand Court Disbands Popular Opposition Party" *New York Times*, February 21.

Buehler, Michael. 2016. *The Politics of Shari'a Law: Islamist Activists and the State in Democratizing Indonesia.* Cambridge, UK: Cambridge University Press.

Crosby, Raphaella Kathyrn. 2018. "Personality and Electoral Fortunes." In *The Rise of Right Wing Populism*, ed. Pauline Hanson, 103-142. New York: Springer.

Elman, Miriam Fedius and Carolyn M. Warner. 2008. "Faith and Security: The Effect of Democracy on Religious Political Parties." *Asian Security* 4(1): 1-22.

Jansen, Robert. 2011. "Populist Mobilization: A New Theoretical Approach to Populism" *Sociological Theory* 29(2): 75-97.

Levitsky, Steven and Daniel Ziblatt. 2018. *How Democracies Die.* New York: Crown Publisher.

Mols, Frank and Jolanda Jetten (2015) "Explaining the Appeal of Populist Right-Wing Parties in Times of Economic Prosperity" *Political Psychology*, vol. 37, issue 2.

Sumaktoyo, Nathanael Gratias. 2020. "A Price for Democracy? Religious Legislation and Religious Discrimination in Post-Soeharto Indonesia." *Bulletin of Indonesian Economic Studies* 56(1): 23-42.

Suryana, A'an. 2018. "Indonesian Presidents and Communal Violence against Non-Mainstream Faiths." *Southeast Asia Research* 26(2): 147-60.

Tanuwidjaja, Sunny. 2010. "Political Islam and Islamic Parties in Indonesia: Critically Assessing the Evidence of Islam's Political Decline." *Contemporary Southeast Asia* 32(1): 29-49.

About the Authors

Christopher Ankersen is Clinical Associate Professor at the Center for Global Affairs, where he teaches in the Transnational Security concentration. Prior to joining NYU, he worked for the United Nations, where he served in Bangkok, Thailand (2012-2017) and at the UN Assistance to the Khmer Rouge Trials in Phnom Penh, Cambodia (2010-2012). He is a member of the Regional Consultative Group for Asia and the Pacific on Civil-Military Coordination in Disaster Relief; a Senior Research Fellow at the German-Southeast Asian Center of Excellence for Public Policy and Good Governance (CPG), Faculty of Law, Thammasat University, Thailand; and a Senior Fellow at the Canadian International Council. He is co-founder of the NYU Project on Armed Forces and Society. His research interests include civil military relations, strategic studies, international security, and crisis/disaster response. He holds a BA (Hons) in International Politics and History from Royal Roads Military College (Canada) and an MSc and PhD in International Relations from the London School of Economics and Political Science.

M. Najib Azca is a lecturer in the Department of Sociology and a researcher at the Center for Security and Peace Studies at the University of Gadjah Mada (UGM) in Yogyakarta, Indonesia. He has served as Vice Dean for Research, Cooperation, Community Services and Alumni Affairs for the Faculty of Social and Political Sciences at the UGM. He holds an MA from Australian National University and a PhD from the Amsterdam Institute for Social Science Research. His research expertise is in the sociology of conflict, with a particular focus on youth radicalization in Indonesia.

Jayeel Cornelio is Associate Professor and the Director of the Development Studies Program at the Ateneo de Manila University. He is also an associate editor of the journal Social Sciences and Missions (published by Brill). The broad theme of his work is religion and social change in the Philippines. His scholarly writings have appeared in a number of edited volumes and leading journals (including Social Compass, Religion, State & Society, and Politics, Religion & Ideology). He is the author of *Being Catholic in the Contemporary Philippines: Young People Reinterpreting Religion* (2016), which has been featured in a book symposium by the Journal of World Christianity. He is also the editor of Rethinking Filipino Millennials: Alternative Perspectives on a Misunderstood Generation (2020).

Amy Freedman is department chair and professor of political science at Pace University, NYC. She is also a senior research scholar at the Weatherhead East Asian Institute, Columbia University. She earned her MA and PhD at New York University. Her work looks at Southeast Asia, with a particular focus on Indonesia and Malaysia. Her most recent book *Nontraditional Security Threats in Southeast Asia* is co-authored with Ann Marie Murphy. She is a co-editor of *Asian Security* and the author of numerous journal articles relating to political economy questions, minority politics, and questions about political Islam. Her work appears in *Journal of Civil Society, Religion and Politics, World Affairs*, and elsewhere.

Hakimul Ikhwan is a lecturer at the Department of Sociology and researcher at the Centre for Population and Policy Studies at the University of Gadjah Mada in Yogyakarta, Indonesia. He holds a PhD from the Department of Sociology at the University of Essex UK (2015) and was a research fellow at the Harvard Kennedy School in 2013-2014.

Wahyu Kustiningsih is a lecturer in the Department of Sociology, Faculty of Social and Political Sciences, University of Gadjah Mada in Yogyakarta, Indonesia. Her research focuses on Social Demography, Migration, Labor, Environment, Social Network, and Mixed-Methods (Quantitative and Qualitative). Since 2018, she has been a manager of the Unit of Research, Publication, and Community Service in the Faculty of Social and Political Sciences at the University of Gadjah Mada.

Danielle N. Lussier is Associate Professor of Political Science at Grinnell College. Her research focuses on democratization, political participation, and religion and politics, with geographic expertise on post-communist Eurasia and Indonesia. She earned her BA in Russian and East European Studies from Wesleyan University and MA and PhD in political science from the University of California, Berkeley. She is the author of *Constraining Elites in Russia and Indonesia: Political Participation and Regime Survival* (Cambridge University Press, 2016) and *The Many Faces of Political Islam: Religion and Politics in Muslim Societies* (with Mohammed Ayoob, University of Michigan Press, forthcoming 2020). Her work has also been published in

Journal of Democracy, Religion & Politics, Journal for the Scientific Study of Religion, Problems of Post-Communism, Post-Soviet Affairs, and *Slavic Review.* She is currently working on a book project that examines the relationship between religious practice and political participation among Muslims and Christians in Yogyakarta, Indonesia.

Ia Denise Arnette Marañon is PhD candidate at Ateneo de Manila University. She is a labor and indigenous rights activist and writer.

Ioana Emy Matesan is Assistant Professor of Government and Tutor in the College of Social Studies at Wesleyan University. Her research focuses on contentious politics and Islamist movements, with a particular interest in Middle East politics, democratization, and political violence. Her book project explores why Islamist groups adopt or abandon violent tactics, with a focus on Egypt and Indonesia. She also works on the impact of inclusion and exclusion on Islamist tactics, the possibility of negotiating with armed Islamist groups, how armed non-state actors respond to mistakes, and Hamas and the Israeli-Palestinian conflict. Her articles have appeared in *Studies in Conflict and Terrorism, Terrorism and Political Violence, Journal of Strategic Security, Nations and Nationalism,* and are forthcoming in *Journal of Global Security Studies* and *International Negotiations.* She holds a BA in Political Science and Economics from Monmouth College, a MA in Political Science from Arizona State University, and a PhD in Political Science from Syracuse University.

William ("Billy") Noseworthy is an Assistant Professor of Asian History at McNeese State University in Lake Charles, Louisiana. After completing his dissertation at the University of Wisconsin-Madison in Southeast Asian History, he has been at work on his current book project, tentatively titled *Gods of the Soil: The Continuous Creolizations of Cham Communities in Southeast Asia.* His research and writing have been supported by programs affiliated with the Mellon Foundation, the Council of American Overseas Research Centers-Center for Khmer Studies, and the Social Science Research Council, as well as the University of Wisconsin and the University of Louisiana systems. Inspired by interdisciplinary collaborative research projects with colleagues in Southeast Asian Studies, his publications include a co-authored article on the role of Vietnamese labor on rubber plantations in southern Laos in the *Singapore Journal of Tropical Geography,* an article on the history of transmission and formulation of Hip Hop movements in the transpacific region in *Transfers: Journal of Mobility Studies,* and a book chapter on Vietnam's deliberations on Biển Đông (the "Eastern Sea" or the "South China Sea") in *China & Southeast Asia in the Xi Jinping Era* (eds. Lim & Cibulka, Lexington Books, 2019).

Susy Tekunan is a lecturer of International Relations at the Universitas Pelita Harapan (UPH) in Tangerang, Indonesia. Prior to (UPH) she worked as an international journalist at the *Voice of America* in Washington, D.C. covering humanitarian and political issues for multimedia publication including TV, radio, and the internet. She holds an MBA from Radford University in Virginia and a MA in Political Science from NYU. Her research interest is on China and the U.S. international politics issues, ASEAN, and Indonesian politics.

Religion and Politics in Southeast Asia
was published in Spring 2020
by Pace University Press

Cover and Interior Layout by Delaney Anderson and Francesca
Leparik
The journal was typeset in Pt Serif and Century Gothic Pro
and printed by Lightning Source in La Vergne, Tennessee

Pace University Press

Director: Manuela Soares
Associate Director: Stephanie Hsu

Graduate Assistants: Delaney Anderson
and Francesca Leparik
Graduate Student Aide: Shani Starinsky